# Professional Practice in Governance and Public Organizations

"Professional Practice in Governance and Public Organizations" offers cutting-edge insights and practical guidance for professionals in the areas of economics, politics, public policy and public administration, and those working at international organizations. The series features concise and accessible books on the latest developments in governance, organizational and political strategies, institutional policies, policy instruments, public management, and finance. Leadership and digitalization issues are a core topic throughout the series. All volumes are written by practitioners, experts and leading authorities from think tanks, non-governmental organizations, and public and international organizations. While the books are explicitly intended for professionals in the above-mentioned fields, students of economics, political science, public policy and public administration will also benefit from these practical guides for their future careers.

Max Rangeley

Editor

# The Age of Debt Bubbles

An Analysis of Debt Crises, Asset Bubbles
and Monetary Policy

 Springer

*Editor*
Max Rangeley
Cobden Centre
Plymouth, Devon, UK

ISSN 2731-9776 ISSN 2731-9784 (electronic)
Professional Practice in Governance and Public Organizations
ISBN 978-3-031-66472-4 ISBN 978-3-031-66473-1 (eBook)
https://doi.org/10.1007/978-3-031-66473-1

This Springer imprint is published by the registered company Springer Nature Switzerland AG
The registered company address is: Gewerbestrasse 11, 6330 Cham, Switzerland

If disposing of this product, please recycle the paper.

# Preface

## The Structure and Intention of the Book

When I first spoke with Springer about the idea for a book on debt bubbles and central banking, there were a number of avenues down which we could have gone. The quantity of publications from within academia commenting on monetary policy is voluminous to say the least. When talking through possible structures for the book, we decided to go with something different to most academic volumes. The first part of this book goes through an outline of the situation in which we find ourselves; first, we examine the nature of how money is created in a modern economy, then we go on to examine how debt bubbles form and their consequences for the economy. The second part of this book then has chapters from senior policy-makers from the world of politics and central banking. This combination of an academic analytical framework in the first half of the book with the experiences and thoughts of those who have worked "at the coalface" means we can develop a fuller understanding of how debt bubbles form, why they are often missed by the economics establishment and the mechanisms through which they are so damaging. This combination of theory, economic analysis, and senior policy-makers discussing their experiences separates this book from others in this domain.

Why do we start the book with a lengthy discourse on the nature of money itself—what it is and where it comes from? Money creation is so misunderstood by the academic establishment that we had to search hard for any institutions which had a correct framework for understanding the monetary system. The vast majority of textbooks teach a completely wrong, and in many ways a back-to-front, model of how money is created. The errors presented in academic textbooks, ranging from undergraduate right up to Ph.D. level, have cascaded through the intellectual ecosystem of economics to the point where hardly any economics professors can lay a claim to understanding how money is created. We cannot expect policy-makers to understand our monetary system if most economics professors do not seem to truly understand it. Hopefully, our chapter in this book on the topic, *How Money is Created in a Modern Economy*, will clear up many of the misunderstandings.

Following the outline of the money creation process, we then go through many of the data relating to the debt bubble phenomena. We do not cover just the last 5 or 10 years, but the last 40 years. For much of the last generation, from the early 1980s onwards, each recession has been responded to by central banks creating a series of larger and larger debt bubbles by setting interest rates lower and lower. In America, for example, when the bubbles of the 1980s burst, leading to the recession of the early 90s, the response from Alan Greenspan was to set interest rates at 3%, the lowest for generations, and then follow this with several years of the so-called "Greenspan Put" whereby expansionary monetary policy would be used to inflate the stock market, and other asset classes, whenever they began to correct back to historically normal prices. This of course generated what became known as the Dot Com Bubble, the peak of which saw a PE Ratio higher than even 1929.

When this bubble burst in 2000, the response from Alan Greenspan was even lower interest rates, of 1% between 2003 and 2004, which then created an even larger bubble—the housing bubble. Then when this burst in 2008, nearly taking down the global financial system with it, the response was, of course, even lower interest rates, in fact the lowest interest rates in history—more than a decade of zero percent interest rates. This policy was followed in much of the rest of the world, and even countries that had hitherto had reasonable debt levels, such as China, suddenly experienced an explosion in corporate and household debt. In fact, in 2008, total global aggregate debt was around $150 trillion; this was, by some margin, already the largest debt bubble in history, both in absolute terms and relative to GDP, but by the time we started writing this book, global aggregate debt had reached around $300 trillion. In other words, far from bringing about a return to prosperity, zero percent interest rates and other "stimulative" monetary policies have served to essentially double the size of the global debt bubble since the 2008 crisis.

The question therefore presents itself, how is it possible that many economists are still blissfully unaware of the dire situation in which we find ourselves? Of course, as has already been touched on, some of this stems from the fact that most economists do not understand the nature of our monetary system, and, in particular, how money is created—in our current system, when banks make loans, they do not take money from depositors and lend out this money to borrowers, they actually create new money ex nihilo. Yet it is this capacity of banks to create money out of nothing combined with central banks setting lower and lower interest rates for a generation has been the engine and fuel for the creation of the series of ever-larger debt bubbles we have seen during this period, culminating in the current $300 trillion debt extravaganza. Economic historians sometimes write with incredulity about historical bubbles such as the South Sea Bubble, Tulip Mania and the Mississippi Bubble. Yet those we have seen over the last 40 years not only match these in volume but are also the consequence of far more predictable policy errors. Interest rates are a pricing mechanism. When the price of butter or fuel or consumer goods is set artificially low, the consequences are obvious and can be predicted by any economics undergraduate; when the government of Venezuela sets the price of food artificially low, we are not surprised when they have food shortages, conversely, when central banks set interest rates artificially low for years on end we should not be surprised that we have a $300 trillion global debt bubble.

In 2018, at the Economic Freedom Summit in the European Parliament, I had a debate with the head of IMF Europe, Jeff Franks, billed as "Central Banks—The Solution or the Problem?" In Jeff's speech, he discussed how central banks had made recessions shorter and easier to bear by setting interest rates low; I talked through how interest rates set artificially low will of course boost GDP, but GDP is merely a measure of economic activity—the real question is what kind of economic activity is stimulated by artificially low interest rates? By understanding the intricacies of the consequences of interest rate manipulation by central banks, economists can make better macroeconomic predictions, much as they can make effective predictions about the consequences of governments setting prices in other areas of the economy such as food or fuel. I hope that this book will go some way to explaining how debt bubbles form and why they are so destructive to the economy, and in so doing allow us to think more deeply about how we might move towards a more rational and prosperous financial and monetary system.

## The Authors

In putting together the plan for this book, I wanted to ensure that we have the best writers available—both the economists for first part and policy-makers for the second part. I've known all of the authors for some time prior to writing this book, and have had many interesting conversations on the problems with the current monetary system and its consequences. In the first part of this book, my co-authors are Roger Koppl, Professor of Economics at Syracuse University in the United States, and Harry Richer, a policy researcher and political advisor in the UK. Roger has written a number of important publications on the failure of technocracy to formulate sound policy, and nowhere has this expert failure been more apparent than within the world of central banking. In 2022, I wrote a book with British member of Parliament Steve Baker on the global debt bubble, for which Harry did excellent work—many of the data from that book have been used for the debt bubbles part of the first part in this work, looking at data from dozens of countries around the world to build a picture of the magnitude of the problem. I co-authored the chapter on money creation in the first part with William White, who also wrote a chapter for second part (see below).

In the second part of this book, we have four authors writing from the policy-makers' perspective on the nature of debt bubbles and modern central banking. William White is the former head of the Economic and Monetary Department at the Bank for International Settlements, the central bank of central banks. Bill has decades of experience of central banking, having worked at the Bank of England and Bank of Canada before going to the BIS, and following the BIS becoming Chairman of the Economic and Development Review Committee at the OECD. Barbara Kolm is the Vice President of the Austrian central bank and is the most prominent Austrian School central banker in the world today; Barbara has also run think tanks focussing on broad areas of economic policy and understands how monetary policy plays into many aspects of a modern economy. Lord Syed Kamall was a member of the European

Parliament for many years, heading the ECR group, at the time the third largest group in the European Parliament; I worked with Syed on the 2016 Blockchain Summit in the European Parliament, where we had the IMF, World Bank, UN and BIS among others discussing the future of money. Having also been a professor of economics, Syed has an excellent knowledge of both the theoretical and practical aspects of how an economy works. Miguel Fernandez Ordoñez is the former Governor of the Bank of Spain and was at the helm when the 2008 crisis hit; Miguel has since become one of the most interesting thinkers in the world when it comes to how we might reform our monetary system. These esteemed authors, all of whom have different perspectives and thoughts on the current monetary system, ensure that this book is a unique contribution in the field of monetary economics.

Finally, I would like to express my gratitude to Johannes Glaeser at Springer—producing novel works in the field of academic literature is far more enjoyable when working with a knowledgeable and enterprising publisher. With Johannes at Springer, we have now produced some of the most innovative books in recent academic history, featuring authors ranging from the prime ministers of major countries to senior central bankers and, for our artificial intelligence book, some of the most interesting AI thinkers in the world.

Plymouth, UK                                                                                          Max Rangeley

# Contents

# Understanding the Monetary System and Debt Bubbles in Modern Economies

# How Money Is Created in a Modern Economy

**Max Rangeley and William White**

The way in which money is created in a modern economy is misunderstood by many academics and practitioners of finance, including in some cases even central bankers. Broadly speaking, the confusion arises from the view that banks lend out depositors' money when they make loans—this is what is taught in the vast majority of economics textbooks. In reality, when a bank makes a loan, it creates that new money ex nihilo—out of nothing. Rather than taking money that it has in the form of deposits from Bob and lending this out to Alice, the bank expands both sides of its balance sheet when it makes a loan to Alice, thereby creating new money. This idea that banks create new money is often called endogenous monetary theory.

While almost all university economics textbooks teach that banks receive money from depositors and then lend it out to customers, a small number of central banks—most notably those in Germany, the UK, Switzerland and Spain—have written the truth about how money is created. Most of these are short papers or speeches; we shall see some of the key points from these central banks, but this chapter will also present a more general outline of how money creation occurs in a modern economy and some of the consequences, as well as pointing out some of the errors in how economics is generally taught.

The Deutsche Bundesbank, in a paper in 2017 (2017b), outlined the money creation process, and how it occurs without the need for lending out deposits, as follows:

> What the stylised example of the creation of money shows particularly clearly is that a bank can grant loans without any prior inflows of customer deposits. In fact, book money is created as a result of an accounting entry: when a bank grants a loan, it posts the associated credit entry for the customer as a sight deposit by the latter and therefore as a liability on the

M. Rangeley (✉)
The Cobden Centre, 61 Pembroke St, Plymouth PL1 4JS, UK
e-mail: maxrangeley@gmail.com; max@cobdencentre.org

W. White
131 Bloor Street West, Unit 615, Toronto, ON M5S153, Canada

liability side of its own balance sheet. This refutes a popular misconception that banks act simply as intermediaries at the time of lending – i.e. that banks can only grant loans using funds placed with them previously as deposits by other customers. (2017, p. 17)[1]

The Banco de España similarly described this simple process through which money is conjured into existence by banks:

> Most of the money we use is created by commercial banks when they lend money. When a commercial bank issues a new loan to its customers and credits their current accounts with the corresponding amount, it is creating "inside money." This money will be used to buy goods or make investments and will eventually end up being deposited in other bank accounts. Conversely, when customers pay off their debts, that inside money is destroyed.[2]

Even within the relatively small community of economists who do understand that new money is created when banks make loans, there is still confusion. Many believe that banks are "reserve constrained"—that the reserves held by banks with the central bank constrain how much money they can create. In reality, most central banks are accommodative, they generate whatever reserves are necessary when banks create new money by making loans. The Bank of England (McLeay et al. 2014) explained this concisely and effectively in one of their papers on the money creation process:

> Commercial banks create money, in the form of bank deposits, by making new loans. When a bank makes a loan, for example to someone taking out a mortgage to buy a house, it does not typically do so by giving them thousands of pounds worth of banknotes. Instead, it credits their bank account with a bank deposit of the size of the mortgage. At that moment, new money is created. For this reason, some economists have referred to bank deposits as 'fountain pen money', created at the stroke of bankers' pens when they approve loans.
>
> While new broad money has been created on the consumer's balance sheet, […] this is without — in the first instance, at least — any change in the amount of central bank money or 'base money'. As discussed earlier, the higher stock of deposits may mean that banks want, or are required, to hold more central bank money in order to meet withdrawals by the public or make payments to other banks. And reserves are, in normal times, supplied 'on demand' by the Bank of England to commercial banks in exchange for other assets on their balance sheets. In no way does the aggregate quantity of reserves directly constrain the amount of bank lending or deposit creation. (p. 16)

This misunderstanding among economists with respect to how money is created leads, by extension, to misunderstandings about the effects of the money creation system on the rest of the economy, in particular how bubbles are inflated and how an inefficient use of resources in the economy propagates.

It is worth looking a little more closely at the erroneous model found in most economics textbooks. It goes something along the lines of the following:

> Someone deposits £10,000 in Alpha Bank. Alpha Bank then keeps 10% of this, or £1,000, in reserve, and lends out £9,000—so-called "fractional reserve banking." That £9,000 is then deposited in Beta Bank, which is similarly lent out with 10% (£900) being kept in reserves.

---

[1] The role of banks, non-banks and the central bank in the money creation process, Deutsche Bundesbank, Monthly Report, April 2017.

[2] This can be found here: https://www.bde.es/wbe/en/areas-actuacion/politica-monetaria/preguntas-frecuentes/definicion-funciones-del-dinero/como-se-crea-el-dinero.html.

The amount of money in the economy, it is posited by the textbooks, is thereby "multiplied out" over time, leading to the oft-used term "multiplier model" to describe this mechanism. Furthermore, when a central bank wants to "stimulate" the economy through credit creation, it engages in open market operations—it buys bonds from banks, which puts cash onto the balance sheets of the banks. The economics textbooks then outline how this cash is then lent out to customers, increasing the amount of credit available in the economy. Once this is lent out, the borrowers will also of course deposit the cash at a bank, thereby continuing the "multiplier effect" once again. The extent to which base money is multiplied up in the economy is a function of the reserve ratio and the demand for credit, for instance if the reserve ratio is 0.10 (10%), then the multiplier effect will be the inverse of this, 10. In other words, for every £10,000 injected into the economy by the central bank through open market operations, this will, over time, be multiplied up into £100,000 over time as, through each iteration, 10% of deposits are kept in reserve and 90% are "lent out."

This is in fact how most textbooks erroneously describe the process of money creation. For example, in *Modern Money and Banking*, a popular textbook by Miller and VanHoose (1993), they write the following[3]:

> In this example, a person went into bank 1 and deposited a $100,000 check drawn on another bank. That $100,000 became part of the reserves of bank 1. Because that deposit immediately created excess reserves, further loans were possible for bank 1. Bank 1 lent the excess reserves to earn interest. A bank will not lend more than its excess reserves because, by law, it must hold a certain amount of required reserves. (p. 331)

In Mankiw and Taylor's (2014) introductory text, *Economics*, they describe how reserve ratios determine how much of customers' deposits are "lent out," which are then "multiplied up":

> Let's suppose that First European has a reserve ratio of 10 per cent. This means that it keeps 10 per cent of its deposits in reserve and lends out the rest. (p. 569)

In Harvey and Jowsey's (2007) *Modern Economics*, they write of how:

> Banks are companies which exist to make money for their shareholders. They do this by borrowing money from their 'depositors' and relending it at a higher rate of interest to other people. (p. 324)

In Hardwick et al.'s (1999) text *An Introduction to Modern Economics*, they describe how central banks push cash onto banks' balance sheets so that it can be "lent out" to the public (note, we shall examine how central bank operations actually work in more detail later in this chapter):

> Conversely, if the central bank wishes to expand the money supply, it will buy securities on the open market and will pay for them with cheques drawn on itself. The sellers of the securities will deposit these cheques with the commercial banks, which will present them for payment to the central bank. The central bank will credit the commercial banks' accounts and this represents an increase in their cash reserves. The commercial banks will now be in a position to undertake a multiple expansion of bank deposits. (p. 441)

Heffernan's (1996) *Modern Banking in Theory and Practice*, popular with MBA and economics Master's courses, describes how:

---

[3] Several of the quotations shown here are taken from Werner (2014). Specifically, Miller and VanHoose (1993), Heffernan (1996), Samuelson and Nordhaus (1995) and Stiglitz (1997).

> To summarise, all modern banks act as intermediaries between borrowers and lenders, but they may do so in a variety of different ways, from the traditional function of taking deposits and lending a percentage of these deposits, to fee-based financial services (p. 18).

Even within institutions there have been differences in the understanding of how money is created. On the one hand, Benes and Kumhof (2012) of the IMF wrote a paper in 2012 correctly describing how banks create money, and how the Chicago Plan provided a possible alternative. On the other hand, the IMF's own videos used for teaching finance on the educational platform EdX taught that banks take money from depositors and lend it out to other customers. Similarly, the IMF, in their series explaining banking and finance to a wider audience, in *Banking: At the Heart of the Matter*, describe banking as follows:

> You've got $1,000 you don't need for, say, a year and want to earn income from the money until then. Or you want to buy a house and need to borrow $100,000 and pay it back over 30 years.
>
> It would be difficult, if not impossible, for someone acting alone to find either a potential borrower who needs exactly $1,000 for a year or a lender who can spare $100,000 for 30.
>
> That's where banks come in.
>
> Although banks do many things, their primary role is to take in funds—called deposits—from those with money, pool them, and lend them to those who need funds. Banks are intermediaries between depositors (who lend money to the bank) and borrowers (to whom the bank lends money). The amount banks pay for deposits and the income they receive on their loans are both called interest.[4]

In Samuelson and Nordhaus's famous work, *Economics* (1995), one of the most used textbooks in the world (both Samuelson and Nordhaus won the Nobel Prize in Economics), they note that:

> Each small bank is limited in its ability to expand its loans and investments. It cannot lend or invest more than it has received from depositors (p. 496)

In Stiglitz's (also a Nobel Prize winner) book, similarly titled *Economics* (1997), he writes that:

> It should be clear that when there are many banks, no individual bank can create multiple deposits. Individual banks may not even be aware of the role they play in the process of multiple-deposit creation. All they see is that their deposits have increased and therefore they are able to make more loans (p. 737)

More recently, Nobel Prize winner Paul Krugman, who wrote another economics textbook that is widely used, has used his position as a journalist at the New York Times to ridicule the idea that banks "just issue checks out of thin air," calling it "banking mysticism" and asserting that "any individual bank does, in fact, have to lend out the money it receives in deposits." We have shown a longer quote below to obviate any risk of accusation that we are using cherry-picked quotes:

---

[4] This outline can be found here: https://www.imf.org/en/Publications/fandd/issues/Series/Back-to-Basics/Banks.

It's obvious that many commenters don't get the distinction between the proposition that banks create money — which every economics textbook, mine included, says they do (that's what the money multiplier is all about) — and the proposition that their ability to create money is not constrained by the monetary base. Sigh.

A bit of a followup on my previous post.

As I read various stuff on banking — comments here, but also various writings here and there — I often see the view that banks can create credit out of thin air. There are vehement denials of the proposition that banks' lending is limited by their deposits, or that the monetary base plays any important role; banks, we're told, hold hardly any reserves (which is true), so the Fed's creation or destruction of reserves has no effect.

This is all wrong, and if you think about how the people in your story are assumed to behave — as opposed to getting bogged down in abstract algebra — it should be obvious that it's all wrong.

First of all, any individual bank does, in fact, have to lend out the money it receives in deposits. Bank loan officers can't just issue checks out of thin air; like employees of any financial intermediary, they must buy assets with funds they have on hand. I hope this isn't controversial, although given what usually happens when we discuss banks, I assume that even this proposition will spur outrage.

But the usual claim runs like this: sure, this is true of any individual bank, but the money banks lend just ends up being deposited in other banks, so there is no actual balance-sheet constraint on bank lending, and no reserve constraint worth mentioning either.

That sounds more like it — but it's also all wrong.

Yes, a loan normally gets deposited in another bank — but the recipient of the loan can and sometimes does quickly withdraw the funds, not as a check, but in currency. And currency is in limited supply — with the limit set by Fed decisions. So there is in fact no automatic process by which an increase in bank loans produces a sufficient rise in deposits to back those loans, and a key limiting factor in the size of bank balance sheets is the amount of monetary base the Fed creates — even if banks hold no reserves.

So how much currency does the public choose to hold, as opposed to stashing funds in bank deposits? Well, that's an economic decision, which responds to things like income, prices, interest rates, etc.. In other words, we're firmly back in the domain of ordinary economics, in which decisions get made at the margin and all that. Banks are important, but they don't take us into an alternative economic universe. (Krugman 2012)

In reality, the multiplier model is not only misleading, but leads to a poor understanding of how credit creation is transmitted through the underlying capital structure of the economy. From an accounting perspective, when Alpha Bank makes a loan, it does not shift cash from one part of its balance sheet (a customer's deposits) in order to make the loan—it actually expands both sides of its balance sheet. When a mortgage for £500,000 is given, the bank creates both an asset (the £500,000 owed to the bank by the borrower) and a liability (the deposit newly created for the borrowed, which they can then spend). At the point of the loan being issued, £500,000 of new money comes into existence in the economy. Conversely, when loans are paid back, that money is destroyed just as easily—it simply ceases to exist in the economy. When that £500,000 mortgage is finally paid off, it does not sit on the bank's balance sheet waiting to be lent out again to another customer, but is expunged from the balance sheet of the bank, and by extension the macroeconomic balance sheet of the economy more widely. Customer deposits sitting on the bank's balance sheet, representing what is owed by the bank to its customers, are therefore a *liability*, not an asset. Note that on the other side of the balance sheet, the loan that the customer owes to the bank is the bank's asset (and, of course, the customer's liability).

One might therefore consider this a "pull" rather than a "push" system, the reverse of what is taught in textbooks. Textbooks generally teach that central banks *push* money into the economy by creating base money, sometimes called "high powered money," which is then lent out into the economy and "multiplied out." In reality, consumers *pull* money into the economy when they borrow money from commercial banks, thereby conjuring new money into existence, which then requires the creation of the requisite amount of central bank reserves. As we shall see in more detail shortly, there are different levels of money in the economy, but the majority of money is *pulled* into existence when credit-worthy consumers demand credit. The Bank of England also clarified some points related to this in an article in their 2014 Q1 Quarterly Bulletin:

> Another common misconception is that the central bank determines the quantity of loans and deposits in the economy by controlling the quantity of central bank money — the so-called 'money multiplier' approach. In that view, central banks implement monetary policy by choosing a quantity of reserves. And, because there is assumed to be a constant ratio of broad money to base money, these reserves are then 'multiplied up' to a much greater change in bank loans and deposits. For the theory to hold, the amount of reserves must be a binding constraint on lending, and the central bank must directly determine the amount of reserves. While the money multiplier theory can be a useful way of introducing money and banking in economic textbooks, it is not an accurate description of how money is created in reality. Rather than controlling the quantity of reserves, central banks today typically implement monetary policy by setting the price of reserves — that is, interest rates.
>
> In reality, neither are reserves a binding constraint on lending, nor does the central bank fix the amount of reserves that are available. As with the relationship between deposits and loans, the relationship between reserves and loans typically operates in the reverse way to that described in some economics textbooks. Banks first decide how much to lend depending on the profitable lending opportunities available to them — which will, crucially, depend on the interest rate set by the Bank of England. It is these lending decisions that determine how many bank deposits are created by the banking system. The amount of bank deposits in turn influences how much central bank money banks want to hold in reserve (to meet withdrawals by the public, make payments to other banks, or meet regulatory liquidity requirements), which is then, in normal times, supplied on demand by the Bank of England. (p. 15)

Given this lack of importance of central bank reserves in the lending process, the question might be asked as to why they exist at all; this also derives from a misunderstanding of the nature of money creation and the banking system. Central bank reserves are used by banks to settle transfers with each other. If Bob sends some money from his bank to Alice's account, the settlement between the two banks is generally done using central bank reserves; all commercial banks hold reserves with the central bank, and when transfers take place between banks this is ordinarily done using these reserves. Settlement could actually be done bilaterally between banks for a small number of transactions, but in a modern economy there may be millions or even hundreds of millions of people and organisations paying each other for products and services, increasingly using electronic transfers rather than physical cash, and this is netted out by the transfer of central bank reserves between banks.

The processing system used by most advanced central banks is called Real Time Gross Settlement, or RTGS, which allows for banks to use real-time settlement with the reserve accounts they have at the central bank. Reserves are also used by banks to exchange with the central bank for notes and cash for customers, although this represents a shrinking use of reserves in most modern economies.

What we therefore have is an order of operations such as the following:

> Jack borrows £10,000 from the bank for a renovation project; at this point £10,000 of new money is created. He pays his builders electronically, and his bank debits his account while the builders' banks credit their accounts; Jack's bank then transfers central bank reserves of the corresponding amount to the builders' banks, thereby netting everything out.

One of the small number of central banks that has discussed the reality of how money is created is the Swiss National Bank. In a speech, *How Money is Created by the Central Bank and the Banking System*, Chairman of the SNB Jordan (2018) summarised the process of money creation and the inter-bank transfer of funds.

> How do deposits at commercial banks, i.e. customer deposits in Swiss francs, come into existence? In our present-day financial system, the creation of deposits by banks is closely linked to the granting of loans. When a bank provides a loan, it credits the amount in question to the borrower in the form of a deposit to his or her account. This leads to an increase in credits on the assets side and in customer deposits on the liabilities side of the bank's balance sheet.
>
> As a rule, borrowers will immediately use their new deposit to acquire the goods or services for which they requested and received the loan. They thereby trigger a payment that reduces their deposits while increasing the deposits on the payment recipient's account. By far the most common form of loan in Switzerland is a mortgage. When a mortgage is taken out for the purchase of a house or an apartment, the deposit does not normally even appear on the borrower's account, since the bank remits the loan amount directly to the seller of the house or apartment in exchange for the mortgage certificate.
>
> To execute the payment, the bank needs to have sight deposits with the SNB. If it holds enough liquidity in the form of central bank money, the payment can be made without delay. If not, the bank needs to obtain liquidity on the interbank market or via credit facilities at the SNB, which only works if the bank has sufficient collateral in the form of securities or if it is prepared to pay a premium. (p. 4)

In addition to creating money when loans are made to customers, banks also create new money when they make purchases, either from individuals or, more commonly, from companies and governments. Specifically, when a bank makes a purchase of government bonds, either directly or from the private sector, it creates new deposits to purchase those bonds. It is worth reiterating this point—*when a bank purchases government bonds, it typically does so by creating new money out of thin air*. Remember, these are profit-making institutions, and all taxpayers contribute each year towards the government paying interest on these bonds. In recent years, governments have become indebted to the point of saturation, meaning the tax paid by the public in order to pay interest on government debt can be quite substantial. In Britain, as of writing, the interest paid on the national debt is roughly £10 billion per month, more than double the entire national defence budget.

## Understanding Different Measures of the Quantity of Money in Circulation

Money that is created through banks making loans, sometimes euphemistically called "fountain pen money," constitutes around 80% of the money in most modern economies, with central bank reserves accounting for around 15–17% and cash and notes making up only around 3–5% of the total. Given that central bank reserves are only for use by banks and the central bank, bank-created money that can be used by regular companies and ordinary people therefore constitutes around 95–97% of the total.

There are, however, different layers of money in the monetary system. At the bottom is central bank money, or "base money" (sometimes called "high powered money") which, as we have seen, is used for inter-bank settlement and is supplied on demand when banks create new money by making loans. When using the multiplier model, this is sometimes erroneously thought to constitute the base of the pyramid from which money is "multiplied out." When a bank requires central bank reserves, it will often borrow them on the interbank overnight (short-term) market. It does this in order to fulfil its obligations with respect to transactions with other banks. Contrary to common assertions, it does not do this borrowing in order to "lend out" this money to customers. Additionally, coins and notes in circulation make up a small and dwindling part of the money supply, and are usually put at the bottom of the pyramid with central bank money. Coins and notes are a liability on the central bank's balance sheet, and an asset on the commercial banks' balance sheets, and they may be exchanged by the banks at any time for central bank reserves.

The most fundamental qualities of money in a modern economy are that it is available at par with central bank money and is immediately available; governments have chosen to maintain the parity between bank-created credit and central bank money, which is what gives the credit issued by banks its quality of being "money." Machlup (1970) used the term "moneyness" to describe how different financial assets assume money-like qualities in different environments. You can't buy a cappuccino at your local coffee shop using gilts, T-Bills or corporate paper, but in financial markets they have a high degree of "moneyness." Since much of the money in the economy is tied up in short-term financial assets or funds of various forms, from money market funds to savings accounts, the terms often used are shown below, from M0 to M4— as the levels progress, the types of money included become broader, encompassing more types of "money."

M0:  Notes and coins and central bank reserves (this is sometimes known as high-powered money, or base money).

M1:  Money in circulation, in other words current accounts (immediately available for spending) plus notes and coins. M1 does not include central bank reserves.

M2:  M1 plus time deposits with up to 3 months notice or 2 years fixed maturity.

M3:  M2 plus repurchase agreements, money market funds with a maturity of more than 24 h, debt securities up to 2 years.

M4:  M3 plus other deposits at UK banks or building societies.

Bank-created money is also sometimes called "inside money" as it is created from inside the banking system ("outside money" is the term used for money from central banks.) As we analyse the nature of credit expansions throughout this book, these different "M" levels will be useful to bear in mind.

Before the 2008 Global Financial Crisis, influencing the overnight interbank lending rate was the main tool of monetary policy. This was accomplished by central banks providing a supply of reserves that slightly exceeded/fell short of the generally low levels demanded by banks to meet their anticipated clearing requirements. However, this "scarce reserve system" (SRS) for influencing short-term rates had to be replaced with a new "abundant reserves system" (ARS) following the 2008 crisis. When the interbank lending market totally froze up in that year, central banks created huge quantities of reserves in order to rebuild confidence and restore market functioning. Subsequently, reserves were further increased during Quantitative Easing for the purpose of stimulating aggregate demand. With central bank reserves now more plentiful, interbank lending markets are less important and therefore so is the interbank interest rate; the interest rate paid on reserves by the central bank has therefore become a more important tool of monetary policy. More recently, Claudio Borio, Head of the Monetary and Economic Department at the Bank for International Settlements, has discussed why we should move back to a scarce reserves systems from the abundant reserves systems, noting three benefits in particular: (1) reducing the central bank's footprint in the economy at large, and thereby its effects on resource allocation, (2) limiting central banks' links with government balance sheets and (3) a "third, often underestimated, benefit of a lean balance sheet is that it maximises the central bank's ability to expand it when the need does arise" (Borio 2023, p. 11).[5]

Some commentators thought that the expansions of central bank reserves following the 2008 crisis would lead to very high inflation or even hyperinflation, but this was based on the misunderstanding that reserves will be "lent out" and then "multiplied up" by the banking system. In the UK, prior to the financial crisis, banks had as little as £1 in central bank reserves for every £100 in deposits, but since then they generally have been around £7–8. Not only has the increase in base money failed to "push" up the creation of deposits, but there is increased evidence (see for instance Acharya et al. 2023) that the demand by banks for reserves has ratcheted up significantly. As will be discussed below, this will likely complicate the process of Quantitative Tightening when the time comes to do so.

## Capital Ratios, Liquidity Ratios and Reserves

Private banks are funded in the first instance by the issue of private equity or capital. In recent decades, the exact definition of capital and how much capital a bank must hold for prudential reasons has been guided by international standards set by the

---

[5] https://www.bis.org/speeches/sp230426.pdf.

Basel Committee on Banking Supervision (BCBS). The fundamental problem is that capital is eaten into when losses take place, such as defaults on loans. Defaults, in other words, reduce both the loans on the asset side of the balance sheet and own capital on the liability side of the balance sheet. If the defaults exceed the capital set aside by the bank, then own capital can become negative, rendering the bank insolvent. In a sense, this is not substantially different from a builders' merchant or a grocery store's balance sheet: if all the assets were sold, and all the debts paid, then equity is what remains, and if this is negative then the company is insolvent (note that equity is on the *liability* side of the company's balance sheet, it is an *asset* of the shareholders).

Before it gets to this level, the diminishment of capital could leave the bank failing to meet the requirements of the Basel capital adequacy ratios. This means that the bank would need to either shrink lending, sell assets or raise new capital through issuing more shares or restricting the distribution of dividends. Since retained earnings are accumulated as capital, profitable loans generate the capital necessary for maintaining capital adequacy ratios. It is worth noting that, in the short term, the interest paid by the customer to the bank actually reduces the money supply in the economy as it then becomes the retained profits of the bank; it is only if that bank pays it out to suppliers or employees or in dividends to shareholders that it re-enters the money supply of the economy.

At this point it is important to establish the difference between banks becoming illiquid and insolvent, since even popular financial commentators frequently get the two confused. A bank becomes illiquid when it cannot fulfil its immediate short-term liabilities, generally when too many customers seek to withdraw their savings at the same time. This is commonly known as a bank run and these days it might well happen digitally rather than with people queuing outside the bank, as happened in the infamous case of Northern Rock in September 2007. In contrast, a bank becomes insolvent when enough of its asset side of the balance sheet—its loans to customers (remember, customer deposits are a *liability*, not an asset)—default, meaning its capital goes below zero. Both illiquidity and insolvency can lead to systemic problems in the financial system with serious negative effects on the real economy. Thus, in the aftermath of the Great Financial Crisis, steps were taken by the Basel Committee to reduce both sets of risks.

To reduce the risk of illiquidity, the BCBS introduced the Liquidity Coverage Ratio (LCR); banks must hold an adequate reserve of high-quality liquid assets (HQLA) so that they can get through 30 days of significant liquidity stress. HQLA is divided into three levels. Level 1 HQLAs are highly liquid low risk assets, including cash, reserves held at the central bank and government bonds from countries with a good credit rating. Level 2A assets include other sovereign, supranational, and corporate bonds and are subject to a 15% haircut. Level 2B HQLAs include higher risk corporate bonds and even mortgage-backed securities; given the events of 2008 and some of the smaller liquidity shocks that occurred since then, it is questionable whether assets such as mortgage-backed securities will be liquid to any degree in the event of a crisis. As a further measure to reduce the risk of illiquidity, the BCBS also introduced the Net Stable Funding Ratio (NSFR) which requires banks to hold enough stable funding to cover their long-term assets, defined as more than one year, thereby reducing banks' reliance on short-term wholesale markets and limiting maturity transformation.

To reduce the risk of insolvency, the BCBS made a number of refinements to their previous capital adequacy requirements. The 2008 crisis revealed that even banks with sufficient HQLA had made loans to customers that were based on overly optimistic assessments of the likelihood of repayment. The Basel Capital Adequacy Ratios are calculated using higher risk weights for loans or investments judged by the supervisors to be more risky. If you have ever wondered why banks are more eager to loan money (create money) in the form of mortgages rather than loans to small businesses—which are often left to die on the vine—then this is an important factor. Loans to small businesses typically have a 100% risk weighting, whereas loans in the form of mortgages have a lower risk weighting, as low as 35% in the Basel III rules. This means that, for instance with a 10% capital adequacy, the capital required to support a £100,000 loan to a business is £10,000, whereas for a mortgage it is only £3,500. The consequence of this is that mortgages are generally more profitable than business loans. The Basel II rules used fixed risk weightings for mortgages, whereas the Basel III rules implemented a sliding scale, from 35 to 100%.

The Capital Adequacy Ratio (CAR) is the ratio of a bank's capital to its risk-weighted assets. The capital a bank holds is generally divided into Tier 1 and Tier 2 Capital. Tier 1 Capital is further divided into Common Equity Tier 1 (CET1), which comprises common stock, retained profits, other comprehensive income, qualifying minority interests and regulatory adjustments, and Additional Tier 1 Capital (AT1), which includes noncumulative, non-redeemable preferred stock and related surplus and qualifying minority interest as well as some other instruments, such as perpetual contingent convertible capital instruments. Tier 2 Capital is more permissive, and includes undisclosed reserves, revaluation reserves, general provisions and subordinated term debt, although more recently Tier 2 Capital also includes hybrid instruments, such as corporate bonds which can be converted to equity in the event of a default.

The new Basel capital rules also require banks to have buffers in addition to their capital requirements, specifically, (1) a capital conservation buffer (CCB) of 2.5% of Common Equity Tier 1 Capital must be maintained, and if a bank dips into this then it faces restrictions on dividend payouts, bonuses and share buybacks, (2) a countercyclical capital buffer, also consisting of Common Equity Tier 1 capital, designed to lean against the build-up phase of the credit cycle across jurisdictions by increasing in times of rapid credit growth; it is outlined by the BIS (2024) as "[the] countercyclical capital buffer is calculated as the weighted average of the buffers in effect in the jurisdictions to which banks have a credit exposure,"[6] (3) a global systemically important bank surcharge (G-SIB) consisting of 1–3.5% of risk-weighted assets, designed specifically to deal with the risk fallout from globally interconnected banks. Under the Basel III rules, banks must hold 4.5% of Common

---

[6] More information on buffers can be found here: https://www.bis.org/bcbs/ccyb/.

Equity Tier 1 capital, with an additional buffer of 1.5%, whereas Basel II only required 4%, with no buffers.

The differences between capital requirements and liquidity requirements are fundamental, being linked to the difference between insolvency and illiquidity. The former governs the amount of loans a bank can issue relative to the amount of capital it holds. The latter governs the amount of liquid assets held by the bank to ensure resilience in the event of a liquidity-constricting event, such as withdrawals of deposits by customers. In a moment, we will consider the degree to which these factors restrict money creation by banks, if at all. In the meantime, it is worth bearing in mind that banks are in a rather extraordinary position. When they make loans—when they create new money in the form of credit—assets are thereby created, but the retained profits from these loans also accumulate as capital, meaning a growth in the bank's balance sheet can be self-sustaining.

The Leverage Ratio (LR) was also introduced under the new Basel rules. The Leverage Ratio is the inverse of the Capital Adequacy Ratio, but calculated without using any risk weighting for the assets; for example, for leverage ratio purposes both mortgage loans and small business loans would have the same risk weighting. Following the 2008 financial crisis, there were a number of reports suggesting that the leverage ratio might be a more effective tool for regulation, at both a microprudential and macroprudential level, than the Capital Adequacy Ratio. While the leverage ratio has the benefit that banks cannot manipulate risk weightings for capital adequacy purposes, much of the commentary on leverage ratios was implicitly based around the idea that banks take money in the form of deposits and lend them out, which thereby increases "leverage," for instance the World Bank, in its 2009 report *The Leverage Ratio: A New Binding Limit on Banks*, noted that:

> Balance sheet leverage is the most visible and widely recognized form. Whenever an entity's assets exceed its equity base, its balance sheet is said to be leveraged. Banks typically engage in leverage by borrowing to acquire more assets, with the aim of increasing their return on equity. (D'Hulster, 2009, p. 1)

But of course in a system of endogenous money creation, when banks make loans they do not borrow and lend, but rather create new money; the interest payments from these loans created from nothing then feed into the bank's capital so the creation of new money/credit during a boom period can actually *reduce* the leverage ratio, at least until assets fall in value and customers start defaulting.

Some readers might ask how it is possible that a bank can become insolvent if it can create money? Remember that when a bank creates money it creates both an asset (a loan to be repaid) and a liability (a deposit/money that can be immediately withdrawn). This means that more money creation will not solve the underlying problem, at least not in the short term, of liabilities exceeding assets on the balance sheet.

## Open Market Operations, Quantitative Easing and Other Monetary Functions

In order to influence the overnight interest rate in the interbank lending market, central banks have traditionally used open market operations. Through open market operations, central banks do not need to lend directly to the banking sector in order to influence interest rates, but rather buy and sell securities, thereby injecting or withdrawing central bank reserves. If the central bank wants to increase the amount of central bank reserves in the system, thereby reducing the interest rate at which banks lend to each other, it usually buys securities (generally government bonds). If the central bank wants to pursue a "tighter" monetary policy, it sells securities in exchange for reserves, thereby withdrawing base money from the system. A number of central banks, including the Bank of England, have tended to use repo loans to achieve this objective rather than overtly buying and selling securities. This has a more targeted approach, but any method that enables the central bank to inject or withdraw reserves from the system would function.

Most of the time, the rate at which banks lend to each other (known as the London Interbank Offered Rate, or LIBOR, which is the average of what ten banks would charge to lend to each other and is calculated each day for ten currencies and fifteen maturities, ranging from one day to one year) is close to the central bank's policy rate, but sometimes, for instance in the event of a credit crunch, a larger delta forms. When this happens, the central bank will generally make additional loans of reserves to the banks, and in the event this does not mollify the situation then the next step will be outright asset purchases. Standing facilities allow a central bank to lend directly in the event of a crisis, generally, to use Walter Bagehot's term, at a penal rate of interest (usually one per cent above the market rate). Sir Tucker (2009) summarised Bagehot's dictum thus: "To avert panic, central banks should lend early and freely (i.e. without limit), to solvent firms, against good collateral, and at 'high rates.'".

Thus far, we have spoken about how banks create money when they make loans. But more recently we have seen another form of money creation, quantitative easing. Once interest rates reach the zero lower bound, the policy tools for central banks become more limited. Quantitative easing, like most other forms of exotic monetary policy, began in Japan several years before the rest of the world. The mainstream financial news often describes QE as putting money on the balance sheets of banks so they "lend it out" in the multiplier process described earlier. Hopefully you can see by now why this is false. Cynics describe it as "free money for banks," yet this is also false. In most countries, the primary objective of QE was to lower longer term interest rates and stimulate investment. If the central bank purchased assets from households or Non-Bank Financial Institutions (NBFIs) such as pension funds, the overall liquidity of their asset portfolio would also rise. It was hoped this latter development would induce a further portfolio rebalancing that would also stimulate investment (known as the *portfolio rebalancing effect*). Through this process, M1 is also increased, and this of course also makes it cheaper for the government to borrow money. The Bank of England created a special body to process these transactions, called the Asset Purchase Facility (APF). As well as the portfolio rebalancing effect, the *wealth effect*, whereby higher valuations of financial assets stimulate investment and spending, and the *liquidity effect*, whereby the extra reserves on the balance sheets of banks make them more confident in lending and thereby creating credit, were the other two objectives of QE in most countries.

The assets purchased under QE programs varied widely across central banks. In the UK, the Bank of England generally purchased low-risk government bonds, with only £20 billion of the £895 billion total consisting of corporate bonds. Other central banks, such as the Federal Reserve, have bought assets of various kinds, such as mortgage-backed securities, directly from banks, which is done through the creation of central bank reserves (M0). In addition to QE, in 2011 the Federal Reserve pursued "Operation Twist," which sold short-term bonds while buying long-term bonds to influence the term structure. This made it cheaper for the US government to borrow longer-term, but also influenced corporate credit markets, which they hoped would generate business investment. The European Central Bank has focussed more on purchasing corporate bonds in order to stimulate investment and economic growth; this is a more targeted approach, injecting money into certain sectors of the economy so that interest rates will fall, making it cheaper and easier for businesses to invest. We shall see in a later chapter whether this has indeed stimulated the economy—or induced chronic malinvestment and stagnation. The Bank of Japan has gone one step further and purchased equities, becoming the largest stock owner in Japan, with nearly half a trillion dollars of stocks; this may seem outlandish, but we must bear in mind that Japan has been the main trendsetter for other forms of exotic monetary policy for the last twenty-five years. When the next phase of the debt bubble bursts, this policy may well become mainstream in the rest of the world.

QE has also brought about changes to how central banks implement further policies. We saw earlier how scarce reserves were an integral mechanism through which central banks influenced interest rates, but with abundant reserves these mechanisms became less relevant. Claudio Borio pointed out three main changes to monetary policy which have taken place following the shift to abundant reserves after the Global Financial Crisis. First, the policy stance can no longer be communicated with only short-term (overnight) interest rates, so central banks' direct influence has extended well beyond just overnight interest rates. Second, the decoupling principle, whereby central banks restrained themselves from influencing market prices, has not only become attenuated but has also proven difficult to resurrect, as has been demonstrated when central banks have tried to reduce their balance sheet. Third, reserves are now more plentiful than are needed, and hence "As a result, they are no longer just a payments or settlement medium but also a store of value, competing with other assets in terms of remuneration" (Borio 2023, p. 3). There have therefore been profound shifts in the nature of monetary policy resulting from QE which are often unappreciated by financial commentators, and which may be more difficult to unwind than is often imagined.

It has been hypothesised that very low interest rates are likely to induce a liquidity trap, where individuals and institutions prefer to hold highly liquid assets such as cash rather than financial assets with a very low, or even negative, return. John Maynard Keynes, in his 1936 *General Theory*, explained it thus:

> There is the possibility...that, after the rate of interest has fallen to a certain level, liquidity-preference may become virtually absolute in the sense that almost everyone prefers cash to holding a debt which yields so low a rate of interest. In this event the monetary authority would have lost effective control over the rate of interest. But whilst this limiting case might become practically important in future, I know of no example of it hitherto.

A liquidity trap, however, is more complex than is often perceived by those who suggest that it can be remedied by central bank asset purchases. Being a consequence of low interest rates, it is generally the result of a system whereby interest rates are set artificially low by central banks rather than allowing interest rates to be set by the market like other prices. We shall see later how allowing interest rates to be set by the market would cure much of this underlying sickness, as financial assets would have a valuation which reflects their underlying value, rather than what central bankers believe is "optimal" for "stimulating" the economy—in 2019 Bloomberg reported that there were 14 *junk bonds* being traded with *negative nominal yields*, which is hardly likely to reflect their underlying risk (Benitez and Vossos, 2019). Another point related to this, which we shall also examine in more detail later in this book, is the extent to which zero (and negative) per cent interest rates bring about malinvestment, thereby reducing the number of investible opportunities as the underlying resources of the economy are misallocated from productive uses to speculative finance and other bubble activities. An underappreciated example would be the large percentage of physics Ph.D.s that go to work in speculative finance during credit bubbles rather than doing something productive. The concept of the liquidity trap, far from being another reason for QE, must therefore be tied into a more general understanding of capital-based macroeconomics, including how debt bubbles distort the capital structure across different sectors.

## Are There Limits to Money Creation, and How Does All This Money Creation Affect The "Boom-Bust" Cycle?

We have already considered some of the more common erroneous beliefs regarding constraints on bank money creation, in particular the belief that central bank reserves are a constraining factor, and the widely held belief that banks must have cash on their balance sheets in the form of customer deposits or high powered money to "lend out." In reality, the new money is created rather than lent out, and reserves are generally supplied on demand by the central bank when loans are made. It would be more correct to say that banks' decision to make loans and create money will be determined by the effect this has on the level of their anticipated profits adjusted for risk. Unfortunately, there can be strongly procyclical elements in these anticipations and in the amount of credit granted at different stages of the credit cycle. In short, absent the constraints imposed by needing to have deposits to lend out, our current monetary system is prone to damaging "boom-bust" cycles. As Mervyn King, then governor of the Bank of England, stated in a speech in New York in 2010: "Of all the many ways of organising banking, the worst is the one we have today" (King 2010, p. 18).

As we have seen, the Deutsche Bundesbank is one of the few central banks that has correctly described how banks create money; in their explanatory outline *How Money is Created* (2017a), they note how money is created by the bank merely making an accounting entry, including when the bank purchases assets (note that "book money" is another term for "inside money," "fountain pen money" or, as we shall see in a moment, "horizontal money"):

> In terms of volume, the majority of the money supply is made up of book money, which is created through transactions between banks and domestic customers. Sight deposits are an example of book money: sight deposits are created when a bank settles transactions with a customer, i.e. it grants a credit, say, or purchases an asset and credits the corresponding amount to the customer's bank account in return. This means that banks can create book money just by making an accounting entry... By the same token, excess central bank reserves are not a necessary precondition for a bank to grant credit (and thus create money).

The question then poses itself—are there any limitations to how much money can be created by banks? Even among those who have a good understanding of how the money creation process works, and the nature of reserves, liquidity and capital, there is much debate about the extent to which banks are restrained in their money creation. The Bank of England (McLeay et al. 2014, p. 17) posited that the constraints to bank money creation fall into three categories:

(1) The demand for credit limits how much banks can lend, specifically the market demand for new credit and the market and regulatory risk associated with more lending, for instance the credit ratings of potential borrowers.
(2) The behaviour of households and businesses; it may well be the case that when individuals receive new money they use it to pay off loans, thereby destroying money.
(3) Monetary policy: through interest rate manipulation, central banks influence the demand for credit, and therefore the likely amount of money creation. As the Bank of England points out, this has both a direct effect on the bank itself as interest rates influence its business, but also an indirect effect as interest rates influence the macroeconomy, which then of course influences the bank in question.

The three areas described by the Bank of England are related—monetary policy (3) influences the demand for credit (1), which also influences the general behaviour of those seeking credit (2), both of which often feed back into monetary policy. Nevertheless, these are not what one might call intrinsic constraints on money creation, but rather are all either on the demand side (including the credit-worthiness of the demand side) or in the case of monetary policy, designed to influence the demand side through the pricing of credit. For this reason, the term "horizontal money" has been used within much of the Post-Keynesian literature (for instance see Moore

1988) to describe the money created by banks when they make loans—if there are no constraints on money creation, then the supply curve of money is horizontal.

Yet the story is somewhat more complex than this. As we have seen, once regulatory factors, specifically the Basel Regulations, are taken into account, we must factor in not only the quantity of money created, but the nature of the sectors to which those loans are being made, the capital adequacy rules and the extent to which the bank may become reliant on its capital as a buffer. As the Basel rules place risk weightings on different types of loans, for instance, small business loans have a far stricter risk weighting than property loans, money is likely to be created in specific areas and the monetary spigot will be more likely to be opened in certain circumstances—such as during property bubbles. During such periods, while assets are increasing in value (and defaults are rare) capital accumulates on balance sheets, propelling another cycle of credit creation. In such circumstances, the limits to money creation by banks, both individual banks and the banking system as a whole, are nugatory. Remember, when consumers receive loans from banks, they *pull* new money into the economy. As the Bank of England explained in one of their papers on this topic:

> The supply of both reserves and currency (which together make up base money) is determined by banks' demand for reserves both for the settlement of payments and to meet demand for currency from their customers — demand that the central bank typically accommodates.
>
> This demand for base money is therefore more likely to be a consequence rather than a cause of banks making loans and creating broad money. This is because banks' decisions to extend credit are based on the availability of profitable lending opportunities at any given point in time. (McLeay et al. 2014, p. 21)

Sooner or later, the credit expansion will reach its apogee and following this there will be a bust and fall in asset values; this is usually following a rise in the policy rate pursued by the central bank, thereby bringing about a slowing or even a contraction in the money supply. As asset values are falling, not only does money creation become limited, but indeed can in some cases be smothered as the capital on balance sheets shrinks to the point where banks cannot lend more, and in some cases must dispose of assets or risk failure. When this happens across the banking system, a negative feedback loop can easily develop. Newton's Third Law states that for every action (force) in nature there is an equal and opposite reaction; something similar might be said for booms resulting from credit expansions.

The collapse when the credit expansion finally falters will therefore be at least the magnitude of the credit expansion, but is often quite a lot worse as during the boom period malinvestment accumulates as resources in the economy are allocated towards asset bubble sectors and must be redistributed back to productive uses. Additionally, when credit bubbles form there is a broader problem related to the gap between consumption and productive investment that develops. Easy money is more likely to stimulate consumption than productive investment; consequently, debts rise without any offsetting increase in productive assets to service them. This is often viewed as "stimulating" the economy as GDP increases, but without an increase in the productive capacity of the capital structure there will be a debt overhang brought about by over-consumption. In the case of malinvestments brought about by the credit expansion, there are indeed assets remaining following the crash but they are not productive as they are the result of credit bubble activities, such as the monstrous amount of housing overproduction in China in recent years and the capital required for the "economic growth" and millions of "jobs created" as a result.

The question of to what extent banks are restrained in their money creation is therefore dependent on what stage in the cycle they are at—during the boom period, there are little to no constraints, while during the bust period, the falling asset prices and consequent defaults combined with regulatory structures place significant constraints on money creation. As we shall see throughout this book, once the inevitable credit crunch happens, the central bank then has a choice between allowing the liquidation of malinvestments or cutting interest rates further and thereby generating another cycle of credit creation. During the 2008 crisis, the culmination of several years of artificially low interest rates, sudden falling asset prices brought about a severe contraction in the credit creation capacity of banks around the world.

The late Minsky (1986) posited that there are three phases which constitute the development of a credit bubble: hedge finance, speculative finance and ponzi finance. In the early stages, hedge finance, people borrow amounts such that they can pay back both the principal and the interest. This economy has low levels of credit and asset prices are low to moderate. As more credit is created over time, the economy gets into a feedback loop and moves into the phase of speculative finance; as people increasingly take loans on which they can only afford to pay the interest but not the principal, they become reliant on asset prices increasing in order to service the loan. Over centuries, this has taken place with respect to stock bubbles, housing bubbles and even in quite obscure areas such as tulips, art and classic cars—classic car valuations grew considerably during the period of QE, so speculators were more likely to take loans on which they could only pay the interest in the hopes that the asset would go up enough to pay off the principal in the future.[7]

In the final phase of the credit bubble, ponzi finance, borrowers increasingly can pay neither the principal nor the interest on the loan. This may sound fanciful, but it indeed happens; in the build-up to the 2007/2008 Global Financial Crisis, people were taking large mortgages, often more than 100% of the value of a house, on which they could not even afford to pay the interest unless the value of the house kept going up. Through "negative amortisation" mortgages, the monthly payment to the bank is *less than just the interest on the loan*, thereby formalising the idea that future payments are reliant on perpetually increasing asset valuations. In 2007, CEO of Citigroup Chuck Prince made the following (Reuters (reporting by Maria Aspan), 2010), now infamous, quip: "As long as the music is playing, you've got to get up and dance. We're still dancing" (a little over a year later, Citigroup would receive the largest TARP bailout of any US bank.)[8] This era of ponzi finance of course had its Minsky Moment in 2008, as the credit bubble house of cards came crashing down. It is also worth noting that, as will be examined in more detail later, this multi-trillion

---

[7] For an excellent overview, see Kindleberger's (1978) classic on the nature of financial crises from several centuries. Also see Schularick and Taylor (2012).

[8] See a 2010 Reuters piece on this here: https://www.reuters.com/article/idUSN08198108/.

dollar credit expansion fuelling the housing bubble took place at a time of historically low saving rates—a case of "endogenously created money" getting out of control if ever there was one. In the coming chapters, we shall examine evidence that over the last forty years we have seen a series of Minsky-esque credit expansions, each one larger than the previous as central banks set lower and lower interest rates.

## The Shadow Banking System

One area we have not mentioned thus far is the so-called "shadow banking system." Mehrling (2010) has called the 2008 crisis a run on the shadow banking system, and indeed a large part of the crisis was caused by a sudden reversal in the demand for securitised mortgages, largely processed by the shadow banking system in the previous years. Shadow banking has not yet been given a universally clear definition; the Financial Stability Board (FSB) defined it broadly as "credit intermediation involving entities and activities outside the regular banking system," (2011) while Bernanke (2013), former Chairman of the Federal Reserve, described it as follows:

> Shadow banking, as usually defined, comprises a diverse set of institutions and markets that, collectively, carry out traditional banking functions—but do so outside, or in ways only loosely linked to, the traditional system of regulated depository institutions. Examples of important components of the shadow banking system include securitization vehicles, asset-backed commercial paper [ABCP] conduits, money market funds, markets for repurchase agreements, investment banks, and mortgage companies.[9]

When looking at money market funds and other such institutions it is clear that they are not creating M1 in the way that commercial banks do. Shadow banks must attract funds (existing M1), but may then carry out all the other functions of banks. In so doing, they take on credit risk, liquidity risk, and duration risk and, as a result, they can also create instability, but are less likely to do so because they must price their liabilities and assets more carefully in the absence of the implicit subsidies given to banks (the right to create M1 and other safety nets). Proposals to extend the current banking safety nets to the shadow banking system would likely bring about some of the moral hazard problems we see in traditional commercial banking, albeit without the capability to create M1.

One of the problems with much of the analysis of the risks pertaining to shadow banking is its conflation with "traditional banking functions," which, as we have seen, are of course very different from what textbooks describe and include creating 97% of all the money circulating in the economy *without the need for prior deposits or reserves.* The IMF, in their outline of shadow banking, conflated shadow banking activities with the borrowing and lending that the *textbooks* teach is the role of banking:

> Commercial banks engage in maturity transformation when they use deposits, which are normally short term, to fund loans that are longer term. Shadow banks do something similar.

---

[9] Bernanke (2013).

They raise (that is, mostly borrow) short-term funds in the money markets and use those funds to buy assets with longer-term maturities.[10]

The IMF also cited the Financial Stability Board definition of shadow banking, which similarly uses an understanding of traditional banking based around the intermediation of savings and loans:

> The Financial Stability Board (FSB), an organization of financial and supervisory authorities from major economies and international financial institutions, developed a broader definition of shadow banks that includes all entities outside the regulated banking system that perform the core banking function, credit intermediation (that is, taking money from savers and lending it to borrowers).

In reality, much of what happens in these credit markets is if anything less prone to volatility than commercial banks as the money circulating is not constantly being created and destroyed when loans are made and paid off, but rather when loans are paid off that money is then available to be lent out again. Indeed, there are lessons to be learned from the shadow banking system. Peer-to-peer lending for instance, which could be regarded as part of the shadow banking system, has provided small businesses with credit that they could not get from banks and facilitates intermediation rather than money creation. Similarly, money market funds engage in intermediation and maturity transformation in a way comparable to how many *believe* (and have been taught by textbooks) commercial banks do. Interest rates in such markets are more likely to reflect genuine underlying risk and other market factors rather than the centrally planned interest rates that result from central banking—in a peer-to-peer lending market, would you lend someone money at zero per cent interest rates, or even negative interest rates? More appropriate terms for what we call shadow banking would be "non-bank credit markets" or "market-based finance" (as Tony James, the President of Blackstone, suggested it should be called) or something similar. (James, 2014) Nevertheless, even without the ability to create M1, some shadow banks may contribute to debt bubbles indirectly; when commercial banks make loans, for instance mortgages, one of the ways they can quickly get the loans off their balance sheets is to securitise them and sell them on. This generally happens through the shadow banking system. The shadow banking sector, rather than creating M1 in the way that commercial banks do, may therefore act as an enzyme for the credit-creation activities within commercial banking and thereby facilitate more endogenous money creation that would have occurred otherwise. It is also worth bearing in mind, however, that were we to move to a financial system where commercial banks did not have the right to create money in the way they currently do, the shadow banking system, or at least parts of it, would provide some examples for how this might occur, whereby there is genuine intermediation and maturity transformation such that the savings of one person becomes credit for others.

---

[10] This can be found here: https://www.imf.org/en/Publications/fandd/issues/Series/Back-to-Basics/Shadow-Banks.

## A Summary of the Money Creation System

The most important point to get to grips with is that the majority of economics textbooks have the money creation system wrong, and in a sense they have it backwards. The textbooks teach that central banks create the base for a pyramid of credit, which is actualised through the multiplier model whereby banks lend out the money they have on deposit which is in turn saved and lent out, with a certain percentage being kept in reserve each time. In reality, banks create new money when they make loans, both sides of the balance sheet are expanded. Additionally, even among those who understand that banks create new money when they make loans, many mistakenly believe that banks are "reserve constrained." In reality, central banks create whatever reserves are necessary to accommodate the credit expansion initiated by the commercial banks. The consequences of this for the economy can be profound; with the most relevant constraints to bank money creation on the demand side, this can lead to feedback loops in which people borrow money to invest in assets, often housing, and then as the houses go up in value this in turn generates a new cycle of credit expansion followed by higher prices. As we shall see throughout this book, however, it is not just the money creation process which does this, but rather money creation by commercial banks combined with the setting of artificially low interest rates by central banks.

## References

Acharya V, Rahul C, Raghuram R, Rajan, Steffen S (2023) Liquidity dependence and the waxing and waning of central bank balance sheets. NBER working paper 31050

Banco de España. How is money created. https://www.bde.es/wbe/en/areas-actuacion/politica-monetaria/preguntas-frecuentes/definicion-funciones-del-dinero/como-se-crea-el-dinero.html. Accessed 21st May 2024

Bank for International Settlements (2024). Countercyclical capital buffer (CCyB). BIS, Basel https://www.bis.org/bcbs/ccyb/. Accessed 21st May 2024

Benes J, Kumhof M (2012) The Chicago plan revisited. IMF working paper No. 12/202

Benitez L, Vossos T (2019) Sub-zero yields start taking hold in Europe's junk-bond market: Bloomberg

Bernanke B (2013) The crisis as a classic financial panic. In: At the fourteenth Jacques Polak annual research conference. Board of Governors of the Federal Reserve System, Washington, D.C.

Borio C (2023) Getting up from the floor: remarks at the Workshop "Beyond unconventional policy: Implications for central banks' operational frameworks". Netherlands Bank, Amsterdam, 10 March 2023

D'Hulster K (2009) The leverage ratio: a new binding limit on banks. The World Bank, Washington DC

Deutsche Bundesbank (2017a). How money is created. Deutsche Bundesbank, Frankfurt. https://www.bundesbank.de/en/tasks/topics/how-money-is-created-667392. Accessed 21st May 2024

Deutsche Bundesbank (2017b) The role of banks, non-banks and the central bank in the money creation process. Deutsche Bundesbank, Monthly Report, April 2017

Financial Stability Board (2011) Shadow banking: scoping the issues. FSB, Basel

Gobat J Banks: at the heart of the matter: international monetary fund. https://www.imf.org/en/Publications/fandd/issues/Series/Back-to-Basics/Banks. Accessed 21st May 2024

Hardwick P, Langmead J, Khan B (1999) An introduction to modern economics, 5th edn. Pearson Education, Essex

Harvey J, Jowsey E (2007) Modern economics, 8th edn. New York, Palgrave MacMillan

Heffernan S (1996) Modern banking in theory and practice. Wiley, Chichester

James T (2014) Shedding some light on shadow banking. Wall Street J, New York

Jordan T (2018) How money is created by the central bank and the banking system: Swiss National Bank, Zurich, 2018 (speech given in German)

Keynes JM (1936) The general theory of employment, interest and money, 2007 edn. Palgrave Macmillan, United Kingdom

Kindleberger C (1978) Manias, panics, and crashes: a history of financial crises, 5th edn. Wiley (October 4, 2005)

King M (2010) Banking: from Bagehot to Basel, and back again. The Second Bagehot Lecture, Buttonwood Gathering, New York City, Bank of England, London

Kodres L Shadow banks: out of the eyes of the regulators. International Monetary Fund. https://www.imf.org/en/Publications/fandd/issues/Series/Back-to-Basics/Shadow-Banks. Accessed 21st May 2024

Krugman P (2012) Banking mysticism, continued. New York Times, New York. https://archive.nytimes.com/krugman.blogs.nytimes.com/2012/03/30/banking-mysticism-continued/. Accessed May 21st 2024

Machlup F (1970) Euro-dollar creation: a mystery story. Banca Nazionale del Lavoro Quarterly Review 94:219–260

Mankiw G, Taylor M (2014). Economics, 3rd edn. Andrew Ashwin, Cengage Learning EMEA

McLeay M, Radia A, Thomas R (2014) Money creation in the modern economy. In: Bank of England quarterly bulletin, vol 54, no 1, pp 14–27

Mehrling P (2010) The new lombard street: how the fed became the dealer of last resort. Princeton University Press

Miller R, VanHoose D (1993) Modern money and banking, international editions, 3rd edn. McGraw-Hill, New York

Minsky H (2008) [1st Pub. 1986] Stabilizing an unstable economy. McGraw-Hill Professional, New York

Moore B (1988) Horizontalists and verticalists: the macroeconomics of credit money. Cambridge University Press

Reuters (reporting by Maria Aspan) (2010) Ex-Citi CEO defends "dancing" quote to U.S. panel. Reuters https://www.reuters.com/article/idUSN08198108/. Accessed 21 May 2024

Samuelson P, Nordhaus W (1995) Economics. McGraw-Hill, New York

Stiglitz J (1997) Economics, 2nd edn. W.W. Norton, New York

Schularick M, Taylor A (2012) Credit booms gone bust: monetary policy, leverage cycles, and financial crises, 1870–2008. National Bureau of Economic Research, Cambridge, Massachusetts

Tucker P (2009) The repertoire of official sector interventions in the financial system: last resort lending, market-making, and capital (90 KB PDF). In: Remarks at the Bank of Japan 2009 international conference on the financial system and monetary policy implementation, Bank of Japan, Tokyo, May 27–28, p 5

Werner R (2014) Can banks individually create money out of nothing?—The theories and the empirical evidence. Int Rev Financ Anal 26(2014):1–19

# Business Cycles, Debt Bubbles and the Monetary System

**Max Rangeley, Roger Koppl, and Harry Richer**

## Prices and Interest Rates in a Market Economy

Government price setting never works the way politicians promise. Most economists would agree. But not all economists apply that lesson to interest rates, which are central to the good functioning of markets. The Austrian school of economics is an exception. They recognise that the general theory of price controls applies no less to interest rates than to the prices of tomatoes or pillowcases. Gasoline prices give us a real-world example of how price controls go wrong. When we turn from gasoline prices to interest rates, we will see that the lessons learned apply only too well.

During the 1973 oil crisis, price controls gave us long lines at the gas pumps in Europe and North America. The price of gasoline was not allowed to rise with the price of oil. It was artificially low, creating an excess demand. Queuing for gasoline is a vivid example of the "non-price rationing" caused by price ceilings. By artificially reducing the price of gasoline, the government simultaneously *encouraged* efforts to buy and *discouraged* efforts to sell. No wonder we had gas lines. If you add in the time cost of all that waiting, a litre of gasoline costs you *more* than the price at which supply and demand meet. Economists understand why gasoline price controls go wrong. But the governments they advise rarely get the message. They flout the logic of supply and demand even when they claim to be pro-market. In the oil crisis, therefore, governments did not go to the root cause of shortages—price controls. Instead, they cast about for additional non-market measures to further restrict what

M. Rangeley (✉)
The Cobden Centre, 61 Pembroke St, Plymouth PL1 4JS, UK
e-mail: maxrangeley@gmail.com; max@cobdencentre.org

R. Koppl
Syracuse University, 721 University Avenue, Syracuse, NY 13244, USA
e-mail: rkoppl@syr.edu

H. Richer
73 Penshurst Gardens, Edgware, London HA8 9TT, UK

**Fig. 1** A German couple improvised a horse-drawn vehicle during the oil crisis of 1973 (Keystone Pictures USA 1973a)

you could do with gasoline. Governments usually attempt to fix the problems created by one set of restrictions, such as what prices you can charge, by piling on yet more restrictions, such as what days you can drive. In the oil crisis, governments answered queuing with various ad hoc prohibitions on vehicle use. Unable to drive, people were driven to seek alternative means of transportation, as Figs. 1 and 2 illustrate. It was a mess.

Resort to price controls is a recurring theme in history from at least the time of Hammurabi about 4,000 years ago. In 301 CE, The Roman emperor Diocletian resorted to price controls, and his contemporary, the Roman thinker Lactantius let him have it (Lactantius 1965). The emperor, Lactantius explains, "attempted to fix by law the price of saleable goods. Then, on account of scarcity and the low grade of articles, much blood was spilled; and because of fear nothing purchasable appeared. Therefore, expensiveness raged much worse." It was a mess, *and* "expensiveness raged much worse" despite a law against it. It was the same with gas prices 1,672 years later. If governments are playing the same games with interest rates, perhaps we should not be surprised if we get a colossal mess complete with lots of raging expensiveness.

Why don't more economists understand that governments create a mess when they interfere with interest rates just as they create a mess when they interfere with other prices? Part of the answer is probably to be found in the difference between microeconomics and macroeconomics. In college textbooks on economics, the manipulation

**Fig. 2** Unable to drive in Amsterdam on a "Car-Free Sunday," these four men decided to use a more traditional mode of transportation (Keystone Pictures USA 1973b)

of interest rates is usually covered in books on macroeconomics, while lessons on the dangers of price controls are covered in the books on microeconomics. Textbooks on microeconomics usually show maximum prices such as rent control tend to create an excess demand while minimum prices such as minimum wages tend to create an excess supply. Usually, the textbook will elaborate on the evils thereby created. Rent controls make it easier for landlords to neglect maintenance, for example. Another important example concerns who suffers most from the evils of price controls. Both minimum wages and rent control give powerful people, employers and landlords, greater freedom to act on any false bigotries they may have, including racial prejudice. The excess supply of labour created by a minimum wage creates unemployment including, for some unlucky souls, chronic unemployment. If some employers are bigots, such unemployment will be greater for unfavored groups such as, in many cases, poor black persons. The excess demand for housing created by rent controls drives some people to live elsewhere, perhaps undertaking a lengthy commute to work. Others may have to live in overcrowded units. Some may end up homeless. And so on. If some landlords are bigots, such housing troubles will be greater for unfavored groups such as, in many cases, poor black persons. Price controls create a mess, and the mess expands. *Microeconomics* textbooks explain why, but none of this inexorable logic makes its way into the typical *macroeconomics* textbook.

Central banks fix short-term interest rates and influence long-term interest rates. Such price fixing creates a mess by distorting the structure of production. Too much of some things get made, too little of others. Importantly, the induced pattern of produce cannot be sustained and calamity looms. Friedrich von Hayek won the Nobel Prize in Economics in 1974 in part for his "pioneering work in the theory of money and economic fluctuations." The cited "economic fluctuations" are also called the "business cycle," which just means the overall ups and downs in output and employment over time. Booms are the ups and recessions, depressions, and panics are the downs. The Great Recession that began in 2007 was a doozy, but not as bad as the Great Depression of the 1930s. Business cycles are bad mostly because of unemployment, although they produce other evils as well. Hayek's pioneering work on business cycles showed what goes wrong when governments, through their monetary authorities, push interest rates below their market-determined values. The "interest-rate mechanism" is the key to his "Austrian business cycle theory" (ABCT), which is discussed below.

Austrian business cycle theory emerged from the Austrian School of economics, which was founded by Carl Menger with his 1871 book, Principles of Economics (*Grundsätze der Volkswirtschaftslehre*). Menger was one of the three "marginalist revolutionaries" of the 1870s. The other two were Leon Walras and William Stanley Jevons. Menger taught at the University of Vienna. Thus, the school he founded came to be known as the "Austrian school." Like the other marginalists, Menger explained value by "marginal utility" rather than costs of production. Drinking clean water is more important to you than owning a beautiful diamond. And yet you can often drink clean water for free, whereas a nice diamond is costly. This logic led Adam Smith to deny that usefulness, "utility," has much to do with market value. The marginalists pointed out that one extra cup of water is less useful than one more diamond. The *marginal* utility of water is less than the *marginal* utility of diamonds, which explains the difference in their market values.

Menger stood out from the other two marginalists because of his emphasis on the evaluating mind. Far more than Jevons or Walras, he emphasised that the marginal utility of something is a judgement made by an evaluating mind. *Value* emerges from an act of *evaluation*. This emphasis on the evaluating mind is the core of Austrian "subjectivism." Your theoretical explanations must clarify who does what. And what they do must be sensible and understandable. Real people would understand the people in your model because they would act the same way in such circumstances. Menger's "subjectivist" economic theory was developed by Eugen von Böhm-Bawerk and Friedrich von Wieser. Their students, Ludwig von Mises and F. A. Hayek, combined Austrian economics with insights from the Swedish economist Knut Wicksell to produce what is now known as Austrian business cycle theory.

Hayek and Keynes first met at the end of a meeting of the London and Cambridge Economic Service in 1928. Hayek recalled that they quickly were into a long heated debate about the effects of changes in the interest rate (Wapshott 2011). Lionel Robbins, the Chair of Political Economy at the London School of Economics, invited Hayek to deliver a series of lectures on the business cycle in January 1931. Robbins brought in Hayek specifically to counter the dominance of the Cambridge School, the home of the economics of Keynes and Marshall. Hayek was invited to the LSE specifically to take down the ideas of Keynes. These lectures later appeared as *Prices and Production*. They were a hit and he joined the university. His 1931 series of lectures could be considered the moment the Austrian School of economics seriously began its entry into academic economic thought in Britain.

The young Hayek was now the *wunderkind* of monetary theory in the UK. In the same year, Hayek reviewed J. M. Keynes's 1931 book, *A Treatise on Money*, which espoused an underconsumption theory of the business cycle. Hayek had carefully studied and rejected the earlier underconsumption theory of William Trufant Foster and Waddill Catchings. Looking back years later, Hayek said, "I had spent a great deal of time and was absolutely ready to criticise any under-consumption theory. When Keynes then produced his, I pounced upon him completely equipped" (Hayek 1994, pp. 76–77). Hayek attacked Keynes's work as so technical and complicated that it was completely unintelligible to most, and focused his substantive criticisms on Keynes's failure to take into account Austrian School views of capital theory. The two engaged in tussles over the work, but it was Hayek who won out.

This was a devastating attack against Keynesian economics. Keynes was eventually forced to abandon the work he espoused on *The Treatise* and to progress with something new. At the same time, Keynes fell out of favour in the corridors of power in Britain as Ramsey MacDonald's new National Government was dominated by Conservative and Liberal MPs who did not take kindly to his ideas (Wapshott 2011). Keynes worked on his ideas and produced his famous 1936 book, *The General Theory of Employment, Interest, and Money*, which launched "macroeconomics" into the world. It was a bigger hit than Hayek's earlier *Prices and Production*, and Keynesian macroeconomics won the battle for dominance against Austrian business cycle theory.

Keynes was hard to understand, and the gist of his message is debated to this day. As if to illustrate the interpretive difficulties, one early Keynesian mused, "[T]here were moments when we had some trouble in getting Maynard to see what the point of his revolution really was" (Robinson 1974, p. 7). However we interpret the turgid original, many economists and policymakers reduced Keynes' message to a simple and gratifying maxim: Government spending saves the day. Hayek's rival theory had its "difficulties" too, as he has admitted (Hayek 1994, p. 78), and they were not resolved at the time. These difficulties were not offset by any gratifying maxims one might impute to the theory. In the depths of the Great Depression, most economists, especially most *young* economists, found the general prescription for *laissez faire* implausible and unattractive. Thus, the difficulties with Hayek's theory caused acolytes to fall away, one after another. Nicolas Kaldor, for example, was at first drawn to Hayek, only to be drawn away by Keynes. Hayek's sophisticated "new theory of industrial fluctuations," Kaldor (1942, p. 359) explained, made England's home-grown theories seem "facile and superficial" by comparison. "There were admitted gaps," however, and "when one attempted to fill these gaps, they became larger, instead of smaller and new and unsuspected gaps appeared—until one was driven to the conclusion that the basic hypothesis of the theory… must be wrong" (Kaldor 1942, p. 359).

After the 1930s Keynesian macroeconomics was triumphant, and the Austrian School was in retreat. Austrian Business Cycle Theory was mostly abandoned and fell into relative obscurity. The 1970s saw a revival of the Austrian School, in part because of Hayek's receipt of the Nobel Prize. It is still a minority school today, and university courses in Austrian economics are uncommon. But we are far from the near total eclipse of earlier years. Recently, the Austrian Business Cycle Theory has been catapulted back into prominence by the 2008 Global Financial Crisis. The crisis fit the pattern of the Austrian theory so well that many non-Austrian economists saw it and said so. The world may finally be ready to learn the "Austrian" lesson that "stimulating" the economy distorts output and makes things worse overall.

## Understanding Hayek-Mises Business Cycle Theory

The gist of the Austrian story can be quickly stated. Money growth creates credit expansion thereby driving interest rates below the levels determined by the free interplay of supply and demand. The low rates discourage saving, thus boosting consumption spending. These same low rates make business borrowing easier, thus boosting investment spending. The extra spending produces a boom. The different pieces of the economy no longer fit together because you can't have investment without saving. At some point, therefore, the boom will be followed by a bust. In this boom-bust cycle, the boom is a bubble, and its bursting is the bust. The boom produces sectoral shifts in production which are reversed in the bust. This back and forth sloshing of production is wasteful and, in the bust phase, painful. Attempts to "stimulate" the economy with expansionary monetary policy are futile and destructive. Better to let supply and demand do their work unmolested. The turn from boom to bust may be brought on by "real" or "monetary" factors as explained below. In either event, it is inevitable. Governments may act to limit the painful reallocation of resources characterising the bust. But if they do, they make the problem worse and only postpone the inevitable reckoning, which gets more costly and calamitous with each postponement. Unfortunately, governments have been growing ever more reckless in their efforts to hold off the day of reckoning. The tragic consequence is that we have inflated the largest bubble in history and are therefore poised for economic calamity.

As Ludwig von Mises put it:

> True, governments can reduce the rate of interest in the short run. They can issue additional paper money. They can open the way to credit expansion by the banks. They can thus create an artificial boom and the appearance of prosperity. But such a boom is bound to collapse sooner or later and to bring about a depression (Mises 1944, p. 251)

At the core of the analysis of debt bubbles which we shall shortly embark on in this book is the idea that interest rates are a pricing mechanism, and when prices are set by a bureaucratic authority, whether this be the price of wheat, fuel, consumer goods or interest rates, it causes distortions to the economy. In a free market, interest rates would reflect the pool of available savings in the economy relative to the demand for credit. This is, therefore, not dissimilar to coffee or other goods—when the demand goes up relative to supply, the price goes up. So in an economy with free market interest rates, if there is a sudden demand for credit, this pushes up interest rates, thereby disincentivising borrowing and incentivising saving and bringing the market back to equilibrium. This is the market's natural mechanism for preventing debt bubbles, in the same way that rises in the price of coffee after a bad harvest actually rectify the problem by incentivising more production and innovation while disincentivising too much consumption while there is a shortage. On the other hand, if people are saving more, this provides a larger pool of savings, which brings down interest rates.

An additional function of interest rates is that of coordinating time preferences. In our previous scenario, if a lot of people are saving, this expands the pool of available savings, bringing down the interest rate—as well as signalling the current demand and supply of credit, this also signals to the economy that time preferences have become extended. People are saving for future time periods and, concomitantly, the lower interest rates allow companies to borrow at a cheaper rate and invest on a longer time horizon. Consequently, as those investments come to fruition in future time periods, and new products are brought to market, the consumers have savings available.

When a government responds to a shortage in, for instance, coffee, by setting the price artificially low, it removes the adaptive mechanisms brought about by higher prices, and instead disincentivizes further production, as the good is no longer as profitable, and incentivises even more consumption through lower prices, even though there is a shortage—the false price signals give the *illusion of abundance*. When central banks set interest rates artificially low the effect is similar; not only does this cause excess borrowing relative to the amount of savings in the economy, but these artificially set interest rates also send false price signals to the economy with respect to time preferences—low interest rates indicate that consumers are deferring consumption to future time periods and therefore that there is a high level of savings. These *ersatz* low interest rates set artificially by central banks, however, actually disincentivise saving, so companies take on more debt and invest on a longer time horizon, but in those future time periods there will be no savings available for consumers to spend.

The increase in the supply of credit is "artificial" because it is created by nothing more substantial than printing money, nothing more substantial than a few government-induced bookkeeping entries. The increase in the supply of credit does not reflect any corresponding increase in saving. No one is postponing yet more present consumption to enable yet more investment and a correspondingly increased future consumption. On the contrary, lower interest rates tell consumers to enjoy more present consumption. Saving now gives you a smaller boost to future consumption, making it less reasonable to abstain today for the sake of tomorrow. Eat, drink, and be merry, for tomorrow we'll have about the same consumption anyway. Thus, the increase in credit is "artificial." Call the supply of credit as it would be without the monetary expansion of the "underlying" supply of credit. The central bank's expansionary policy has driven the interest rate below the level that equates the demand for credit with the underlying supply of credit. In this sense, there is an excess demand for credit, just as there was an excess demand for gasoline during the 1973 oil crisis. The monetary injection drives interest rates below their "market equilibrium" levels. In other works, it drives interest rates below the level that would have been reached by the interaction of unmolested supply of credit with unmolested demand for credit. Trouble is brewing.

When central banks attempt to stimulate the economy with expansionary monetary policy, consumers get the message to indulge in present consumption and let tomorrow take care of itself. Investors are getting the message to draw resources away for present consumption to boost what's available tomorrow. The pieces of the economy no longer fit together. More precisely, the plans of the different actors in the economy are no longer consistent. Admittedly, they are never perfectly consistent. The economist's model of overall economy-wide equilibrium is an "imaginary construction" and not, somehow, a photograph of reality. But when supply and demand are mostly unmolested, the system does tend to hammer out a rough and ready harmony across decision-makers. The adjustments decision-makers will have to make are distributed across different sectors and point in different directions. One farmer has planted too much wheat because they underestimated the price of corn. Another farmer has planted too little wheat because they overestimated the price of barley. The market doesn't have room for all the competitors working on new technologies for making, say, silicon wafers; a shakeout is coming. And so on. Sure. But these inconsistencies across market plans do not add up to a systemwide distortion. How different the situation is when central banks "stimulate" the economy by creating money!

We saw that the low interest rates brought on by the central bank's monetary expansion give investment a boost. But not every productive sector gets the same boost. The relatively interest-sensitive sectors expand during the boom more than the relatively interest-insensitive sectors. The more interest sensitive a sector is, the greater will be the flow of resources into it during the boom. The less interest sensitive a sector is, the smaller will be the flow of resources into it during the boom. When the bubble bursts, the relatively interest-sensitive sectors will contract more than the relatively interest-insensitive sectors. The more interest sensitive a sector is, the greater will be the reflux of resources flowing back out of it during the bust. The less interest sensitive a sector is, the smaller will be the reflux of resources flowing back out of it during the bust. The movement of resources first into and then out of relatively interest-sensitive sectors of the economy is the painful "sloshing" of resources mentioned above.

The bust and its reflux of resources are inevitable. There will be an "upper turning point" at which boom turns to bust. The turn is inevitable because, as we have seen, the different plans in the economy no longer mesh. But the trigger could be either business failures, which are "real factors" or a reduction of the money supply relative to trend, which is a "monetary factor." As Koppl has noted elsewhere, "In practice, the real and monetary factors go together, and it can be hard to decide which came first in a given bust" (Koppl 2014, p. 33). It helps keep our thinking straight, however, if we consider them separately when working out the Austrian Business Cycle Theory.

Real factors alone would cause a bust. As we have seen, the low interest rates of the boom discourage saving while encouraging investment. Decision-makers in the economy are trying to purchase more consumption goods and more investment goods. Households may be trying to buy more kitchen tables made of wood, while investors are trying to buy more lumber for making, say, houses. The resulting increase in the prices of wood products, including lumber will put financial strain on table makers and house builders. If house builders are in the more interest-sensitive sector, then they will have expanded more during the boom. They will be put in greater distress by the increase in lumber prices, and some of them will fail. The bust has come. The failures in the housing sector will put construction workers out of work. Their demand for automobiles and kitchen tables will fall, precipitating business failures among automakers and furniture makers and thrusting many woodworkers and auto workers into unemployment. And so on. For a period, there will be round after round of business failures and corresponding increases in the ranks of the unemployed. "The rot snowballs," as Leland Yeager once put it (1983, p. 306). Once the bust is on, monetary factors will kick in. The bust drives businesses to ruin, especially in the more interest-sensitive sectors, which prevents them from repaying their boomtime loans. Increased loan default rates will drive up bank reserve ratios, thus causing a contraction of the money supply, at least relative to the trends prevailing before the bust.

Monetary factors alone would cause a bust. The increase in the supply of credit will be reversed and precipitate a bust if the monetary authorities do not continue to expand the money supply briskly enough to prevent such reversal. If the supply of credit falls back, then interest rates will bounce back. In this scenario, it is the increased interest rates and not the increase in input prices that drives businesses to ruin. Some businesses will fail because they are no longer able to obtain cheap credit. Such failures will be concentrated in the interest-sensitive sectors. And we will get the same snowballing rot just described.

It can be hard for the monetary authorities to keep the money supply growing enough to prevent a fallback in the supply of credit. At some point, money growth causes inflation. The boomtime expansion of output may hold off inflation for a time. Sooner or later, however, the general price level will rise. Yet to prevent a decline in the artificially boosted supply of credit, the central bank must expand the money supply at an ever higher pace and tolerate ever higher rates of price inflation. When the central bank finally gives up the fight, the supply of credit will fall back. At that point, the postponed bust will finally arrive. Should the central bank never give in, but always choose yet higher rates of money growth the economy will enter hyperinflation and the currency will eventually collapse altogether. If currency collapse is to be avoided, then at some point the money supply must fall relative to its ever-accelerating trend. No way out.

Once the Rubicon of monetary expansion has been crossed, there will be no escape from the subsequent bust. The immediate precipitating cause of the bust might be some real factor or set of real factors. It might be monetary contraction relative to trend. But the bust will come sooner and less painfully or later and more painfully.

## The Formation of the Super Bubble

Austrian Business Cycle Theory shows that danger lurks when central banks act to artificially suppress interest rates. Unfortunately, such state suppression of supply and demand has been practised for over thirty years in the UK, US, Europe, Australia and other parts of the developed world. Interest rates have been forced further and further down. Since the 1980s recessions have been answered with a new round of monetary expansion meant to hold off the ill effects of the last round of monetary expansion. Interest rates have bumped clumsily downward recession-by-recession. Each round of monetary expansion inflates the bubble anew, and the bubble grows larger with each iteration of this sorry sequence of "corrective" interventions. In the US, the bubble of the late 1980s burst in the recession of 1990. The Federal Reserve System inflated the currency, thereby inflating the larger Dot Com Bubble, which burst in 2000. To address *this* crisis the Fed expanded some more, driving interest rates to 1% in 2002–2004. The resulting bubble was again bigger than its processor. This time it was concentrated in housing as Koppl (2014) and others have discussed. When this bubble burst, the US was tossed into the Great Recession of 2007–2009. Time for more monetary expansion. And interest rates were driven to zero. Some countries even had negative interest rates. Global debt hit the stellar height of $157 trillion in 2007. Austrian economists everywhere felt their ears bleeding. Zero-interest and negative-interest policies drove global debt to $250 trillion by 2017 and something close to $300 trillion today. We are likely in the biggest bubble in history and the bursting of it promises to be more painful by far than the Great Recession. As Geena Davis's character said in The Fly, "Be afraid. Be very afraid."

## Appendix 1: The Structure of Production Austrian Cycle Theory

It is relatively simple and straightforward to discuss the Austrian theory's resource sloshing in terms of more and less interest-sensitive sectors. Unfortunately, this straightforward approach somehow evaded Hayek and other Austrian economists until recently. Hayek tried to get at the Austrian sloshing by speaking of "earlier" and "later stages of production" (Hayek 1931/1935, p. 53). He assumed for expository purposes that the structure of production was arranged in a linear sequence of stages. In that simple world you can count the number of days between the application of, say, the farmer's labour when planting wheat and the eventual transformation of those planted seeds into, say, a slice of birthday cake on a child's plate. You can do that for all the "original factors of production" (Hayek 1931/1935, p. 148) and then compute an "average period of production." With Hayek's simplified structure of production, the boomtime movement of resources into interest-sensitive sectors is movement towards the higher stages of production. Resources may even move into new stages that are higher than those previously existing. This flow of resources up the structure of production is an increase in the average period of production, which is reversed in the bust. The reversal may cause the very highest stages of production, which opened up in the boom, to be abandoned altogether. Hayek explains, "Such an abandonment of early stages will, of course, mean that the average period for which the current supply of original factors is being invested, is shortened" (Hayek 1931/1935, p. 139). Boomtime investments in the highest reaches of the structure of production are revealed as pure waste, because they had to be abandoned when the bust hit. This is captivating stuff for an economist.

Hayek's use of the "average period of production," which he attributed to Böhm-Bawerk, was *at first* every bit as impressive as Kaldor (1942) said. But it was too simple, as Kaldor claimed and Hayek later acknowledged. We might imagine that bauxite mining is an early stage of production, while shoemaking is a late stage. You can't eat a chunk of bauxite or wear it as a hat, but you can put on a pair of shoes to keep your feet warm and dry. The trouble is that mine workers wear shoes on the job. Are the shoes, then, "really" later in the structure of production than bauxite, as we at first imagined? Now it seems like shoes come "before" bauxite. Which is "really" the earlier stage of production, mining or shoe making? The question cannot be answered. It represents the sort of "gap" in Hayek's theory that we saw Kaldor complain of earlier. Instead of a linear sequence of stages of production, we have a complex dynamic web of mutually supporting productive activities. "Even in a dynamic evolving economy, coal and iron make coal and iron" (Hordijk, Kauffman, & Koppl, MS). Hayek came around to the view that his lectures in 1931 employed a "grave simplification" (Hayek 1994, p. 77). He said, "I became aware later that the question of a single average period of production was a complex structure; if I had been aware of this in 1931, I could not have given a beautiful simple exposition, but I could have confused everybody" (Hayek 1994, pp. 77–78). Hayek tried to salvage something from the notion of an average period of production with his 1942 book The Pure Theory of Capital (Hayek 1994, p. 141). The idea was to "introduce much more complex assumptions. Once you do this," however, "the things become so damned complicated it's almost impossible to follow it."

And while we're at it, what is an "original" factor of production anyway? The farmer we imagined earlier is not, somehow, "pure labour." They had to learn how to farm, which means someone, the farmer's parents perhaps, invested in the farmer, thus producing "human capital." Nor is "land" on which the farm sits an "original" factor of production. It had to be cleared, the soil turned up and the rocks carted off. The farmland is also a product, in part, of prior investment. There are no "original" factors of production.

Austrian Business Cycle Theory was caught by its horns in the thickets of capital theory and Hayek could not extricate it. Only recently have Austrian economists released the theory from its tangles thanks to Lewin and Cachanosky (2016). The theory was explained above entirely in terms of more or less "interest-sensitive sectors." It does not require any notion of "stages of production" arrayed from "earlier" to "later." All it needs is a precise meaning of "interest sensitivity." Lewin and Cachanosky have found such a meaning in the notion of "duration" from modern finance. (Macaulay's duration is the discount-factor elasticity" of present value, as explained in Appendix 3.) Duration formulas measure interest sensitivity and let the whole Austrian story be told in terms of such "interest sensitivity" as has been done above. Koppl (2014) uses, in effect, duration without formulas by speaking of "interest-sensitive sectors" rather than "stages of production." Lewin and Cachanosky (2021) were right to say that "much of the controversy surrounding capital theory and the business cycle might have been avoided if duration had been incorporated into the discussion." Their work develops the analytics of duration and works out its relationship to the Austrian theory.

If Hayek had been able in the 1930s to rely on Macaulay's duration instead of "stages of production" the epic battle between Hayek and Keynes might have turned out differently. Figures such as Kaldor might not have been "driven to the conclusion that the basic hypothesis of the theory… must be wrong." Keynes' interventionist prescription would still have appealed to politicians and many economists. But the Austrian story might not have faded so completely from the scene.

The Austrian theory shows that once central banks have caused a false boom by setting interest rates artificially low, the only way to bring about a re-coordination of savings and borrowing is to allow interest rates to be set by the market. Setting interest rates even lower is counterproductive. Hayek said, "to combat the depression by a forced credit expansion is to attempt to cure the evil by the very means which brought it about" (1933, p. 20) Don't cure your hangover by getting drunk.

## Appendix 2: What About the Increase in Bond Prices?

We are imagining the central banks to be buying bonds. That's an increase in the demand for bonds. Are the resulting changes in bond prices consistent with the overall (artificial) increase in the supply of credit created by such bond buying? By buying bonds, the central bank increases the demand for them and drives up their prices. Those price increases do not increase the payouts to bond holders, however. A bond's payout will include its "maturity value," which is also called its "par value" or its "face value." That's the final payment the bond makes, which happens on its "maturity date" or "at maturity." For some bonds, so-called "zero-coupon bonds," that's the only payment they make. The bond might promise to pay, say, $1,000 in two years. If the relevant interest rate is 5%, you would have to pay $907.03 to buy it today. In college finance classes they call that the bond's "present value." In this case, the equation for present value reduces to the following expression.

$$PV = \frac{\$1,000}{(1+0.05)^2}$$

The $47.62 difference between the purchase price and the maturity value is 5% of the purchase price. Your money has grown at a 5% annual rate. The principle is the same, but the math is a bit more complicated for bonds that make additional payments along the way. Such payments, typically made every six months, are called "coupon payments." They are often said to be interest payments. But coupon payments are fixed money amounts that do not vary with interest rates. Whether a bond makes coupon payments or not, what the bond pays to the bondholder is not affected by the price of the bond. Thus, if you go out and buy a now more expensive bond and keep it through to maturity, your return will be lower than it would have been without the price increase. But higher purchase price implies a lower return from buying the bond and holding it to maturity. More money invested in the bond plus the same money paid out by the bond equals a smaller rate of return on the bond. In our example of a zero-coupon bond, the price might jump to, say, $961.54, which implies an interest rate of 4%, which is less than the 5% we imagined to prevail earlier. The ultimate payout, $1,000 one year from today, is the same; the price to get that payout has risen. The bond's interest rate is correspondingly reduced. This idea is expressed by saying that a bond's "yield to maturity" goes down when its price goes up. But the yield to maturity is an interest rate. When central banks expand the money supply by purchasing bonds, the yield to maturity—the interest rate of the bond—goes down. Thus, when central banks launch a program of bond buying, the changes in bond prices are consistent with both the increase in demand for them and decrease in interest rates created by monetary expansion.

## Appendix 3: Why Do Interest-Sensitive Sectors Expand More?

More interest-sensitive sectors expand more in the boom and contract more in the bust. This point is best seen by imagining that you are in the business of treasure hunts, such as dredging up gold coins from old shipwrecks. You are considering an investment that would yield, say, one million dollars in precisely one year. At an annual interest rate of 10%, you would be willing to spend up to $909,091. You would be willing to pay only $826,446 for a million-dollar payout coming *two* years from now. These numbers are relatively easy to compute because we have the simple case of one sum in today and one sum out at a fixed date in the future.

Consider first the one-year case. If you invested $909,091 for a year and if it were to grow at 10% per year, you'd have a million dollars at the end of the year. In equation form, we have the "present value" of $PV = \$909,091$ growing at an annual rate $r = 0.10$ to reach a "future value" of $FV = \$1,000,000$.

$$(1 + 0.10)(\$909{,}091) = \$1{,}000{,}000.$$

In symbols:

$$(1 + r)(PV) = FV.$$

Solving for $PV$ gives us a relatively simple version of the present value equation, which works in this case:

$$PV = \frac{FV}{1 + r}.$$

Consider now the two-year case. If you invested $826,446 for two years and if it were to grow at 10%, you'd have $909,091 at the end of one year and a full million at the end of two years. In equation form, we have the "present value" of $PV = \$826{,}446$ growing at an annual rate $r = 0.10$ to reach the intermediate value of $909,091 at the end of the first year.

$$(1 + 0.10)(\$826{,}446) = \$909{,}091.$$

We have been imagining a 10% *annual* rate of interest and one year has passed. For the following year, therefore, we will earn interest on the accumulated sum of $909,091.

And we have already seen that when the annual rate of interest is 10%, it takes precisely one year for this value ($909,091) to grow to a cool million. In equation form, we have the "present value" of $PV = \$826{,}446$ growing at an annual rate $r = 0.10$ to reach the intermediate value of $IntV = \$909{,}091$, which then grows at the same rate to reach a million dollars two years from today.

In symbols we have first:

$$(1 + r)(PV) = IntV.$$

Then we have:

$$(1 + r)(IntV) = FV.$$

Putting these two steps together by we get

$$(1 + r)((1 + r)(PV)) = FV$$

and, therefore,

$$(1 + r)^2 PV = FV.$$

Solving for $PV$ gives us a slightly more complicated version of the present value equation that is appropriate to this case:

$$PV = \frac{FV}{(1+r)^2}.$$

The present value of the two-year project is less than the present value of the one-year project. If the interest rate for your treasure-hunting business falls to 5% because of a monetary "stimulus," you'd be willing to spend more on each project: $952,381 for the one-year project and $907,029 for the two-year project as we can now confirm by plugging into our two simple versions of the present value equation.

$$\$952,381 = \frac{\$100,000}{1+0.05}$$

$$\$907,029 = \frac{\$100,000}{(1+0.05)^2}$$

Notice the key thing for the Austrian cycle theory: The present value of the two-year project grows more than the present value of the one-year project whether we calculate in dollars or percentages. The present value of the two-year project grew by $80,583 or 9.75%. The present value of the one-year project grew by only $43,290 or 4.76%. If your treasure-hunting business had $910,000 to invest, you'd pick the one-year project when interest rates are high and the two-year project when interest rates are low. The two-year project is more interest sensitive. Its value to you goes up by more when interest rates go down, and it goes down by more when interest rates go up. Low interest rates tilt the economy more towards relatively interest-sensitive projects. Monetary stimulus tends to move resources into the more interest-sensitive sectors.

Unsurprisingly, present value equations are more complicated for more complicated cash flows. A "cash flow" is just a sequence of expected cash payments. Some might be inflows and others outflows. When you get the bill in a restaurant, there has been no cash flow. When you pay the cashier, that's a cash flow. It's an outflow and thus a negative cash flow. When you put in your time at work, there has been no cash flow. When you collect your paycheck, that's a cash flow. It's an inflow and thus a positive cash flow. A more complicated cash flow has such flows happening at different times. A bond with coupon payments, for example, has a sequence of coupon payments before it makes its final payout.

The following equation gives you the present value of a discrete set of payments when the interest rate is unchanging.

$$PV = c_0 + \frac{c_1}{1+r} + \frac{c_2}{(1+r)^2} + \frac{c_3}{(1+r)^3} + \cdots$$

In this equation $r$ is the interest rate, $c_0$ is the cash flow happening right now, $c_1$ is the cash flow expected one period from now, $c_2$ is the cash flow expected two periods from now, and so on. A few fussbudgets may wonder about "continuous compounding," whereby interest is paid in a theoretically continuous flow. That's fun stuff if you like higher maths, but not important for Austrian Business Cycle Theory. In any event, the assumption of a discrete set of payments lets us dispense with such arcane stuff.

## Appendix 4: Duration

As we first saw with the example of a treasure-hunting business, the value of an investment option is the present value of the corresponding cash flow. In the treasure hunting examples, you were expecting a one-time payment at some point in the future. But the same logic works for more complicated cash flows too. For example, an investment that is expected to pay 100,000€ every year for ten years is worth 772,173€ if the interest rate is 5%. At that interest rate, you'd be willing to invest up to 772,173€ in it. It's the same for the value of a business. The value of a business to you is the present value of the cash flows you expect the business to generate. Duration measures how sensitively the value of a business or an investment opportunity responds to a change in the rate of interest. It measures, roughly, the percent change in the present value of a cash flow over the percent change in the "discount factor," which is one plus the interest rate. Such percent ratios are called "elasticities" in economics. Thus, duration is the elasticity of present value with respect to the discount factor. Duration is sometimes discussed as if it is applied only to bonds. But the formula (given below) works for any cash flow and thus for the values of businesses and investment opportunities.

It is good and appropriate for the duration formula to use the discount factor, $1 + r$, rather than the interest rate, $r$. Economists sometimes say that interest is the "price of waiting." That statement conveys the general idea, but it is a little loose. Let's say your cousin has a coffee shop and wants to buy a new espresso maker costing 10,000€. You agree to lend your cousin's business the required sum for one year at a 5% interest rate. Your cousin is "paying" you to wait. You will get 10,500€ in exchange for 10,000€ today. You are metaphorically "selling" present consumption to your cousin, who must "pay" with 10,500€ of future consumption. Just as the price of an orange is the number of euros per orange, the price of present consumption is the number of future euros per euro of present consumption. In our examples that's the ratio $\frac{10,500€}{10,000€}$ or 1.05. Thus, the "price" of your "waiting" is the "discount factor" 1.05 and not 500€ or 5%. The price of waiting is $1 + r$. It makes sense, then, to measure how interest sensitive a cash flow is by computing the elasticity of its present value with respect to the discount factor.

Duration was defined above as *roughly* the percent change in the present value of a cash flow over the percent change in the discount factor. Why "roughly"? The ratio of the percent change in present value to percent change in discount factor will be different for different percent changes. A 1% increase in the discount factor might induce, say, a 2% decrease in present value giving us an elasticity of $-2$. But imagine something silly like a 1,000,000% increase in the discount factor. Such an increase would cause the present value to fall by almost 100% giving us an elasticity of about $-0.0001$. The bigger the imagined increase in the discount factor the smaller the computed duration of the cash flow. To eliminate such unwanted variations in "the" duration of a cash flow we consider only infinitesimal changes in the discount factor. A little calculus then brings us to the following formula for duration, $D$.

$$D = \frac{\left(\frac{c_1}{1+r}\right) + 2\left(\frac{c_2}{(1+r)^2}\right) + 3\left(\frac{c_3}{(1+r)^3}\right) + \cdots}{PV}$$

Duration so defined is "Macaulay's duration." Some writers, including Lewin and Cachanosky, also discuss modified duration, MD, which is simply

$$MD = -\frac{D}{1+r}$$

and Osborne's duration, which assumes a changing interest rate.

# References

Hayek FA (1933) Monetary theory and the trade cycle. Jonathan Cape, London

Hayek FA (1931/1935) Prices and production, 2nd edn. Augustus M. Kelley, New York

Hayek FA (1994) Hayek on Hayek: an autobiographical dialogue. Cambridge University Press, Cambridge

Kaldor N (1942) Professor Hayek and the concertina effect. Economica 9(36):359–382

Keystone Pictures USA (1973a) Carless Sunday in connection with the oil boycott on horseback. https://www.alamy.com/carless-sunday-in-connection-with-the-oil-boycott-on-horseback-by-the-jordaan-date-4-november-1973-location-amsterdam-noord-holland-keywords-car-free-sun days-oil-boycott-oil-crisis-horses-riders-image341214320.html. Accessed Aug 2024

Keystone Pictures USA (1973b) Alternate ways of transport - two horses pulling a Volkswagen. https://www.alamy.com/alternate-ways-of-transport-two-horses-pulling-a-volksw agen-image69474835.html. Accessed Aug 2024

Koppl R (2014) From crisis to confidence: macroeconomics after the crash. Institute of Economic Affairs

Lactantius (1965) The deaths of the persecutors. In: Lactantius: the minor works, translated by Sister Mary Francis McDonald. Washington, D.C.: The Catholic University of America Press

Lewin P, Cachanosky N (2016) Financial foundations of Austrian business cycle theory. Adv Austrian Econ 20:15–44

Lewin P, Cachanosky N (2021) Capital and finance: theory and history. Routledge, London

von Mises L (1944) Omnipotent government: the rise of the total state and total war. Yale University Press, New Haven, Conn.

Robinson J (1974) What has become of the Keynesian revolution? Challenge 16(6):6–11

Wapshott N (2011) Keynes Hayek the clash that defined modern economics. W.W. Norton & Company, New York

Yeager L (1983) Stable money and free-market currencies. Cato J Cato Institute 3(1)

# Analysis of the Formation of the Super Bubble

**Max Rangeley, Roger Koppl, and Harry Richer**

## An Overview of 40 Years of Credit Expansions

From the 1980s onwards, each recession has been responded to by central banks setting lower and lower interest rates, thereby creating larger and larger debt bubbles. In the US, for instance, when the bubbles of the 1980s burst, bringing about the recession of the early '90s, the response from Alan Greenspan, then Governor of the Federal Reserve, was to set interest rates at 3%, the lowest for decades. This, combined with several years of the Greenspan Put, whereby expansionary monetary policy would be implemented whenever the stock market wobbled, then served to create an even larger bubble—the Dot Com Bubble. When this burst in 2000, the response was even lower interest rates, reaching 1% from 2003–2004, which then served to create a yet larger bubble, the Housing Bubble. When this burst in 2008 the response from the Federal Reserve and other central banks was the lowest interest rates in history, more than a decade of 0% interest rates, which has served to create an even larger bubble. In 2008, total global aggregate debt was roughly $150 trillion; this was already by some margin the largest debt bubble in history, both in absolute terms and relative to GDP, but in the years of 0% interest rates that followed, global aggregate debt would eventually reach $300 trillion. In other words, far from bringing about a return to prosperity, 0% interest rates and other policies from central banks have served to essentially double the size of the global debt bubble.

M. Rangeley (✉)
The Cobden Centre, 61 Pembroke St, Plymouth PL1 4JS, UK
e-mail: maxrangeley@gmail.com; max@cobdencentre.org

R. Koppl
Syracuse University, 721 University Avenue, Syracuse, NY 13244, USA
e-mail: rkoppl@syr.edu

H. Richer
73 Penshurst Gardens, Edgware, London HA8 9TT, UK
e-mail: harryjamesricher@outlook.com

Some economists at the IMF and elsewhere have made the argument that lower interest rates are driven by demographic trends. For example, they have stated that in societies with an ageing demographic, such as Japan, there is an increase in the amount of retirement savings while a weak outlook leads to investment being limited; they argue that this drives low interest rates in order to incentivize financial institutions to invest in riskier assets "in a continuing search for higher returns" (IMF 2020). However, this argument does not hold strong for several reasons. First, savings rates, as we shall shortly see, have been historically low in most countries and have fallen with each phase of lower interest rates. Second, the pattern observed in the Fed Funds Rate since 1980 often shows rising or steady interest rates until a recession hits; only then do central bankers turn to a policy response of lower interest rates, rather than decisions made in response to an overall trend of demographic ageing. Third, if ageing populations have driven lower interest rates, then why have similar trends been observed in countries without populations that are ageing or that have not aged as significantly. For example, in 2019 only 6.3% of India's population was over 65% compared to 18.5 and 16.2% in the UK and US respectively (Koop 2021) but it has also seen a similar trend of lower iterations of interest rates (Reuters 2019) (Fig. 1).

It is also interesting to note that, to the extent that there is a correlation between lower interest rates and low birth rates, the causation may well go in the other direction: lower interest rates bring about ever increasing house prices which then causes young people to put off having children due to unaffordable house prices. An Adam Smith Institute study found that 157,000 children were not born in the UK between 1996 and 2014 due to the continuously rising cost of housing (Sabisky 2014). The situation has continued to deteriorate since then. In this chapter we shall take a close look at the asset bubbles, including housing, brought about by loose monetary policy (Fig. 2).

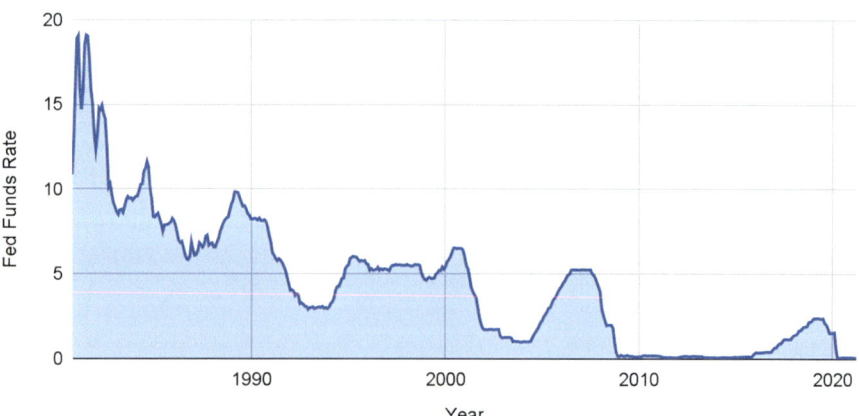

**Fig. 1** Fed Funds Rate. *Source* Federal Reserve. (Rangeley and Baker 2022). © Max Rangeley 2022. All Rights Reserved

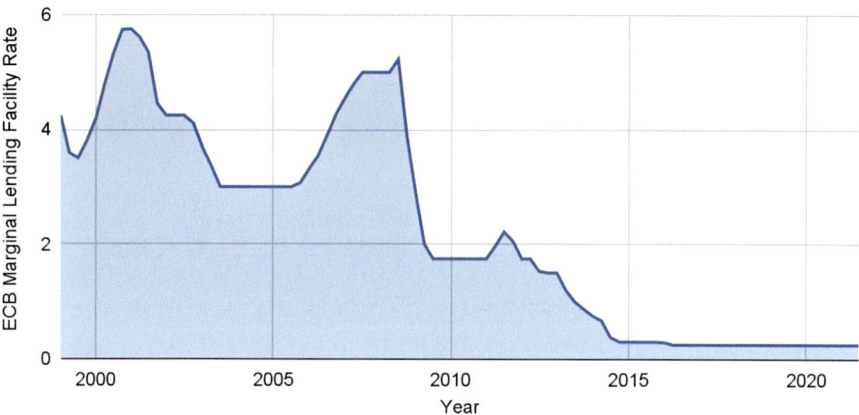

**Fig. 2** ECB marginal lending facility rate. *Source* European Central Bank. (Rangeley and Baker 2022). © Max Rangeley 2022. All Rights Reserved

Hayek made clear that when interest rates—a reflection of the consumption time preferences of individuals—are set artificially low by a central body, the false price signals that are transmitted across the economy will cause debt to grow out of proportion to savings. This is one of the first indicators of distortions in an economy. Rather than interest rates actually reflecting the preferences of present and future consumption, they transmit false information to businesses, who then borrow more despite actual consumer demand not reflecting these decisions. Modern money-creation mechanisms have only worsened this.

It is worthwhile to note the context in which Hayek's life-long economic views started to become a complete theory. The 1920s saw Germany experience hyperinflation and at the end of the decade, the US experienced the stock market crash and the Great Depression. Hayek sought the causes of the Great Depression and opposed explanations given by economists such as John Maynard Keynes. Rothbard sees the Austrian theory of the business cycle as beginning with eighteenth-century economist David Hume and early nineteenth-century economist David Ricardo who saw that, just as the industrial system developed, so had the institution of banking with its capacity to expand the supply of money and credit. Hume and Ricardo saw banking as the key to the great puzzle of the time: the boom-bust cycle. Ludwig von Mises would come to fully develop the Austrian Theory of the business cycle (Rothbard 2011).

The US, during the 1920s, experienced a period of economic prosperity. The price level remained constant which was taken by those setting monetary policy to suggest that their actions were correct. But output was growing, which should have caused prices to fall, as they had in the 1890s. Hayek argued that monetary policy had actually been too expansionary and that the prices that were being observed suggested that the interest rate was being artificially lowered below the natural rate of interest. Investment during this period was at a greater level than could be funded by savings

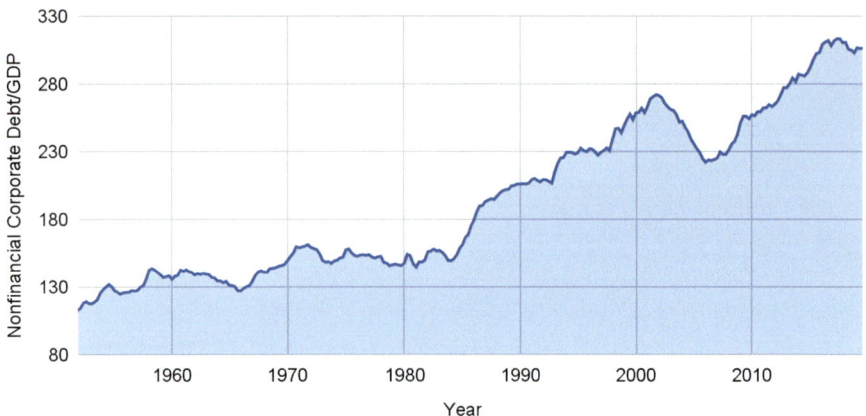

**Fig. 3** Nonfinancial corporate debt/GDP (US). *Source* US Bureau of Economic Analysis (Rangeley and Baker 2022). © Max Rangeley 2022. All Rights Reserved

and so the banking system was keeping the economy going in an unsustainable way—the first indication of distortions in an economy. As we all know, the Great Depression would shortly engulf the US. The structures of production had been distorted by monetary policy at the time transmitting false signals across the economy (Feser and Blackhouse 2008).

During the period of our analysis, from roughly 1980, as saving rates have fallen, larger debt bubbles have been initiated with each iteration of lower interest rates. Previous to this, from the mid-1960s onwards, the Great Inflation period began in the US which saw inflation reach over 14% in 1980 (Bryan 2023). This period was, of course, not isolated to the US. In 1975, the UK saw an annual inflation rate of over 24% in 1975 and nearly 18% in 1980 (World Bank). However, credit creation would begin to outpace economic growth from the mid-1980s onwards (Figs. 3 and 4).

As each phase of the Super Bubble progressed, bringing lower interest rates with each iteration, the saving and borrowing gap grew. As the economy became more dependent on debt, lower interest rates became necessary to support the increased debt load and have therefore never returned to the level of previous iterations. Figure 5 illustrates this correlation over the last generation.

Analysis of debt bubbles from a Hayekian perspective would posit that credit creation during this period was largely endogenously created—Fig. 6 shows the increase in domestic credit created by the US financial sector during the period of our analysis.

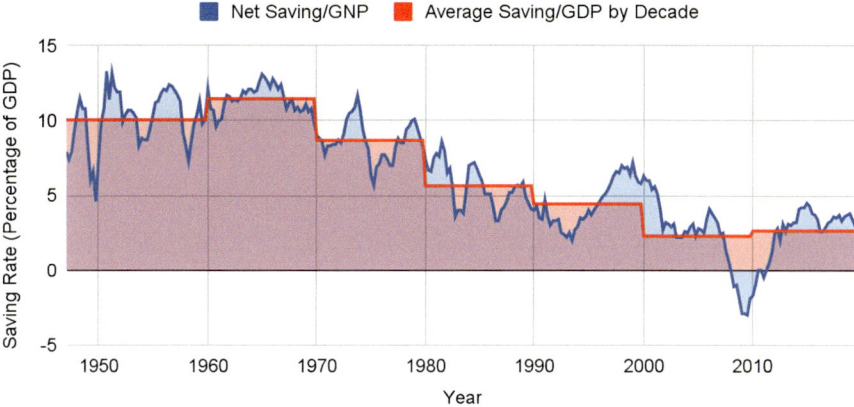

**Fig. 4** Net saving rate/GDP (US). *Source* US Bureau of Economic Analysis (Rangeley and Baker 2022). © Max Rangeley 2022. All Rights Reserved

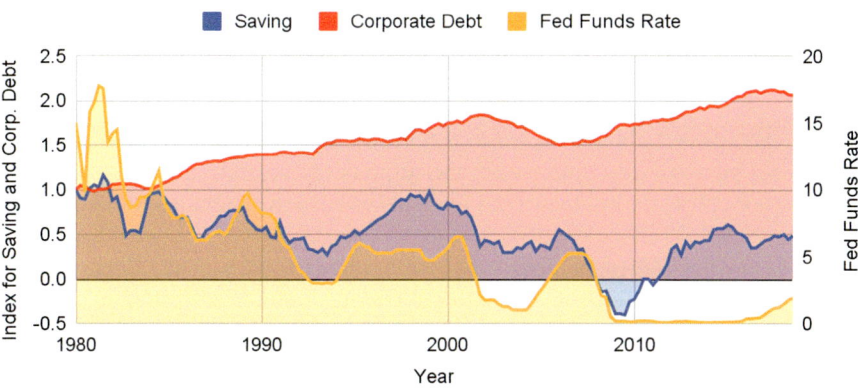

**Fig. 5** Saving rate, corporate debt (non-financial)/GDP (US) and Fed Funds Rate. *Source* U.S. Bureau of Economic Analysis, Federal Reserve (Rangeley and Baker 2022). © Max Rangeley 2022. All Rights Reserved

## Asset Bubbles During the Credit Expansions

The Austrian School has long argued that the result of a central body setting interest rates artificially low is excess credit, which tends to create and inflate asset bubbles. It doesn't matter whether the central body is a central bank or is a political committee. The economic calculations made by markets and businesses are distorted by these artificial interest rates, and decisions that appear profitable are made when they wouldn't have been otherwise. The artificially low interest rates that were seen in the 1920s in the lead-up to the Great Depression created not only stock market bubbles,

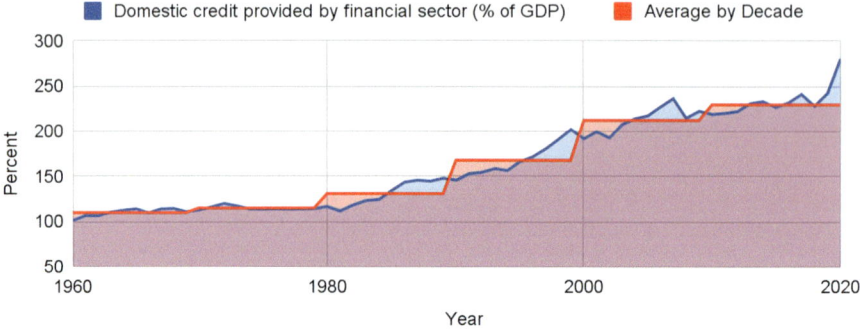

**Fig. 6** Domestic credit provided by financial sector (US, % of GDP). *Source* World Bank (Rangeley and Baker 2022). © Max Rangeley 2022. All Rights Reserved

but also bubbles in housing and other asset classes.[1] The bubble of the 1920s—fuelled by the Fed artificially lowering interest rates and the easing of credit requirements to "stimulate the economy" which created hundreds of millions of dollars of new money and turned America into a debt-fueled economy—built up over the course of a decade. In comparison, the Super Bubble has been almost continuously inflated over the course of an entire generation; when natural market mechanisms have led the aggregate asset bubble to begin to deflate, the response from central banks has been to set interest rates even lower: the response of central banks to the market naturally correcting the bubbles it has inflated has been to generate even larger asset bubbles.

During the past 40 years, across the world, different parts of the Super Bubble manifested itself in different asset classes. Given the trend in almost all parts of the world, the current situation has arisen where almost all asset classes can be classed as in a bubble. This can be seen through looking at net worth in relation to GDP. In the 30 or so years following World War 2, net worth varied from 3.2 times GDP to 3.9 times GDP. The former represents a low for it in 1978 and the latter a high for it in 1961. From the period of mass credit expansion of the 1990s onwards, it would never drop below 3.9 times GDP—the peak that previous generations experienced. For the period our analysis focuses on, in 2007 it would reach 4.9 times GDP and reach even higher at 5.4 times GDP in 2019 (Board of Governors of the Federal Reserve System). The trends for net worth in relation to GDP can be seen to largely follow savings rates at this time. From 1950 to 1980, the standard deviation for net worth over GDP was 0.179; it rose to 0.555 during the 40-year period of our analysis. It must be appreciated just how historically unprecedented these patterns in asset price appreciation are. There are no other periods that compare (Fig. 7).

---

[1] A good overview is provided in Rothbard (1963).

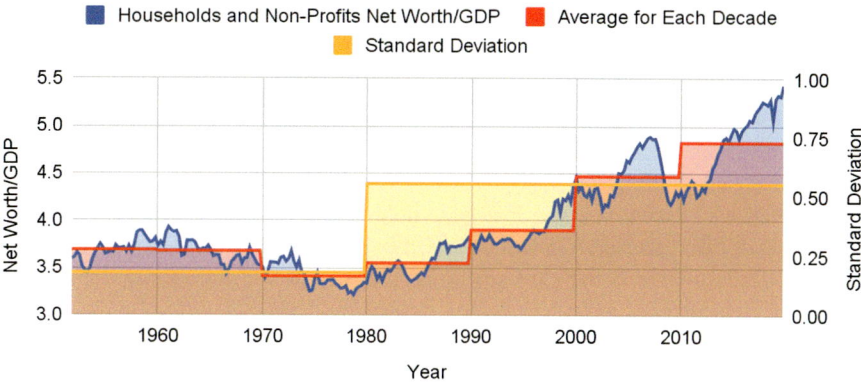

**Fig. 7** Households and non-profits net worth/GDP, average for each decade and standard deviation (US). Source *Federal Reserve* (Rangeley and Baker 2022). © Max Rangeley 2022. All Rights Reserved

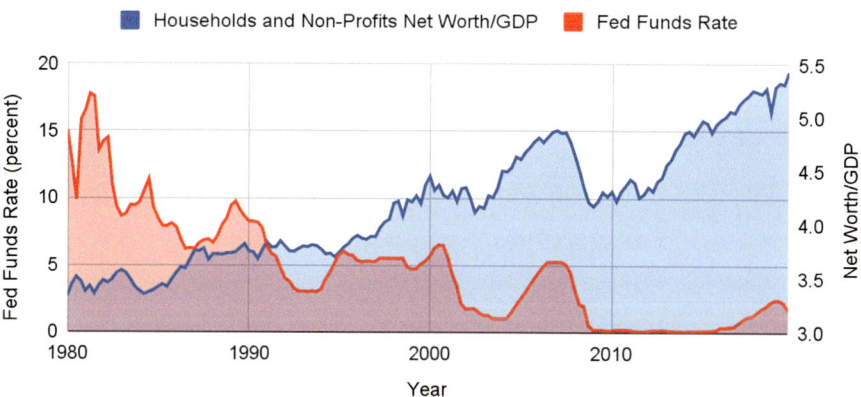

**Fig. 8** Households and non-profits net worth/GDP (US) and Fed Funds Rate. Source *Federal Reserve* (Rangeley and Baker 2022). © Max Rangeley 2022. All Rights Reserved

Similarly, the comparison in Fig. 8 of the Fed Funds Rate with net worth in relation to GDP over the past 40 years illustrates the pattern of the four phases of monetary policy generating successively larger bubbles.[2]

Three of the most important indicators of equity valuations are Tobin's Q, the Wilshire 5000 over GDP, and the Shiller P/E Ratio. Tobin's Q—which was actually developed in 1966 by Kaldor (1966a, b) but its use and attention was increased by Tobin and Brainard (1977)—measures the market value of an asset or index with its replacement value; the Wilshire 5000 over GNP—also known as the "the Buffett Indicator" which famed investor Warren Buffett called "probably the best single

---

[2] A useful analysis of monetary factors in almost a century of business cycles can be found in Bordo and Landon-Lane (2013).

measure of where valuations stand at any given moment" (Loomis 2001)—compares stock market value to GDP; the Shiller P/E Ratio—which has risen in use in recent years—compares the value of company or index with 10 years earnings data adjusted for inflation.

The decade averages and standard deviations shed more light on the systemic bubbles that have built up during our period of analysis. While some have compared the P/E Ratios of recent years to 1929, the bubble of the 1920s was short and sharp whereas every decade average from the 1990s onwards has been higher than any previous decade—this is the case since the series begins in the 1870s (Figs. 9, 10 and 11).

It is worthwhile noting that during the third phase of the Super Bubble, the Federal Reserve setting 1% interest rates in 2003–2004, did not lead stock markets to grow

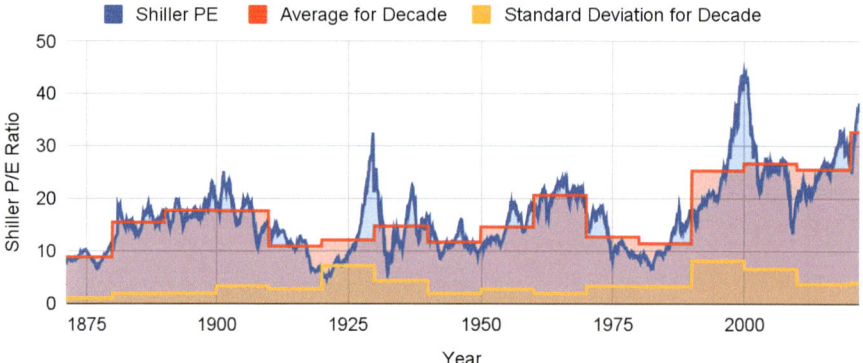

**Fig. 9** Shiller PE, with decadal averages and standard deviations. *Source* Robert Shiller, Calculations our own (Rangeley and Baker 2022). © Max Rangeley 2022. All Rights Reserved

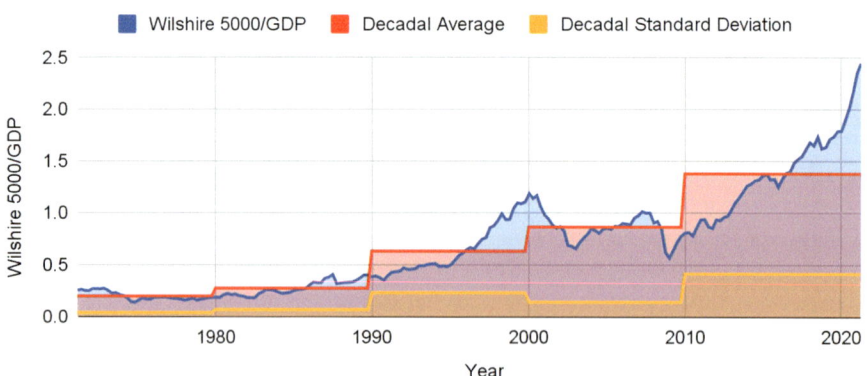

**Fig. 10** Wilshire 5000/GDP (The "Buffet Indicator") with decadal averages and standard deviations. *Source* U.S. Bureau of Economic Analysis; Wilshire Associates (Rangeley and Baker 2022). © Max Rangeley 2022. All Rights Reserved

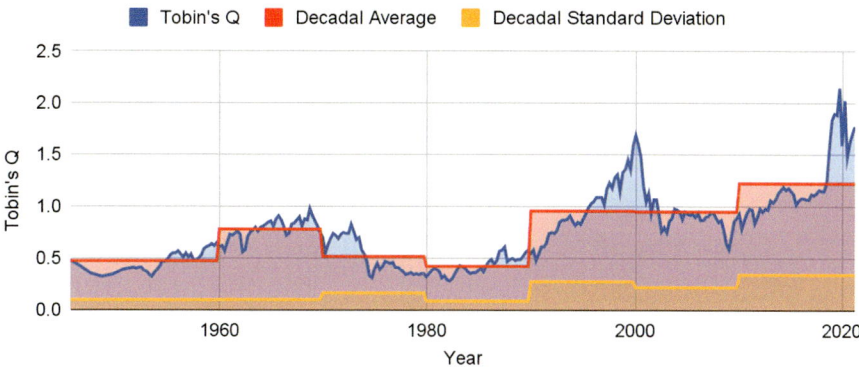

**Fig. 11** Tobin's Q, with decadal averages and standard deviations. *Source* GuruFocus, calculations our own (Rangeley and Baker 2022). © Max Rangeley 2022. All Rights Reserved

in the same outsized manner as they did in other phases of the Super Bubble even though the aggregate asset bubble metric shows assets ballooning; credit creation during this time largely went into the housing market and other property sectors—most notoriously into subprime mortgages. The bursting of this phase led to a long phase of 0% or near to 0% interest rates. From the end of 2008 to 2017, the federal funds rate did not rise above 0.10% (Federal Reserve Bank of New York 2023). In the UK, the Bank of England did not set the Bank Rate above 1% from 2009 to 2022 (Bank of England 2023a, b). Following the bursting of the third phase of the Super Bubble and the implementation of 0% or near to 0% interest rates in response, both stocks and all other asset classes resumed their joint upward trajectory.

The latter phase of the Super Bubble saw Quantitative Easing (QE) play a large role in economies across the world. In the UK, the Bank of England introduced its QE Programme in response to the Global Financial Crisis with £200 billion in 2009; this was increased by the Bank of England to £445 billion in response to the result of the UK's referendum on membership of the European Union in 2016. In response to the Covid-19 pandemic, the level of QE by the Bank of England reached £895 billion in 2021, before the Bank of England began to unwind its QE program in November 2022 (Bank of England 2023a, b).

In the US, prior to the Global Financial Crisis, the Federal Reserve held approximately $800 billion in assets on its books. By 2014, QE had increased this to over $4,000 billion. The Federal Reserve's balance sheet stayed at around this level until the Covid-19 pandemic which saw the Federal Reserve launch another round of QE in March 2020. Its assets would reach a peak of nearly $9,000 billion in March 2022 (Federal Reserve 2023).

This increase in the use of QE, alongside super-low interest rates, has played a large role in inflating already growing bubbles. From the Federal Reserve's QE programs in response to the Global Financial Crisis to the relative tightening of monetary policy in 2015, the correlation for the Federal Reserve balance sheet and the Nasdaq was 0.983, as illustrated below. Even during this period of stagnant or

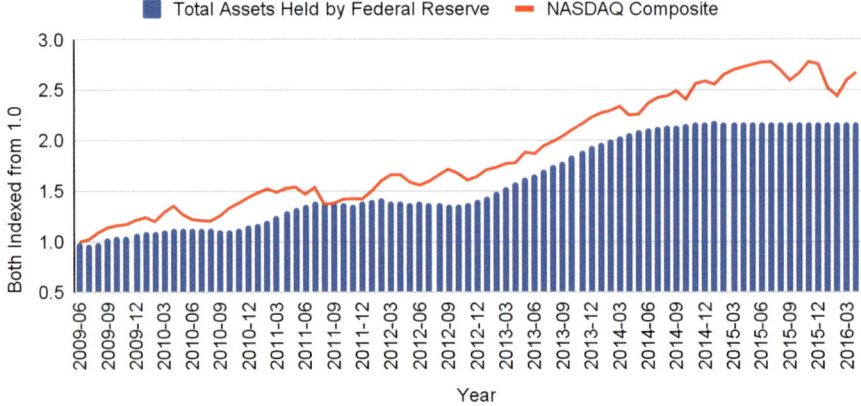

**Fig. 12** The effects of the Fed Balance Sheet on the Nasdaq. *Sources* Federal Reserve, Nasdaq OMX Group (Rangeley and Baker 2022). © Max Rangeley 2022. All Rights Reserved

falling productivity and wages, the Nasdaq rose by a factor of more than 2.5—this was certainly a positive development for those who rely on assets rather than wages for their wealth (Fig. 12).

These stock market bubble metrics should not be focused on in isolation; indeed, some may argue that these valuations mirror expected innovations (Ahrend et al. 2008). McGratton and Prescott's work at the Federal Reserve Bank of Minneapolis has even supported Fisher's 1920s hypothesis that equity valuations in the '20 s were a reflection of innovations (McGrattan and Prescott 2003). This should lead us to look more closely at the extent to which artificially cheap credit fuels equity valuations. John Kenneth Galbraith in *The Great Crash, 1929* (1954) argued for the importance of looking at margin debt to indicate stock market bubbles. However, since the publication of his book in 1955 we have seen periods where healthy economic expansions have been accompanied by growing margin debt.[3]

An Austrian School analysis would hypothesise that if artificially low interest rates drive increases in margin debt, it would lead to false price signals being transmitted to credit markets and, as a result, contribute to bubbles and other systemic economic distortions.[4] Price signals induce individuals, groups, and organisations to respond to information that they do not possess. When interest rates fall because of central body interference rather than changing time preferences and increased savings, businesses and groups still react as they must to changing market signals. Projects that previously seemed unsuitable become profitable even though they still remain unsuitable for the economic conditions of the time. Only through undistorted price signals can they respond appropriately to variables that they do not have knowledge of; without

---

[3] Margin debt as a driver of bubbles is given considerable attention in Galbraith (1954); see in particular pages 46 and 49.

[4] Kindleberger's 1978 classic *Manias, Panics, and Crashes. A History of Financial Crises* also discusses the importance of margin debt.

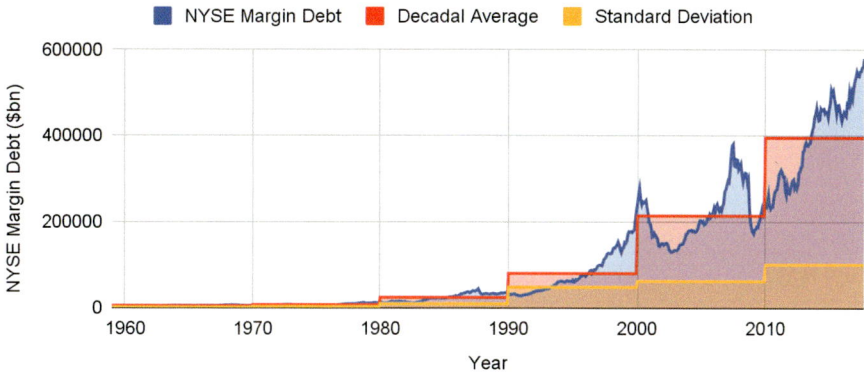

**Fig. 13** NYSE investor margin debt with decadal averages and standard deviations. *Source* NYSE/Gurufocus, calculations our own (Rangeley and Baker 2022). © Max Rangeley 2022. All Rights Reserved

undistorted price signals, malinvestments, resource misallocation, bubbles and many other economic distortions occur. All of which cannot go on forever. These bubbles and distortions must eventually be corrected but the more bubbles and distortions that occur and the longer period of time that they exist, the harder the eventual correction will be.

The highest margin debt reached prior to the phases of our analysis was in 1963 when it peaked at 0.87% of GDP—this approximately matched the peak in that cycle of aggregate asset valuations. Margin debt to GDP would never fall below 1% from the 1990s phase onwards. This means that every year from then onwards it exceeded the previous post-WW2 peak. In 1980, at the start of the Super Bubble, total NYSE margin debt was $24 billion; it rose to $279 billion at the peak of the 1990s phase; it rose by over one-third to $381 billion by the end of the 2008 phase of monetary expansion; the Covid monetary bonanza of economies propped up by ultra-cheap credit and record-high QE programs saw margin debt more than double to $822 billion (Fig. 13).

Hayek and Mises argued that in order to keep the façade going, following a crash, those with the levers controlling monetary policy will reach for an even larger credit expansion as this is required to preserve the bubble. Accumulated malinvestments mean that the only other option is to allow self-corrections in the market to occur.[5] Further money creation or even lower interest rates may seem to fix the problem in the short-term but self-corrections cannot be avoided forever and each round of monetary stimulus and lower interest rates only makes this eventual correction worse. For those who control monetary policy, whether it is because of genuine belief in the monetary orthodoxy or concern for the political and societal ramifications of not preserving the bubble, this is an option that is often inconceivable to them until they are confronted with the reality that monetary policy has become ineffective.

---

[5] Mises' *The Theory of Money and Credit* (1912) discusses the problems associated with responding to debt bubbles with more expansionary monetary policy.

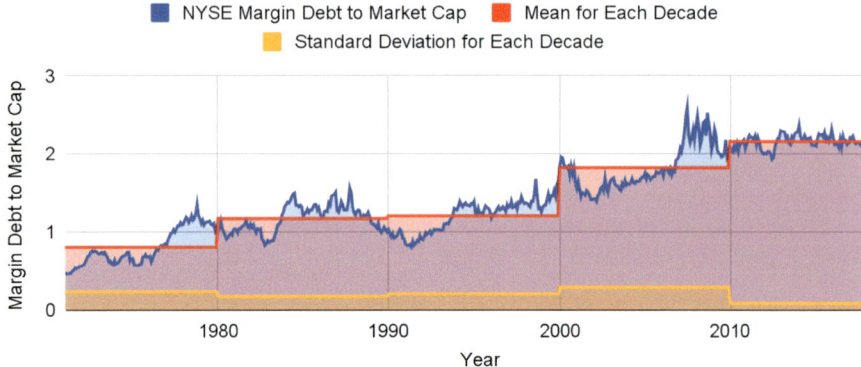

**Fig. 14** NYSE margin debt % of market cap, with decadal averages and standard deviations. *Source* NYSE/GuruFocus, Calculations our own (Rangeley and Baker 2022). © Max Rangeley 2022. All Rights Reserved

Figure 14 illustrates, for the phases of the Super Bubble, the extent to which each phase saw total market capitalisation reliant on margin debt. As a Hayekian analysis would predict, each phase of the Super Bubble would require more margin debt to preserve the bubble. The early 2000s needed 32.6% more margin debt to sustain the bubble than what was seen in the Dot Com phase. The Dot Com phase, in turn, required 24.8% higher margin debt than the 1987 peak.[6]

The monograph "Are We in The Largest Bubble in History? An Austrian School Analysis" (Rangeley and Baker 2022) combined equity valuations with a form of credit dynamics to create a useful metric for stock market bubble analysis from an Austrian School perspective. It created a composite index through combining margin debt as a percentage of market cap with the "Buffett Indicator." This composite index measures the size of the stock market relative to the economy and amount of the stock market that is fueled by credit. From an Austrian School perspective, the danger to the economy comes from both artificial credit expansions and outsized and disconnected asset valuations; for this reason both components are given equal weight in the composite index. As seen in Fig. 15, this composite index illustrates the increased effects that each stage of credit expansion brings.

Ever-increasing credit expansion has been the trend in much of the developed world, but each country has seen this new money flow into different areas.[7] As Hayek argued, the influx of new money into an economy will always reach some individuals and groups quicker than others—it may be directed towards public projects, increasing the salaries of public workers, securities, housing, investment goods, consumer goods, etc. Those who receive the additional money first will direct that money towards a certain area and then the next recipients of the additional money in

---

[6] Some of the predictions from Ludwig von Mises in the 1920s can be found in *The Causes of the Economic Crisis, and Other Essays Before and After the Great Depression* (2006).

[7] Shiratsuka (2003) provided a good outline of the Japanese bubble(s) and the associated monetary factors.

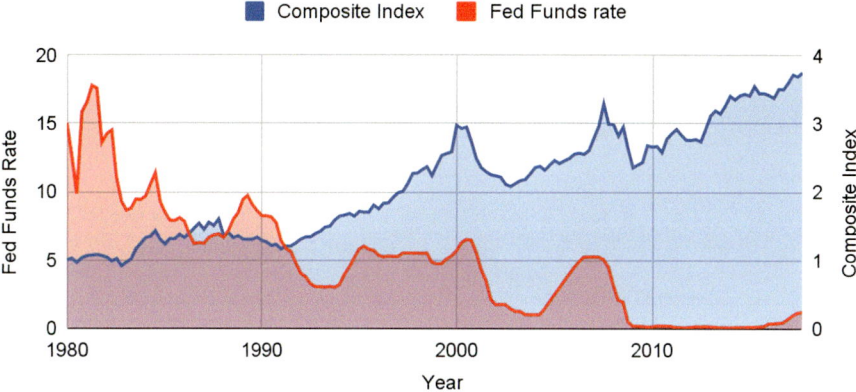

that area will direct it towards other areas and so the process continues. We expand on this point below when we describe "Cantillon effects." Hayek was clear that the process will take different forms in different places. How the new money is created and cultural differences between countries contribute to this (Ebeling and Hayek 1997). For example, stock trading in the US is more popular among the public than in other countries; whereas in the UK over 70% of the money that banks have created has been through mortgages. The economic distortions can be seen in each countries' relevant asset classes.

It has been suggested by several think tanks that the primary factor driving house prices in the UK is a shortage of suitable, permitted land. For example, the British left-wing think tank Institute for Public Policy Research argues this in their 2018 paper the Invisible Land (Murphy 2018) and the British Centre-right think tank Policy Exchange make the same argument in their 2023 policy paper Home for Growth (Vitali 2023).

However, larger bubbles when house prices are compared to average incomes are seen in Australia, Canada, and other countries with far greater land masses. With each phase of the Super Bubble, housing bubbles across the world have grown in similar patterns. Not only does this create the standard problems that come with economic distortions, but housing bubbles can be connected with greater inter-generational strife; owning a house brings the foundations for further developing in life, an identity and a space in which an individual can start a family and have security. Many young people are unable to afford to buy a house without coming from a wealthy family, while older generations who are likely to have bought homes at the beginning of the Super Bubble have seen the value of their houses skyrocket.

While the number of those aged 65 and over who own their own houses outright has risen from 55% in 1993 to 74.2% in 2017 in England, the number of those aged 16 to 64 who own their own houses with a mortgage has decreased from 56.2% in 1993

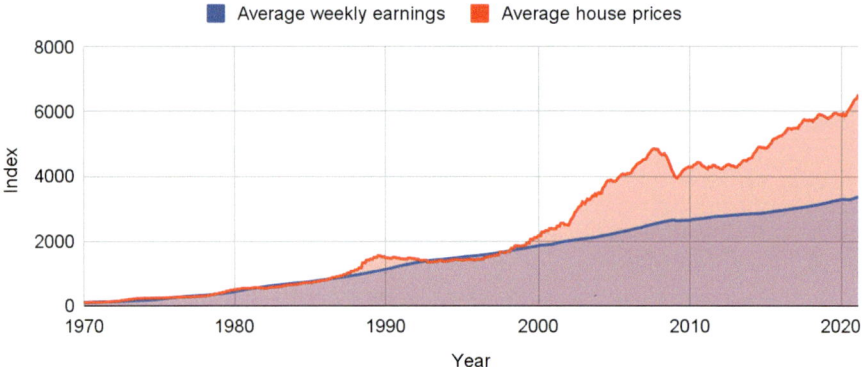

**Fig. 16** Average weekly earnings and average house prices in the UK both indexed from 100. *Source* Office for National Statistics (Rangeley and Baker 2022). © Max Rangeley 2022. All Rights Reserved

to 40% in 2017 (Office for National Statistics 2020).[8] In the US, home ownership among those aged under 35 had fallen by 7 percentage points from 2006 to 2017 and home ownership among those aged 35–44 years old had fallen by 10 percentage points from 2006 to 2017 (Moore 1988). In Fig. 16 we can see that house prices, just like the other assets we have looked at, grew more excessively with each phase of lower interest rates over the last generation.

It is unlikely that many of the bubbles we observe in this analysis, and indeed the overall Super Bubble, would have formed in an economy where interest rates are set by the market as there would be numerous self-correcting mechanisms that would have prevented such large growth. In an economy where interest rates are set by the market, a dramatic increase in the demand for debt relative to the pool of available savings would have driven a proportional rise in interest rates. We observe this with other goods on the free market and interest rates are no different.

In an economy with free market interest rates, the rise in interest rates would have made borrowing less attractive and so lowered the demand for credit. This would have the effect of deflating the emerging debt bubble. As a result, the overall resources in the economy, in terms of both time resources and monetary value, would be directed towards more efficient investments. Similarly, as lenders would be more selective in who they lend to, lending would be more focused on more productive outfits. It should not be thought that free market interest rates will mean that serious bubbles will never form. No single change could ever make the free market perfect, and self-correction measures will often not be pleasant for those operating in the market. However, allowing self-correction measures to operate is vital in preventing more distortions, larger bubbles, and the need for bigger self-correction measures in the future.

---

[8] Those aged 16–64 who own their own houses outright has stayed relatively stable only rising slightly from 14% in 1993 to 17.4% (Office for National Statistics 2020).

Vitally, free market interest rates would ensure that genuine time preferences are transmitted across the economy, reflecting the extent to which people are saving for future time periods. By allowing the demand and supply of credit to move towards an equilibrium, real signals on consumer consumption, business investment, and productive resource allocation would be delivered through interest rates—the market's most important pricing mechanism. Stock valuations, a principal pricing mechanism in any economy, would reflect the genuine time preferences of the overall economy.

Self-correction mechanisms will continue to try to function even as distortions grow, and bubbles inflate. It should have been appreciated at the time that the decline of asset valuations that occurred in 2000 and 2008 were signals from the market that the bubble needed to deflate. However, these self-correction measures were not allowed to operate as central banks responded by manipulating interest rates even further leading to greater distortions and an even larger debt bubble. There is almost a circular effect to how the trend has operated.

As each phase of the Super Bubble developed, the response from monetary policymakers has been to manipulate interest rates further away from the natural rate and thereby induce even more debt to the economy. This has resulted in the bloating of most asset classes. According to Hayekian monetary theory, the result of this when combined with effects that this book will discuss later—malinvestment and bond degradation for example—is that malinvestment will eventually reach a saturation level where monetary policy becomes ineffective and as such asset valuation bubbles will inevitably burst. Allowing free market self-correction mechanisms to kick in and correct the emerging bubbles would have led to much less economic misery than when these super-inflated bubbles eventually burst. Similarly, it would have allowed for resources in the economy to be more efficiently distributed and thus increase prosperity for all.

## Artificially Low Interest Rates and Bond Quality

As we have seen, interest rates have been sinking for the last 40 years or so. These declines are attributable in part to the stimulatory zeal of central banks. Every time the economy wakes up with a hangover, the central bank administers another dose of monetary hooch to the patient. We thus career from crisis to crisis, growing progressively more dependent on artificially cheapened credit. We have been staggering through a kind of pseudo-equilibrium for over a generation now. There has been a stability in this stop and go staggering. And the world's leading monetary authorities seem content with the situation because they have not changed their ways.

This stagger stability of the last 40 years does not seem consistent with Austrian Business Cycle Theory—at first. Consider, for example, the warning delivered by Ludwig von Mises in his 1949 classic, Human Action. After noting "the attempts, repeated again and again, to lower the gross market rate of interest by means of credit expansion," Mises delivered his grave warning. "There is no means of avoiding the final collapse of a boom brought about by credit expansion. The alternative is only

whether the crisis should come sooner as the result of a voluntary abandonment of
further credit expansion, or later as a final and total catastrophe of the currency system
involved." How have they been able to put off "total catastrophe" for 40 years? Part
of the answer is that catastrophe has not been fully averted, as illustrated by the Great
Recession of 2007–2009, which imposed great hardships on many. Someone pays the
price in every recession. Businesses go bust, workers are fired, and the central bank
administers another dose of monetary stimulus. This produces cycles of economic
pain and loss, just as the Austrian theory predicts. But the Austrian theory in its
canonical form cannot explain how the ghoulish game could go on for so long. We
need to take account of some facts of recent economic history to see how the "final
and total catastrophe" Mises warned of was averted for so long.

The disinflation of the Volcker years was the last recession to follow the traditional
Austrian script. The inflation of the 1970s was brought on (of course!) by monetary
expansion. In the summer of 1979, when inflation was running hot at about 13% per
year, US President Jimmy Carter nominated Paul Volcker to head the Federal Reserve
System.[9] Volcker brought inflation down, which brought on the double-barreled
recessions of 1980 and 1982.[10] Volcker had the US economy pay the unavoidable
price for the Fed's prior sins. And he was right to do so. The US was facing the
very choice Mises had flagged so many years earlier: pain now or total catastrophe
later. Since then, the system has changed in ways that enabled the stagger stability
of recent decades. The changes had begun before 1980, but they didn't change the
fundamentals of the game until after the Volcker disinflation.

So, what happened? Corporations were domesticated.

The years since the Volcker disinflation have seen the increasing domestication
of corporations. No longer the feral beasts of an untamed market, big corporations
have become pets of the state. Not wild wolves, but obedient lap dogs. Like the
real wolves who first came skulking around human campfires, feral firms of the free
market were only too happy to give up the hunt for value to become domesticated
beasts fed by their master the state. And like our ancestors who first threw some
skulking wolf a scrap of charred meat, governments have been only too happy to
draw feral firms away from the hunt for value and put them to work on the ends of
their master the state. The people and their interests were not part of this mutually
beneficial exchange. They have been left out of the co-evolution of the corporatist
state and the statist corporation.

The domestication of corporations did not begin in the 1980s. Antitrust measures
of the Progressive Era in America, for example, were always part of the symbiosis

---

[9] On 27 July 1979, the front page of The New York Times ran the headline "Inflation is rising by
13.2% annually; June prices up 1%." There are multiple measures for "inflation." Thus, different
legitimate sources will report different values for "the" inflation rate in June or July of 1979. In
any event, the annual rate was in the double digits and generally perceived to be "high" (New York
Times 1979).

[10] Here again, there are different ways to decide when an economy is "in recession." The most
common marker for the US is probably the NBER dating, which says the first Volcker recession
was February to August 1980 and the second Volcker recession was August 1981 to December
1982 (Federal Reserve Bank of St. Louis 2023).

between state power and corporate power. In 1953, the former CEO of General Motors, Charles E. Wilson, gave assurances to the US Senate that his appointment as Secretary of Defense posed no conflict of interest because, "for years I thought what was good for our country was good for General Motors, and vice versa" (Unattributed 1953). This equation of national and corporate interests reflects the emergence of the "military-industrial complex" Eisenhower warned of in his farewell speech of 1961. And the machinations of this "complex" produced mutual dependency between corporations and governments.

The great turning point in the US was the 1971 bailout of Lockheed Corporation. The market system is a system of profit **and loss** in which losses provide an essential check on business decision-making. If the potential for profit is tied to the risk of loss, market forces are strong. Once that cord has been cut, market forces are weak. Once the potential for profit no longer comes with a risk of loss, market forces have no force.

The American government generally allowed the risk of loss to accompany potential profits when the defence contractor Lockheed Corporation was bailed out. At the time Admiral Rickover damned it in the strongest terms. "We let them privatize profits and socialize losses." He warned, "Corporations cannot expect to be free of Government control if they come to rely on Government beneficence." In the time since Rickover spoke, large corporations have grown increasingly dependent on government beneficence and decreasingly free of government control.

The co-evolution of the corporatist state and the statist corporation has a different arc in each country. But it has brought them all to about the same place, wherein the distinction between "private" and "public" is largely without meaning. As Richard Wagner and his co-authors put it, nominally private and nominally public entities are "entangled" (Smith et al. 2011).

The Lockheed bailout opened the floodgates of government beneficence and control. The list of bailouts has grown as long as it is tiresome. The 1984 bailout of the Continental Illinois National Bank and Trust Company is significant because it brought the bailout habit to the financial sector. In Congressional hearings on the matter, Representative Stewart McKinney growled, "let us not bandy words. We have created a new kind of bank. It is called too big to fail. TBTF, and it is a wonderful bank"(Hearings Before the Subcommittee on Financial Institutions Supervision, Regulation, and Insurance of the Committee on Banking, Finance, and Urban Affair, 1984, p. 300). By 2013 too-big-to-fail had become too-big-to-jail. In a Senate hearing on March 6th Senator Grassley complained of a "mentality of 'too big to jail' in the financial sector." Attorney General Eric Holder responded by admitting that "the size of some of these institutions becomes so large that it does become difficult for us to prosecute them." Should criminal charges be brought, he explained, "it will have a negative impact on the national economy, perhaps even the world economy." After his remarks induced howls in the press, Holder tried to walk it back by saying, "Banks are not too big to jail." But this fig leaf was applied too late to obscure the truth, which had been exposed for all to see: Some businesses are too big to fail and too big to jail.

The mutual dependence of big finance and big government has been facilitated by the peculiar phenomenon of mutual funds that own each other. As the Wall Street Journal has noted, "Three of the largest investment shops in the U.S.—BlackRock, Vanguard and State Street… own each other and themselves." These "Big Three" funds "collectively hold the largest voting blocs for nearly the entire S&P 500." The nature of the problem is best conveyed with an imaginary example involving three companies: A, B, and C. Company A holds, let's say, 30% of B's stock and 30% of C's stock. Company B holds 30% of A's stock and 30% of C's stock. Finally, we may imagine, C holds 30% of A's stock and 30% of B's stock. For each of the three companies, most of its stock is held by the other two companies. Such "levitating firms" will not do what is in the stockholders' interests, but what is in management's interest. For example, management may sacrifice profits for growth in hopes of making the firm too big to fail and themselves too big to jail.[11]

A 2011 study found that levitating firms are a widespread global phenomenon. The study found that transnational corporations (TNCs) own each other. A "large portion of control flows to a small tightly-knit core of financial institutions." And "nearly 4/10 of the control over the economic value of TNCs in the world is held, via a complicated web of ownership relations, by a group of 147 TNCs in the core, which has almost full control over itself." Moreover, "3/4 of the core are financial intermediaries." In the early days of the Soviet Union, the famous Bolshevik revolutionary, Nikolai Bukharin called on the Soviet state to "get a hold upon the chief commanding heights of industry and commerce, then by means of commercial competition conquer private capitalism." He had in mind heavy industry with its big factories and billowing smokestacks. Today, big financial intermediaries have become the "commanding heights of industry and commerce." They are too big to fail and too big to jail.

The co-evolution of the corporatist state and the statist corporation explains why 40 years of interest-rate suppression has not yet resulted in the "total catastrophe" Mises warned of. When markets are mostly unmolested by state control the bursting of the bubble means that many profit-seeking enterprises go bust. But domesticated firms don't go bust and we stagger on to the next and still larger bubble. When the corporatist state props up statist corporations, market discipline is attenuated. As Oliver Hartwich (2020) has said, "We are living in the economic equivalent of a Potemkin village. It all looks pretty—but it is too good to be true."

Over the last 40 years or so, market discipline has been continually eroded by bailout, bailout, bailout. It's been a long, slow slide. And it has produced a long, slow slide in bond quality.

As we have seen, expansionary monetary policy increases the supply of credit. Borrowers who would otherwise have been excluded get loans. They get loans that would not have been made without the new credit. More monetary hooch means more lending and less excluding. Because risk is an important reason for exclusion,

---

[11] Some economists will protest that all concern over the separation of ownership and control has been permanently boxed and buried by the literature on "the market for corporate control." But you need real human stockholders for that market to work. When firms own each other they control themselves.

some of the new credit will go to riskier borrowers, to borrowers less likely to pay it back. Loan quality goes down.[12] And we have seen a general decline in the quality of corporate debt since about 1980.

Corporations have different ways to borrow money, including going to a bank. Bond issues are an important form of corporate debt. And because bonds are traded publicly, they provide information on the credit worthiness of their issuers. Bonds are rated by rating agencies. Bond ratings are supposed to indicate how great the risk of default is. US financial regulations recognise only ten rating agencies. In the American government's regulatory language a rating agency is called a "nationally recognized statistical rating organization" (NRSO). Most ratings are performed by only three of these ten: Moody's, Standard and Poor's, and Fitch, with Fitch a distant third behind the other two. Standard and Poor's ratings, from best to worst, are AAA, AA, A, BBB, BB, B, CCC, CC, C, and D. Sometimes a plus (+) or a minus (−) is added to provide a more refined risk judgement. Bonds in one of the top four categories are "investment grade" (IG). The others are "speculative grade." These riskier assets are sometimes called (perhaps unjustly) "junk bonds." Some investors such as money market mutual funds cannot buy junk bonds. Capital requirements are higher for institutional investors holding junk bonds. For the issuing firm, a brisk demand for its bonds will not be forthcoming unless their bonds are rated investment grade. Thus, it is important for bond issuers to get a good rating. Rating agencies do not get their ratings from a fixed computer program or anything like that. Instead, they formulate an expert opinion that may or may not be validated by future events.

The OECD has a numerical measure of "bond quality" that roughly corresponds to these rating categories. The higher the number, the better the bond. A rating of 14 roughly corresponds to a BBB+ rating.

Rangeley and Baker (2022) contain Fig. 17, which covers the period from 1980 forward. It shows the Federal Funds Rate in red and bond quality as measured by the OECD in blue. The Federal Funds Rate is the overnight rate charged to banks when they borrow from the Federal Reserve. The OECD measure of bond quality was, Rangeley and Baker (2022) explain, averaged across "60,712 bond issuances from 105 countries." The figure shows bond quality and the Federal Funds rate sinking together over time. As the Federal Reserve and other central banks have pursued a policy of monetary expansion, the short-term interest rates have fallen and dragged bond quality down with them.

Figure 18 shows the average bond quality sinking decade by decade. Rangeley and Baker (2022) report that it fell from 15.058 in the 1980s, to 14.555 in the 1990s, to 13.717 and then 13.211 in the following two decades. The OECD reports that in 2019, "the average corporate bond issued has a rating of approximately BBB" (Çelik

---

[12] The link between monetary policy and loan quality is called the "risk-taking channel." Borio and Zhu (2012) coined the term and drew economists' attention to it. Jiménez et al. (2014) is an important study confirming the effect for short-term rates such as the Federal Funds Rate in the US. Long-term rates don't seem to exhibit the effect. Bauer et al. (2014) is a recent discussion. Borio and Zhu (2012) suggest that the risk-taking channel has grown more important "[o]ver the last three decades," i.e., since about 1982. While they tell a different story than given above, it is notable that they give about the same date for the turning point.

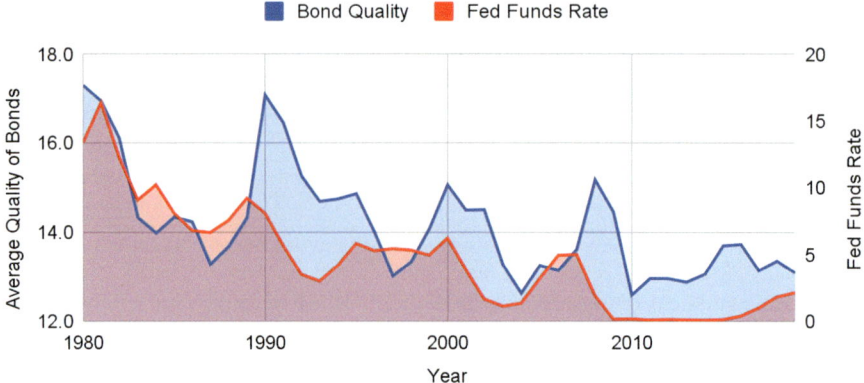

**Fig. 17** OCED global corporate bond rating index and Fed Funds Rate. *Source* OECD capital markets dataset, Federal Reserve (Rangeley and Baker 2022). © Max Rangeley 2022. All Rights Reserved

et al., 2020, p. 14). That's investment grade, but close to speculative grade. Monetary laxity has been dragging bond quality down.

The overall average quality of corporate bonds has been falling. But among junk bonds, the movement has been upward. In other words, the distribution of bond issues has been clustering in the middle, straddling the line between "investment grade" and "junk bond." Rangeley and Baker (2022) note that "BBB rated debt was only 17.4% of IG debt in 1990, but would eventually come to constitute 53.8% in 2019," as shown in Fig. 19. This clustering is also reflected in Rangeley and Baker's (2022) Fig. 20. Figure 20 also shows that bonds are clustering in the categories least likely to be downgraded. If your bonds are rated BBB-, they are barely hanging on to investment-grade status. Lucky for you, however, they have the lowest chance of

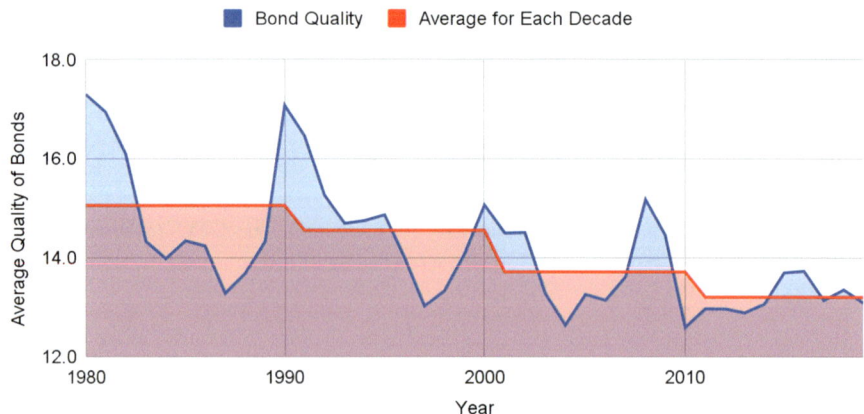

**Fig. 18** Bond quality and phase average. *Source* Constructed from OECD capital markets dataset (Rangeley and Baker 2022). © Max Rangeley 2022. All Rights Reserved

being downgraded by the rating agencies. If your bonds are rated BB+, they missed investment-grade status by only a small margin. In this unhappy case, you may at least console yourself that they have a low chance of being downgraded.

This curious clustering may reflect the global domestication of corporations. It may reflect the increasing role of government in determining profit and loss. We have seen Admiral Rickover's complaint that we "privatize profits and socialize losses." The more likely it is that your losses will be socialised the less likely it is that you will default on your bonds. But there is a cost for this protection from the financial

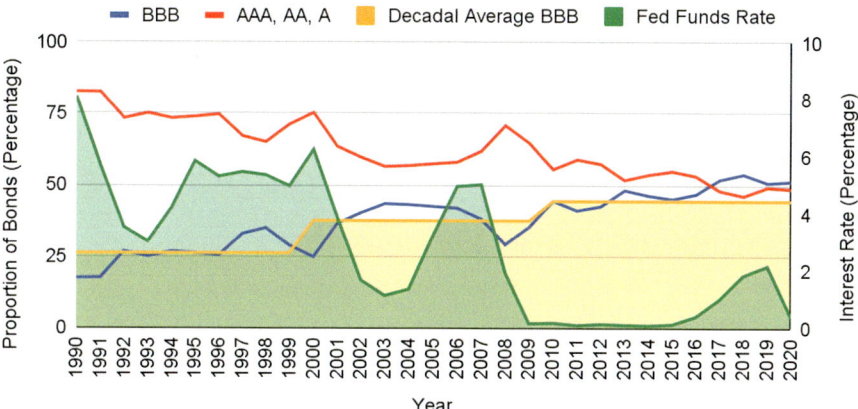

**Fig. 19** Fed Funds Rate and investment grade bonds. *Sources* Constructed from OECD capital markets dataset, Federal Reserve (Rangeley and Baker 2022). © Max Rangeley 2022. All Rights Reserved

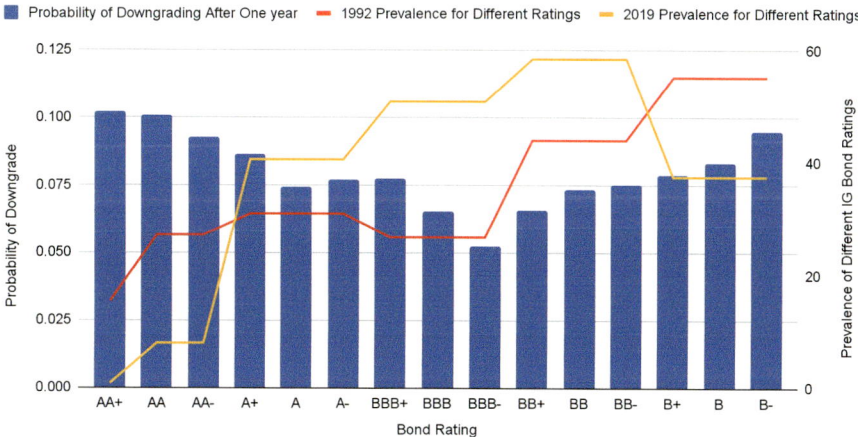

**Fig. 20** Probability of downgrading and prevalence of different ratings. *Source* Constructed from OECD capital markets dataset (Rangeley and Baker 2022). © Max Rangeley 2022. All Rights Reserved

consequences of your bad business decisions. The cost is a system-wide instability that itself creates a risk of default. The risk of default, then, comes to depend more and more on the behaviour of government entities such as the United States Congress and regulatory bodies and less and less on good business judgement about relative scarcities and customer needs. As Koppl (2002, p. 121) said, "when discretionary policymaking thus reduces the knowability of markets and the reliability of expectations, it devalues skill and makes luck count for more."[13] The overall average riskiness of corporate debt grows, but the portion of such risk attributable to the business decisions of bond issuers goes down. The consequence is a clustering of bond ratings around the middling levels, which have the lowest chance of subsequent downgrading. It is worrisome that over half of investment-grade bonds are BBB. A so-called "macroeconomic shock" could send many of them into default. Think of the 2008 recession. When the inevitable bust kicked in, many investment-grade bonds defaulted. What will happen next time?

## Systemic Risk and the Bond Risk Ratio

We have seen that monetary easing tends to reduce credit quality. Greenwood and Hanson showed that the decline in credit quality—the increase in the riskiness of loans—is a better measure of future troubles than the aggregate level of available credit (Greenwood and Hanson 2013). They "show that a significant decline in issuer quality is a more reliable signal of credit market overheating than rapid aggregate credit growth." To measure "issuer quality" they look at "the fraction of corporate bond issuance that is rated speculative grade" for each year of their study, which is "particularly useful for forecasting bond returns." Rangeley and Baker (2022) updated their analysis "with 63,705 corporate bond issuances from 105 countries." Their results are summarised in Fig. 21, which is reproduced here. They note that "Greenwood and Hanson's metric indeed has good predictive capacity."

They generated their own measure of bond quality, which they dub the "Bond Risk Ratio." This measure looks at the ratio of "risky" to "safe" bonds, where a bond is "risky" if it has a BBB rating or below. The higher the Bond Risk Ratio, the lower is bond quality. For this measure, then, higher is worse and lower is better. The Bond Risk Ratio removes the lowest category of investment grade bonds, BBB, from the rest of the investment-grade bonds and lumps it in with the junk bonds. It then takes the volume of risky to safe bonds. Moving the BBB bonds over to the "risky" side of the ledger makes sense given the clustering we noted earlier. In equation form:

$$\text{Bond Risk Ratio} = (\text{Non-Investment Grade Bonds} + \text{BBB})/$$
$$(\text{Investment Grade Bonds} - \text{BBB}).$$

---

[13] The theory of Big Players also helps to explain why discretionary and interventionist policies make it harder for rating agencies to judge credit worthiness.

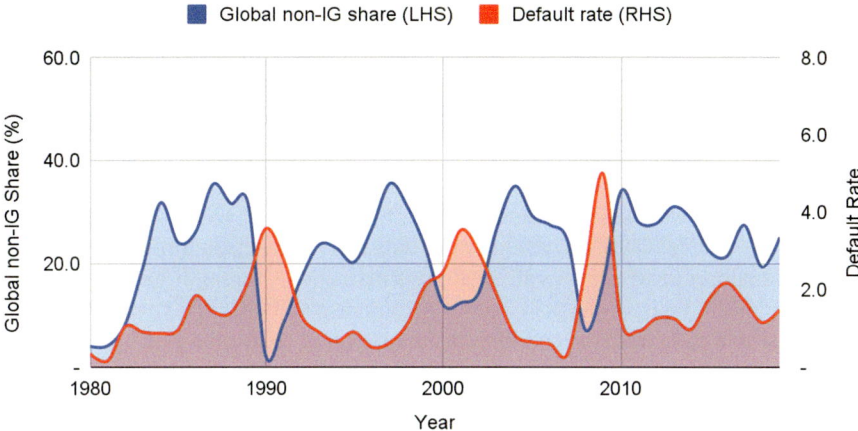

**Fig. 21** Non-IG bonds and default rates. *Source* Constructed from OECD capital markets dataset (Rangeley and Baker 2022). © Max Rangeley 2022. All Rights Reserved

Figure 22 shows the Bond Risk Ratio "constructed from 60,712 bond issuances from 105 countries." Unsurprisingly, it goes up and down. But the red line reveals the terrible trend. Corporate bonds are growing riskier as governments continue to provide routine bailouts, in the context of ongoing monetary expansion.

The Bond Risk Ratio and the pioneering Greenwood and Hanson metric are both useful. It seems only reasonable to keep them both in our analytical toolkit. The value of the Greenwood and Hanson metric for spotting ongoing "overheating" in credit markets seems clear. The Bond Risk Ratio, however, spiked more dramatically than the Greenwood and Hanson metric during both the dot-com bubble of the 1990s and the housing bubble of the 2000s. In those two episodes, the Ratio did a better job

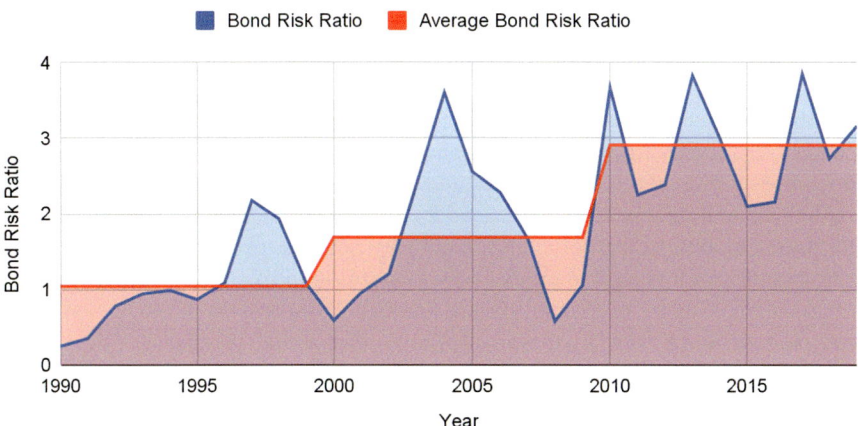

**Fig. 22** Bond risk ratio. *Source* Constructed from OECD capital markets dataset (Rangeley and Baker 2022). © Max Rangeley 2022. All Rights Reserved

of indicating the magnitude of the problem well in advance of the crashes. And in the future, it may prove helpful as an early warning system. Alarmingly, the Ratio continues to hit new highs. We may well fear another large collapse, one that may be even larger than its predecessors.

Comments made by Alan Greenspan in May of 1994 illustrate the gap between the Austrian theory and the thinking of monetary authorities. Testifying before the Senate, he said, "we moved short-term rates lower in a long series of steps through the summer of 1992, and we held them at unusually low levels through the end of 1993." He subsequently says with seeming satisfaction, "strength has been particularly evident in interest-sensitive sectors" (Greenspan 1994). This "strength" was chimerical and reflected, instead, the artificially induced sloshing of liquidity into relatively high duration projects. The "strength" Greenspan noted was a classic "Austrian" sign of monetary laxity.

Greenspan's successor, Ben Bernanke, bragged of the "Great Moderation," just when the Bond Risk Ratio was spiking in the housing bubble. He foolishly boasted, "improved monetary policy has likely made an important contribution not only to the reduced volatility of inflation (which is not particularly controversial) but to the reduced volatility of output as well" (Bernanke 2004).[14] The illusion of macroeconomic solidity was shattered by the financial crisis of 2008.

In the wake of the 2008 crisis, Alan Greenspan said that he had "found a flaw" in his model of capitalism. "[T]hose of us who have looked to the self-interest of lending institutions to protect shareholder's equity (myself especially) are in a state of shocked disbelief. Such counterparty surveillance is a central pillar of our financial markets' state of balance. If it fails, as occurred this year, market stability is undermined" (Greenspan 2008). But domesticated firms have no incentive to conduct meaningful "counterparty surveillance" when they can rely on bailouts. The market forces work better when they have not been destroyed by bailout, bailout, bailout.

The years since about 1980 have seen a long march from the market discipline of profit and loss to levitating firms and regular bailouts. This long march has left us with a phantom market. Corporate enterprises practice double-entry bookkeeping and regularly strike the balance to compute a nominal profit or loss. But losses are often socialised and, as we saw with levitating firms, even profits are not fully privatised. Prices are growing increasingly meaningless. In this faded-market environment, artificially low interest rates have given us high debt levels and a capital structure ever more disconnected from underlying scarcities and risk levels. At some point it will no longer be sustainable, and it will collapse. If asset values slide, as they did in the bursting of the dot-com and housing bubbles, pension funds will shrink correspondingly. It is hard to predict how long this game can go on before it finally collapses, much as the old Soviet system finally collapsed in the 1980s.[15] Just as the collapse of the old Soviet Union was catastrophic, the eventual collapse of the current

---

[14] The term "Great Moderation" was coined by Stock and Watson (2003) and popularized in speech by Bernanke (2004).

[15] No one date is "the" day of collapse. But the system was already teetering when the Soviet leader Mikhail Gorbachev came into office in 1985 and initiated a reform effort that was, in the end, futile. The ongoing collapse of the Soviet system resulted in the fall of the Berlin Wall in 1989. The Soviet

bubble will be catastrophic—unless we decide to make a purposeful exit from an unsustainable system. The sooner we decide to restore reasonable economic order including, vitally, market-determined interest rates, the less painful will be the exit from an unsustainable system.

## Malinvestment

Artificially low interest rates induce bad investments, which Austrians call "malinvestment."[16] A bad investment made during the boom is "a manifest malinvestment, a squandering of the means available" because it can only "withdraw scarce factors of production from employments in which they could satisfy wants considered more urgent by the consumers" (Mises 1949, p. 526). The problem of malinvestment arises in both the standard Austrian trade cycle of the sort Mises and Hayek described long ago and in the more recent world of unending monetary ease and regular bailouts.

In a standard Austrian trade cycle from before 1980, the boom induces investments that are unwound in the bust. These long-term projects are "malinvestment" because they were too long-term given the time preferences of households and because they are unwound in the bust anyway. Resources are wasted by resources sloshing, resources flow into high-duration projects during the boom only to flow right back out during the bust.

The situation changed after about 1980 as market forces became increasingly compromised. In the new situation post-1980, boom-induced investments are not unwound because central banks drive interest rates even lower to stop or prevent the bust. And in many cases bailouts have saved firms that were teetering on the edge of collapse. The resource reflux that used to be inevitable is blocked by the combination of renewed monetary easing and bailouts. But the artificially induced, not-to-be-unwound projects nevertheless "withdraw scarce factors of production from employments in which they could satisfy wants considered more urgent by the consumers." In this vital sense, they are "a manifest malinvestment, a squandering of the means available." Several indicators suggest that the problem of malinvestment is real and important in today's world of levitating firms and bailout, bailout, bailout.

---

Union was officially dissolved by a vote of the upper house of the Supreme Soviet on 26 December 1991.

[16] "Malinvestment" may be used as either a mass noun, that is, a word indicating the general phenomenon or as a count noun, that is, a word denoting discrete units that may be counted. Thus, we may say, "Monetary expansion causes malinvestment." And we may also say, "Their drive-through barber shop was a malinvestment."

## Delinquency Rates

Figure 23, taken from Rangeley and Baker (2022), shows that delinquency rates have been falling in recent decades. This decline might at first seem to be a sign of strength. The situation looks more ominous, however, if we recall that central banks have been pushing interest rates ever lower and big corporations are bailed out on a regular basis. Because central banks have been pushing interest ever lower, the "natural" resource reflux of the bust has been blocked. High-duration projects have been under less pressure than they would have been if interest rates had been permitted to go to their supply-and-demand levels. And high-duration projects that have nevertheless created losses may be saved when big corporations are bailed out on a regular basis.

The economist Joseph Schumpeter emphasised the "creative destruction" of the market process. Successful innovations may produce profits for the innovator. Profits may also go to at least some of the firms that imitate the innovator. But successful innovations generally rain destruction on the incumbent firms that are outcompeted by the innovator and the innovator's imitators. Many makers of horse-drawn carriages, for example, were ruined by the internal combustion engine. The market, once again, is a process of profit **and loss**. The market produces a continuous stream of innovations that make life better and better. A wave of business failures is the flip side of those wonderful innovations. Schumpeter's "perennial gale of creative destruction" has two sides. The "creative" side is innovation. The "destruction" side is business failure. When we see delinquency rates falling over time, the explanation is not that entrepreneurs are getting smarter and smarter. The explanation is the one just given: Continued suppression of interest rates and bailout after bailout prevents the resource reflux that used to be an inevitable part of the business cycle. High-duration projects are kept on life support when they should have died long ago. The economy comes

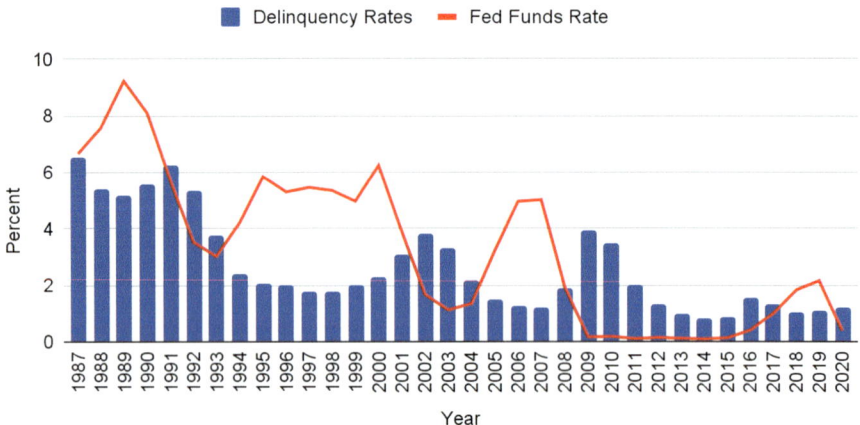

**Fig. 23** US delinquency rates and Fed Funds Rate. *Source* Federal Reserve (Rangeley and Baker 2022). © Max Rangeley 2022. All Rights Reserved

to be populated by "zombie firms" that should have died a natural death but staggers on in the faded-market economy of ever lower interest rates and ever more routine bailouts.

The term "zombie firm" was coined in 2008 by Ricardo Caballero and his co-authors in the context of Japan, where, they say, big banks, "often engaged in sham loan restructurings that kept credit flowing to otherwise insolvent borrowers (which we call zombies)." The general idea was neatly expressed in a 2017 article by Andrews and Petoulakis who say, "zombie firms" are "firms that would typically exit or be forced to restructure in a competitive market."[17]

In an article from 2016, Ryan Decker and his co-authors find, "Since the early 1980s, various measures of entrepreneurial activity in the United States have seen a secular decline." They marshal evidence of a general decline in economic dynamism, with some measures of decline kicking in about the year 2000. It is significant that Decker and his co-authors pinpoint "the early 1980s" as the beginning of "secular decline." As we saw in Chap. 4, "The changes had begun before 1980, but they didn't change the fundamentals of the game until after the Volcker disinflation." Recall that the structure of the American economy began to shift with the bailout of Lockheed in 1971. While the Lockheed bailout was a momentous event, its full impact was not felt until about 1982 when the last trade cycle to follow the traditional Austrian script bottomed out.

In 2017, Gita Gopinath and her co-authors found evidence of reduced dynamism in Europe beginning about 1990. They "demonstrate how the decline in the real interest rate, often attributed to the euro convergence process, led to an increase in the dispersion of the return to capital [across countries] and to lower total factor productivity (TFP) as capital inflows were directed to less productive firms operating within relatively underdeveloped financial markets." Low interest rates induced investment projects that were less productive as revealed by the decline in "total factor productivity," which is the ratio of outputs to inputs.[18] (Thus, total factor productivity grows when you get more output for the same input.) And the allocation of capital came to be more arbitrary as revealed by the increased dispersion in rates of return across countries. Capital was less likely to go to the projects with the highest prospective return. The random component to capital allocation was larger and, therefore, the returns were more arbitrary. The increased dispersion of returns reflects this arbitrariness.

Also in 2017, Andrews and Petoulakis (2017) noted the important phenomenon of "zombie firms," which they attribute in part to "bank forbearance." Recall that zombie firms are "firms that would typically exit or be forced to restructure in a

---

[17] This definition gives us the idea. It does not, however, let us apply a formula to numerical data to distinguish which firms are and are not zombies. Different studies use different "operational" definitions of zombie. Banerjee and Hofmann (2018, p. 1) define zombies as "firms that are unable to cover debt servicing costs from current profits over an extended period."

[18] It is not easy to measure "total factor productivity." Different studies employ different measures, each with its own strengths and weaknesses. It would be inappropriate to dive into the details here, but a few questions may suggest that there are some intricacies. How, for example, shall I measure "output"? How shall I measure "inputs"? Is it legitimate to use a production function for the whole of a national economy? The list of such questions goes on and on.

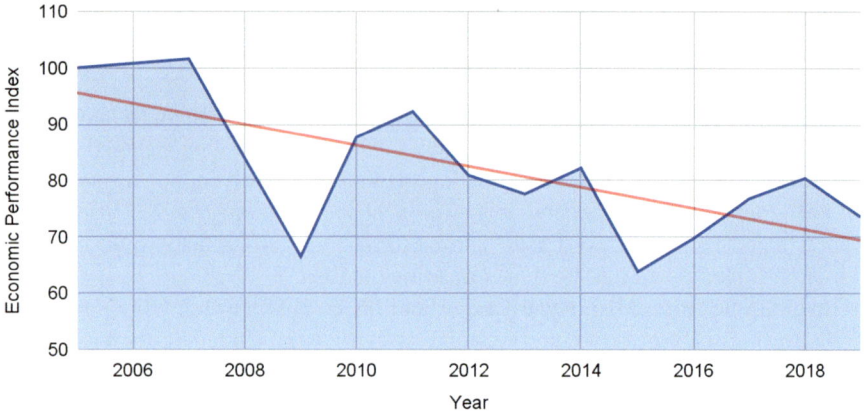

**Fig. 24** Economic performance index. *Source* Constructed from OECD capital markets dataset (Rangeley and Baker 2022). © Max Rangeley 2022. All Rights Reserved

competitive market." They attribute the rise of the zombies to "bank forbearance," which is more likely to come from weak than strong banks. They show that "zombie congestion" makes it harder for "productive firms to attract more capital." The greater the share of capital bound up in zombies, the less able the system is to get capital into the hands of strong firms.[19] They further showed that weak banks worsen the problem of poor capital allocation.

Rangeley and Baker (2022) compute the "Economic Performance Index," which "combines the Asset Turnover Ratio, Return on Assets and Return on Equity into a single metric, which we can analyse relative to growth in debt over time." Crudely, it shows how much output bang you get for your input buck. Its recent performance is shown in Fig. 24, which was "constructed using 49,607 companies in 131 countries" and setting the index to 100 for 2005. The figure reveals that we are getting less and less output bang per input buck.

Rangeley and Baker (2022) note that most econometric studies of the sluggish macroeconomic performance of recent years "conclude that monetary stimulus is the antidote rather than the poison." Fig. 25 adds corporate liabilities to the plot of the Economic Performance Index using the same 49,607 companies in 131 countries. Both indices were set to 100 for 2005. Corporate debt is growing, but "economic performance" is declining. The dismal performance of the Economic Performance Index gives us further evidence that today's faded-market economy is generating ever greater amounts of malinvestment.

Building on this insight into debt growth and economic performance from Fig. 25, Fig. 26 shows the Economic Performance Index divided by liabilities, giving an indication of how productively—or unproductively—debt has been used during the

---

[19] As Andrews and Petoulakis note, the result was also reached by Müge Adalet McGowan and her co-authors. See McGowan et al. (2018), which appeared earlier as OECD Economics Department Working Papers, No. 1372.

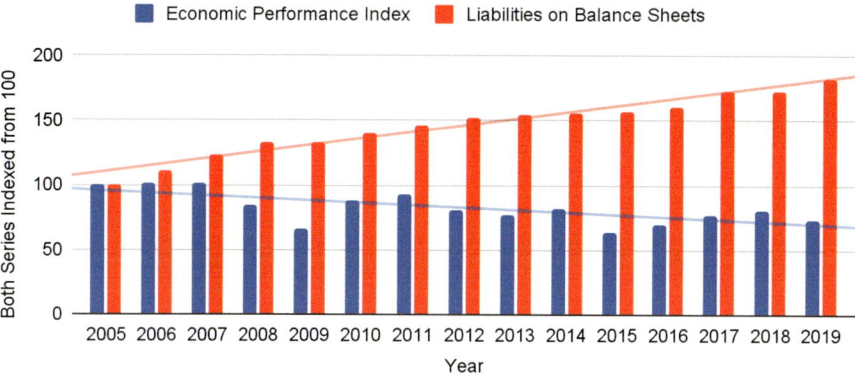

**Fig. 25** Economic performance index and liabilities on balance sheets. *Source* Constructed from OECD capital markets dataset (Rangeley and Baker 2022). © Max Rangeley 2022. All Rights Reserved

phases of artificially cheap credit. Figure 27 then takes this same metric and displays it alongside the growth in the balance sheet of the European Central Bank during the same period.

While the average productivity of debt has been shrinking, the balance sheet of the European Central Bank (ECB) has been growing. Growth in the ECB's balance sheet helps explain Europe's relatively weak and lack-lustre economic performance. The ECB policy of "quantitative easing" (QE) has included a variety of asset-buying programs that get switched on and off as conditions change. These programs include the public sector purchase programme (PSPP), which buys up bonds issued by government entities and the corporate sector purchase programme (CSPP), which buys up corporate bonds. The bank announced in July 2022 that it will "tilt" its

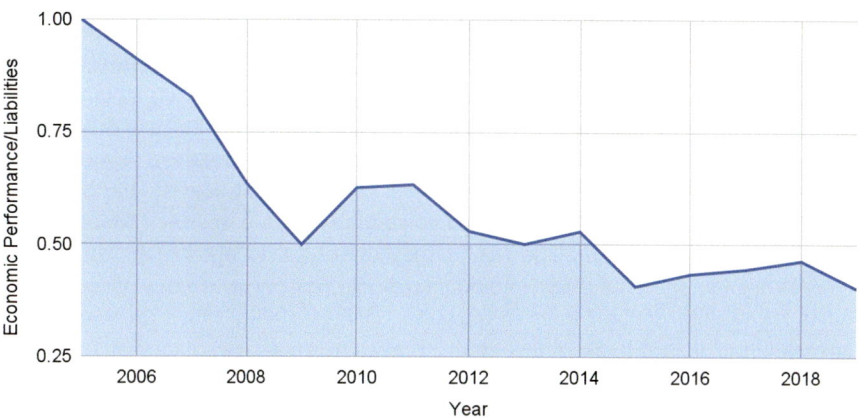

**Fig. 26** Economic performance index/Liabilities ratio. *Source* Constructed from OECD capital markets dataset (Rangeley and Baker 2022). © Max Rangeley 2022. All Rights Reserved

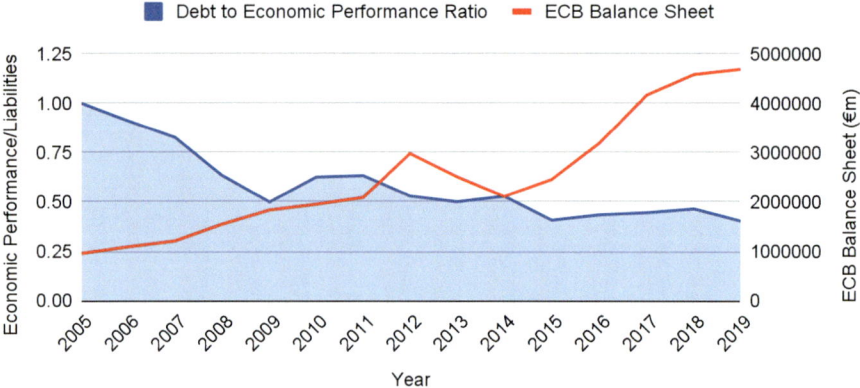

**Fig. 27** Economic performance index/liabilities ratio and ECB balance sheet. *Source* Constructed from OECD capital markets dataset, ECB (Rangeley and Baker 2022). © Max Rangeley 2022. All Rights Reserved

corporate holdings "towards issuers with better climate performance" (ECB, 2022). Thus, as Bernoth and Dietz have emphasised, the ECB does not practice market neutrality, whereby "a central bank tries to keep the relative prices of all assets equal so as to not give individual Member States or selected corporate sectors a financial advantage and to not hamper competitiveness and market discipline" (Bernoth and Dietz 2023). It's picking winners and losers. By early 2023, these programs, especially CSPP, made the ECB "Europe's largest purchaser of corporate bonds" (Webb 2023). The ECB's intrusive role in Europe's corporate bond market helps to explain the area's economic sluggishness. QE does give a temporary boost to GDP, but at the cost of long-run degradation in the quality of the investments being made.

The ECB corporate sector purchase programme is bad for the economy overall. But it is just fine for the corporations favoured by the program. They get their credit on the cheap and before prices have a chance to rise. Such inequalities in how new money is spread through the economy are "Cantillon effects." Richard Cantillon wrote an "Essay on the Nature of Trade in General" (*Essai sur la Nature du Commerce en Général*) in 1755. In it, he noted that new money comes to some first and others later. "If the increase of actual money comes from Mines of gold or silver," for example, the owners of these mines will increase their spending first as will "the Smelters, Refiners," and others closely connected to mining. Then come the "Mechanicks" and others who serve them. The new money drives prices up, which "diminishes of necessity the share of other inhabitants of the State who do not participate at first in the wealth of the Mines in question" (Higgs 1964). Much the same thing happens when central banks inject credit. It goes to some first, others later. The net effect, while damaging overall, is beneficial to those close to the font of new funds. In Europe, that means those whose bonds are purchased by the ECB. As Rangeley and Baker (2022) say, there is "a transfer of wealth towards the receivers of newly created money, but they will also thereby pull resources from the rest of the economy, bringing about distortions."

We have seen good evidence that the current policy regime in the US, UK, Europe, and elsewhere is suppressing the Schumpeterian forces of creative destruction. The salutary forces of creative destruction have been suppressed in part by an ongoing policy of driving down interest rates even to negative values. Schumpeterian dynamics have also been suppressed by routine bailouts. The presence of levitating firms has contributed to the problem by preventing capital from flowing to higher valued uses. Recall that levitating firms have an incentive to increase firm growth and become too big to fail and too big to jail. Thus, levitating firms will reinvest their profits ("retain earnings") beyond the profit-maximising level.[20] Schumpeterian gales of creative destruction are further suppressed when central banks do as the ECB has done: pick winners and losers in the game of market competition.

Further evidence on the suppression of Schumpeterian creative destruction is provided by Rangeley and Baker (2022)'s Figs. 28 and 29. The figures show that the importance of first-time bond issuers has been falling relative to incumbent issuers. Figure 28 shows that as the Federal Funds Rate has shrunk, the fraction of American bond issues from new issuers has shrunk. Figure 29 shows that as the ECB discount rate has shrunk, the fraction—and, lately, the number—of European bond issues from new issuers has shrunk. In the US, Rangeley and Baker (2022) report, the number of bond issues rose from 510 in 2000 to 924 in 2020. They elaborate, "the percentage of active issuers expanded from 55 to 71% while first-time issuers almost halved from 39 to 20% Despite an initial surge following the Financial Crisis, the rate of first-time issuers in Europe fell from 43 to 24%." This shrinkage in virgin bond issues is just what you would expect from a zombified economy. We have seen that firms are being kept alive by artificially low interest rates, bank forbearance, and routine bailouts. And we have seen Andrews and Petoulakis explain that "zombie congestion" makes it harder for "productive firms to attract more capital." Virgin issues are being crowded out by zombies and other incumbents in the corporate bond market.

The phenomenon of zombie firms has been noted repeatedly in this chapter. The faded-market economy keeps them going when they would not survive in a more competitive economy. We saw that the term "zombie company" was coined to describe the situation in 1990s Japan. As Rangeley and Baker (2022) note, "it may well not be coincidental that Japan was the first country to implement zero percent interest rates and other exotic monetary policy and then experienced the rise of zombie companies during their lost decade, which has since become a generation." A 2018 BIS study concluded, "lower rates boost aggregate demand and raise employment and investment in the short run. But the higher prevalence of zombies they leave behind misallocate resources and weigh on productivity growth" (Banerjee

---

[20] While it is customary to speak of "maximizing profits," that phrase can have an ambiguous meaning. Is it better to have a profit of 12 units today and 2 units tomorrow or 3 today and 14 tomorrow? This sort of question cannot be answered by invoking the maxim "maximize profits." A firm that acts in the interests of its shareholders will maximize their *wealth*. It will maximize the present value of the total payouts that will be made to shareholders in the future.

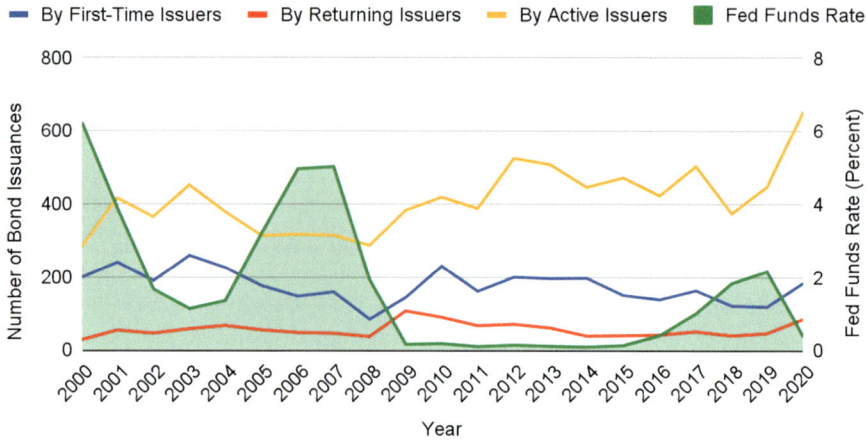

**Fig. 28** Fed Funds Rate and bond issuer incumbency. *Source* Constructed from OECD capital markets dataset (Rangeley and Baker 2022). © Max Rangeley 2022. All Rights Reserved

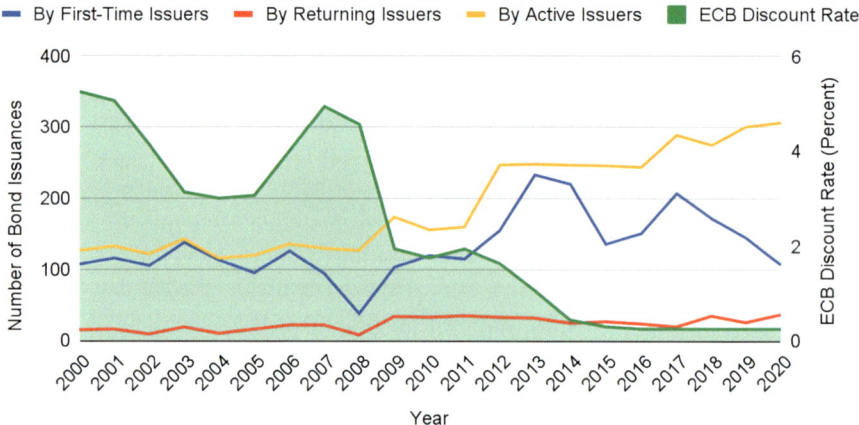

**Fig. 29** ECB discount rate and bond issuer incumbency. *Source* Constructed from OECD capital markets dataset (Rangeley and Baker 2022). © Max Rangeley 2022. All Rights Reserved

and Hofmann 2018, p. 77). Rangeley and Baker's Fig. 30 chronicles the rise of the zombies since about 1980. They used data from 14 countries to study the link between interest rates and zombie-hood; we can see below how each phase of lower interest rates over the last generation corresponds to a commensurate increase in zombies.[21]

The descent into today's faded-market economy has been a long march towards the sort of system described by the famous economist János Kornai in his theory

---

[21] The fourteen economies' data integrated into this metric are those of Australia, Belgium, Canada, Denmark, France, Germany, Italy, Japan, the Netherlands, Spain, Sweden, Switzerland, the United Kingdom and the United States; 32,000 companies in total were used.

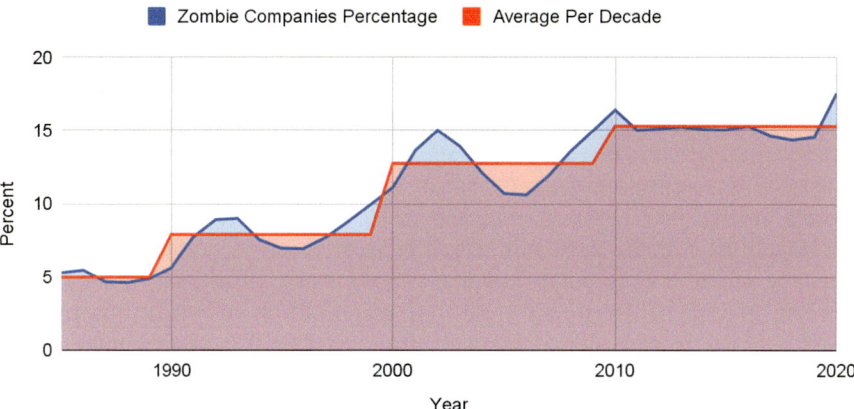

**Fig. 30** Zombie companies percentage for 14 economies. *Source* Bank for International settlements (Rangeley and Baker 2022). © Max Rangeley 2022. All Rights Reserved

of "The Soft Budget Constraint" (Kornai 1986). The theory concerns the budget constraints of firms. But the idea might best be introduced by thinking of one's personal budget constraint, which defines the limits of what you can spend. You are generally *constrained* to spend no more, on average, than your income. Your budget constraint will not allow you, for example, to rent an apartment whose monthly rent exceeds your monthly income. If you have a "hard" budget constraint and can't pay your rent, you'll be tossed out on the street.[22] But if family and friends are willing to help, your budget constraint is softened. How soft it will be depends on the finances and good will of those you might call upon for help. It is much the same with firms. In a market economy with relatively hard budget constraints, to paraphrase Kornai (1986, p. 4), firms must cover their expenses from the income generated by selling their output or otherwise earning a return on their assets.

Kornai notes two conditions for a budget constraint to be softened. First, "the strict relationship between expenditure and earnings has been relaxed, because excess expenditure over earnings will be paid by some other institution, typically by the State" (Kornai 1986, p. 4) Think bailouts and creditor forbearance. Second, "the decision-maker expects such external financial assistance with high probability and this probability is firmly built into his behavior." If you are too big to fail and you know it, then you have a soft budget constraint. Recall the theory of "entangled political economy" noted in Chap. 4. Kornai (1986, pp. 8–9) anticipates this theory by saying, "Our firm has horizontal relationships with his customers and suppliers, and at the same time a very special vertical relationship with the State." When budget constraints are soft, it takes three to tango: buyer, seller, government. "The notion of the soft budget constraint," Kornai (1986, p. 9) explains, "refers to a trend in

---

[22] The "if" in the claim just made is important. Laws governing eviction relax budget constraints to different degrees in different countries. Domurath and Mak (2020) note, for example, that Italian landlords have "encountered problems enforcing the terms of their rental agreements and evicting tenants". Such problems soften the budget constraints of Italian renters.

modern society: the relaxation of financial discipline, the weakening of the feeling that spending, survival, expansion depend on earning capability and not on external assistance."

Kornai identifies three broad consequences of soft budget constraints. First, the firm becomes less price sensitive. When the price of an input goes up, the firm responds less promptly and less fully than it would have with a hard budget constraint. Second, precisely because it has become insensitive to prices, the firm is less efficient than it would have been with a hard budget constraint. "Allocative efficiency cannot be achieved when input–output combinations do not adjust to price signals" (Kornai 1986, p. 10) Importantly, the firm becomes a more political beast. "The attention of the firm's leaders is distracted from the shop floor and from the market to the offices of the bureaucracy where they may apply for help in case of financial trouble (Kornai 1986, p. 10). As Kornai notes, soft budget constraints protect firms from Schumpeter's creative destruction. Finally, Kornai tells us that soft budget constraints create a "shortage economy." If you expect to be bailed out or to enjoy your creditors' forbearance, then "there is no compulsory limit on demand for inputs, and particularly, on investment (Kornai 1986, p. 11). Today, shortages are often called "supply chain problems." And recently we have had "supply chain problems." Their persistence is illustrated by a Reuters story from May of 2023: "US supply chain woes shift and persist in 2023 (Baertlein 2023)."

When budget constraints are generally soft, Kornai points out, there is nothing to coordinate the plans of the different firms. Each charges off in its own direction, and no discipline of potential losses constrains them to bring their actions into alignment with other firms such as the suppliers of their inputs and demands of their outputs. And in this sort of an environment, Kornai tells us, "The transmission between a tighter monetary policy and the micro-response becomes unreliable" (Kornai 1986, pp. 12–13). Thus, tight monetary policy no longer causes a reflux of resources out of high-duration projects.

It is revealing that the primary application of Kornai's theory was to socialist economies. But the theory applies to the mixed economies we tend to see today as well. Budget constraints were softer in the old socialist economies of Central and Eastern Europe than in the democratic West. But they were not hard in either case. In 1986 Kornai warned his readers, "It would be a grave mistake to overate the similarities between socialist and non-socialist economies" with respect to soft budget constraints. As we have seen, however, budget constraints have been growing progressively softer since 1980 or so. The budget constraints of today's mixed economies are harder than the budget constraints of the old Soviet system. But they are softer today than they were in 1982, the bottom of the last classical Austrian cycle in the US. And they are softer than they were when Kornai wrote in 1986.

The classical statements of Austrian business cycle theory assumed hard budget constraints, which was the right assumption when Hayek and Mises worked it all out. Monetary expansion causes interest rates declines and a false credit boom. Resources flow into high-duration projects, which Hayek somewhat mistakenly called "earlier stages of production." The boom is "false" because it is not sustainable. The bubble will burst sooner or later, whether the immediate cause is "real" or "monetary."

Once the bust is on, resources will flow back out of higher-duration projects and into lower-duration projects. This resource reflux is inevitable in the world of hard budget constraints. The world of the classical Austrian business cycle theory is shrinking in the rearview mirror. Since the bailout of Lockheed in 1971 the US has been moving slowly at first, but with increasing speed towards ever-softer budget constraints. After about 1980, budget constraints were soft enough to somewhat qualify the classical Austrian story in America. The story is different in other countries. The UK and New Zealand both had significant episodes of economic liberalisation. But they were temporary episodes. Today, budget constraints in Europe, the UK, the US, New Zealand and Australia are all quite soft and seem destined to grow only softer in the future. The classical Austrian business cycle theory cannot be applied to this new world of soft budget constraints and the faded-market economy without strong amendments. The key point is that resource reflux is no longer inevitable. Mises warned that "catastrophe" was the inevitable result of continued monetary expansion meant to avoid "the final collapse of a boom brought about by credit expansion." And he was right for a world with hard budget constraints. In the mushy world of soft budget constraints, the game can go on for a long time. Economic activity grows progressively more arbitrary and inefficient without a final day of reckoning. For as long as technological progress advances rapidly enough, we can even enjoy increases in the average level of material comfort. But such progress is itself impeded by soft budget constraints.

Interest rates should be free to move to their supply and demand levels. This "laissez faire" prescription repudiates the all-too-common macroeconomic posture of twiddling. The macroeconomist imagines themself outside the system, controlling it by twiddling a few dials. Figure 31 illustrates. It shows the famous macroeconomist A. W. Phillips in front of his MONIAC computer in about 1950.[23] MONIAC was not a modern digital computer. It was an old-fashioned analogue computer that used water rushing through tubes and resting in tubs to model the macroeconomy. It may have been this machine that induced Alan Coddington to coin the term "hydraulic Keynesianism" (Coddington 1976). As we can see in the photo, Phillips stands outside the system ready to twiddle the dials and move the system to its full-employment equilibrium. Standard approaches to macroeconomic policy, including monetary policy, take this twiddling posture. The expert stands outside the system and adjusts the dials. They imagine themself almost literally dialling up a strong economy.

One problem with this way of thinking about the policy expert is that it makes them a "Big Player."[24] A Big Player has three defining characteristics. They influence the market in question and are in this sense "big." They are largely immune from the discipline of profit and loss. And, finally, they are not bound by rules, but act on their discretion. A central bank that practices discretionary monetary policy is the quintessential Big Player. It seems at first that discretion is more rational than being bound to a potentially arbitrary rule of monetary policy. As conditions

---

[23] Phillips (1950) describes several such machines in his article.

[24] See Koppl (2002, 2014).

**Fig. 31** The economist as outside expert (LSE 2009)

change, shouldn't policy change too? What this would-be rational attitude overlooks, however, is the difficulty of predicting what a Big Player will do.

Precisely because the Big Player exercises discretion, they are unpredictable. And that unpredictability creates uncertainty among business investors. Creative destruction takes another hit. And we have seen the disastrous consequences of a largely unconstrained governmental apparatus free to twiddle the dials and fuss and bother and intervene. The result has not been an ever stronger economy. The result has been declining economic performance and a zombified economy. A monetary constitution is an alternative to Big Players, continuous suppression of interest rates, and routine bailouts. The government should be unable to practice discretionary monetary policy, to bailout favoured firms, to compel interest rates ever lower, to buy up corporate bonds, to pick winners in the marketplace. Calling for a policy of "laissez faire" is calling for the economic doctors to stop bleeding the patient to death.

We have, then, two choices. We can continue to bleed the patient to death with policies that suppress interest rates and soften budget constraints, or we restore a meaningful market economy. Our first option is to continue on the path of ever softer budget constraints. It is hard to predict how much longer that choice will be feasible. But it is certainly the path of decreasing economic efficiency and increasing discoordination among the plans of economic actors. That inefficiency and discoordination will eventually overwhelm the beneficial forces of technological progress and we will find larger and larger segments of the population growing poorer and poorer. America's "deaths of despair" chronicled by Case and Deaton show that the proportion of the population growing poorer is itself growing (Case and Deaton 2020) It would be kinder, and more just to find a better option. Our second option is to face up to the situation and make the necessary changes. We should abandon the delusion that economic experts can stand outside the system, twiddle a few knobs, and dial up economic strength. We should return to the system of profit *and loss* by refusing to socialise losses anymore. We should prevent corporations from owning *voting* shares of other corporations, thus ending the unhappy phenomenon of levitating firms. We should put a stop to bailout, bailout, bailout. And, finally, we should restore honest money, which would allow interest rates to move to their supply and demand levels.

The right choice is clearly the second option. The right choice is to restore market prices, hard budget constraints, honest money, and economic liberalism. It is not the easy choice, but it is the only choice.

# References

Ahrend R, Cournede B, Price R (2008) Monetary policy, market excesses, and financial turmoil. OECD Economics Department working paper no. 597

Andrews D, Petroulakis F (2017) Breaking the shackles: zombie firms, weak banks and depressed restructuring in Europe. OECD Economics Department working papers, no. 1433

Baertlein L (2023) US supply chain woes shift and persist in 2023, Reuters. https://www.reuters.com/business/retail-consumer/reuters-events-us-supply-chain-woes-shift-persist-2023-2023-05-17/. Accessed September 2023

Banerjee R, Hofmann B (2018) The rise of zombie firms: causes and consequences. BIS Q Rev September

Bank of England (2023a) Interest rates and bank rate. https://www.bankofengland.co.uk/monetary-policy/the-interest-rate-bank-rate. Accessed April 2023

Bank of England (2023b) Quantitative easing. https://www.bankofengland.co.uk/monetary-policy/quantitative-easing. Accessed April 2023

Bauer M, Rudebusch G, Wu J (2014) Term premia and inflation uncertainty: empirical evidence from an international panel dataset: comment. Am Econ Rev 104(1):323–337. https://doi.org/10.1257/aer.104.1.323

Bernanke B (2004) The great moderation speech at the meeting of the Eastern Economic Association, Washington, D.C., Federal Reserve, 20 February

Bernoth K, Dietz S (2023) Selective bond purchases—may the ecb chose winners and losers. The Economists' Voice

Board of Governors of the Federal Reserve System (US). Households and nonprofit organizations; Net worth, level [TNWBSHNO], Federal Reserve Bank of St Louis

Board of Governors of the Federal Reserve System (US). Nonfinancial corporate business; debt securities; liability, level [NCBDBIQ027S], Federal Reserve Bank of St Louis

Board of Governors of the Federal Reserve System (US). Effective federal funds rate [FEDFUNDS], Federal Reserve Bank of St Louis

Board of Governors of the Federal Reserve System (US). Delinquency rate on business loans, all commercial banks [DRBLACBS], Federal Reserve Bank of St Louis

Bordo M, Landon-Lane J (2013) Does expansionary monetary policy cause asset price booms; some historical and empirical evidence. NBER, working paper 19585

Borio C, Zhu H (2012) Capital regulation, risk-taking and monetary policy: a missing link in the transmission mechanism? J Financ Stab 8(4):236–251. Also available as BIS working paper 268

Bryan M (2023) The great inflation. Federal Reserve History. https://www.federalreservehist ory.org/essays/great-inflation#:~:text=Inflation%20began%20ratcheting%20upward%20in,lat ter%20half%20of%20the%201980s. Accessed 21 May 2023

Caballero R, Hoshi T, Kashyap A (2008) Zombie lending and depressed restructuring in Japan. Am Econ Rev 98(5):1943–1977

Case A, Deaton A (2020) Deaths of despair and the future of capitalism. Princeton University Press, Princeton

Çelik S, Demirtaş G, Isaksson M (2020) Corporate bond market trends, emerging risks and monetary policy. OECD Capital Market Series, Paris

Coddington A (1976) Keynesian economics: the search for first principles. J Econ Lit 14(4):1258–1273

Deb HC (2014) Vol 588. https://hansard.parliament.uk/commons/2014-11-20/debates/141120480 00001/MoneyCreationAndSociety. Accessed 24 May 2022

Decker R, Haltiwanger J, Jarmin R, Miranda J (2016) Changing business dynamism: volatility of shocks vs. responsiveness to shocks. Working paper

Domurath I, Mak C (2020) Private law and housing justice in Europe. Mod Law Rev 86(3):1188–1220

Ebeling RM, Hayek FA (1997) Can we still avoid inflation? In: The Austrian theory of the trade cycle and other essays. Ludwig von Mises Institute of Auburn University, Auburn, pp 93–110

Federal Reserve (2023) Federal Reserve Board—Recent balance sheet trends. https://www.federa lreserve.gov/monetarypolicy/bst_recenttrends.htm. Accessed April 2023

Federal Reserve Bank of New York (2023) Effective federal funds rate. https://www.newyorkfed. org/markets/reference-rates/effr. Accessed April 2023

Federal Reserve Bank of St. Louis (2023) NBER based recession indicators for the United States from the period following the peak through the trough. Federal Reserve Bank of St. Louis. https://fred.stlouisfed.org/series/USRECD. Accessed September 2023

Feser E, Blackhouse R (2008) Hayek on money and the business cycle. In: The Cambridge companion to Hayek. Cambridge University Press, Cambridge, pp 34–50

Galbraith J (1954) The great crash 1929. Houghton Mifflin Company, Boston

Gopinath G, Kalemli-Ozcan S, Karabarbounis L, Villegas-Sanchez C (2017) Capital allocation and productivity in South Europe. Q J Econ 132(4):1915–1967

Greenspan A (1994) Federal reserve bulletin: July 1994, vol 8, no 7. Board of Governors of the Federal Reserve System, Washington D.C. Publications Committee

Greenspan A (2008) Testimony of Dr Alan Greenspan prepared for committee of government oversight and reform given, 23 October 2008

Greenwood R, Hanson SG (2013) Issuer quality and corporate bond returns. Rev Financ Stud 26(6):1483–1525

Hartwich O (2020) Why this is the biggest global bailout in history. Dr Oliver Hartwich. https://oliverhartwichcom/2020/09/15/why-this-is-the-biggest-global-bailout-in-history/. Accessed September 2023

Higgs H (trans, ed) (1964) Essai sur la Nature du Commerce en Général. Augustus M Kelley, New York

IMF (2020) Japan: demographic shift opens door to reforms. https://wwwimforg/en/News/Articles/2020/02/10/na021020-japan-demographic-shift-opens-door-to-reforms. Accessed May 2023

Jiménez G, Ongena S, Peydró J-L, Saurina J (2014) Hazardous times for monetary policy: what do twenty-three million bank loans say about the effects of monetary policy on credit risk-taking? Econometrica 82(2):463–505

Kaldor N (1966a) Marginal productivity and the macro-economic theories of distribution: comment on Samuelson and Modigliani. Rev Econ Stud 33(4):309–319

Kaldor N (1966b) Causes of the slow rate of economic growth of the United Kingdom. Cambridge University Press, Cambridge

Koop A (2021) Mapping the world's youngest and oldest countries. visual capitalist. https://wwwvisualcapitalistcom/worlds-youngest-and-oldest-countries. Accessed May 2023

Koppl R (2002) Big players and the economic theory of expectations. Palgrave Macmillan

Koppl R (2018) Expert failure. Cambridge University Press, Camrbidge

Koppl R (2014) From crisis to confidence: macroeconomics after the crash. Institute of Economic Affairs

Kornai J (1986) The soft budget constraint. Kyklos 39:3–30

Loomis C (2001) Warren Buffett on the stock market fortune magazine, December 10, 2001

LSE (2009) Professor A.W.H (Bill) Phillips with Phillips Machine c1958–67. https://www.flickr.com/photos/lselibrary/3833724890/. Accessed Aug 2024

McGowan MA, Andrews D, Millot V (2018) The walking dead: zombie firms and productivity performance in OECD Countries. Econ Policy 33

McGrattan E, Prescott E (2003) The 1929 stock market Irving fisher was right. Federal Reserve Bank of Minneapolis, Research Department Staff, Report 294

Moore B (1988) Horizontalists and verticalists: the macroeconomics of credit money. Cambridge University Press, Cambridge, UK

Murphy L (2018) The invisible land. Institute for Public Policy Research

Office for National Statistics (2020) House price to workplace-based earnings ratio. Office for National Statistics, London

Phillips AW (1950) Mechanical models in economic dynamics. Economica 17(67):283

Rangeley M, Baker S, (2022) Are we in the largest bubble in history. The Cobden Centre

Reuters (2019) Timeline-changes to India's repo rate since June 2000. https://www.reuters.com/article/india-cenbank-timeline-repo-idUKL3N21M2RT. Accessed May 2023

Rothbard M (1963) America's great depression. Van Nostrand, Princeton

Rothbard M (2011) Economic depressions: their cause & cure auburn: Mises Institute

Sabisky A (2018) Children of when: why housing is the solution to Britain's fertility crisis. Adam Smith Institute, London

Shiratsuka S (2003) The asset price bubble in Japan in the 1980s: lessons for financial and macroeconomic stability. BIS Papers, No 21

Smith A, Wagner R, Yandle B (2011) A theory of entangled political economy, with application to TARP and NRA. Public Choice 148:45–66

Stock J, Watson M (2003) Has the business cycle changed and why? In: Gertler M, Rogoff K (eds) NBER macroeconomics annual 2002. MIT Press, Cambridge, MA, pp 159–218

Hearings before the subcommittee on financial institutions supervision, regulation, and insurance of the committee on banking, finance, and urban affairs, house of representatives, ninety-eighth congress, second session, September 18, 19 and October 4 (1984). U.S. Government Printing Office, Washington

Tobin J, Brainard WC (1977) Asset markets and the cost of capital. Economic progress, private values, and public policy

Unattributed (1953) Excerpts from two Wilson hearings before senate committees on defense appointment. The New York Times, 24 Jan 1953, p 8

Unattributed (1979) Inflation is rising by 13.2% annually; June prices up 1%. The New York Times, 27 July 1979, p 1

Vitali J (2023) Homes for growth. Policy Exchange

Webb D (2023) ECB deepens green tilt in corporate bond purchase programme. Responsible Investor, 3 February 2023. https://www.responsible-investor.com/ecb-deepens-green-tilt-in-corporate-bond-purchase-programme. Accessed Sep 2023

World Bank. Inflation, consumer prices (annual %)—United Kingdom. https://data.worldbank.org/indicator/FP.CPI.TOTL.ZG?locations=GB. Accessed May 2023

# Policy Makers and the Age of Debt Bubbles

# Why the Monetary Policy Framework in Advanced Countries Needs Fundamental Reform

**William White**

## Introduction

I have been working in or around central banks for almost sixty years.[1] To my regret, as I look back on my career, I can now see that I was often guided by an evolving set of false beliefs about how an advanced economy works and how monetary policy might contribute to its better functioning. I was first an advocate of monetary policy targeting the exchange rate, then of targeting the natural rate of unemployment, then of targeting monetary aggregates and, more recently, of pursuing the near-term stability of some index of consumer prices. Indeed, a summing up of my career, prior to joining the Bank for International Settlements (BIS) in 1994, might well have been "I'm sorry, it seemed like a good idea at the time".[2]

---

[1] My Ph.D thesis at the University of Manchester, begun in 1965, focussed on UK monetary policy in the post-war period. After beginning my working life at the Bank of England in 1969, I spent 22 years at the Bank of Canada, ending as Deputy Governor (International). From 1995 I had the post of Economic Adviser at the Bank for International Settlements in Basel, the meeting place for central banks globally. After retirement from the BIS in 2008, I served until 2018 as the Chair of the Economic Development and Review Committee at the OECD in Paris. This committee conducts country surveys and provides policy advice on both macroeconomic and structural issues.

[2] For an overview of my evolving beliefs, and indeed much of conventional macroeconomics, see White (2013).

---

W. White (✉)
131 Bloor Street West, Unit 615, Toronto, ON M5S1S3, Canada
e-mail: whitewilliam7188@gmail.com

© The Author(s), under exclusive license to Springer Nature Switzerland AG 2024
M. Rangeley (ed.), *The Age of Debt Bubbles*, Professional Practice in Governance and Public Organizations, https://doi.org/10.1007/978-3-031-66473-1_4

The fundamental objective underlying the more recent of these policy prescriptions was strongly suggested by the inflationary crises of the 1970s and early 1980s. It seemed obvious in the aftermath that monetary policy should seek to prevent such crises by maintaining projected inflation at some low level.[3] Since inflation was believed to respond to unemployment, this also implied a primary focus on labour market and output "gaps" in the real economy.[4] Financial sector developments, including the evolution of credit and debt, were thought to be of no great importance in the setting of monetary policy.[5]

This focus on the "real" economy urgently needs rethinking, as the BIS suggested for many years.[6] Monetary policy should be guided much more by financial sector developments (credit and debt) and much less by near-term targets for inflation. The pursuit of stable prices remains important but policy should focus on success over a much longer time period than the two year horizon that has become fashionable in recent decades.[7]

Perhaps the most effective way of showing the need for fundamental monetary reform is to point out the negative implications of the monetary policies followed by the major central banks in the advanced economies over the last few decades.

First, the general adoption of a positive (+2%) inflation target has prevented the downward adjustment of prices that would be the natural product of increases in productivity and positive supply shocks. As a result, prices have been drifting upwards (and significantly) for decades. Second, the recurrent use of monetary easing to spur demand and raise inflation has become increasingly ineffective. Current monetary policy faces a fundamental problem of temporal inconsistency: solving today's problems also makes tomorrow's problems worse. Third, stimulative monetary policy has had a variety of unintended and unwelcome consequences that seem likely to continue worsening; credit "booms and busts", potential financial instability, fiscal unsustainability, a progressive loss of central bank "independence", growing inequality of wealth and opportunity and a slower growth rate of potential output. Fourth, as the threat posed by these unintended problems has cumulated over time, "exit" and the "renormalization" of policy has become ever harder to achieve.

To sum up, the current monetary system has trapped us on a path we do not wish to follow because it leads inevitably to ever bigger problems. This is why fundamental reform is needed.

---

[3] Broadly speaking, the projection horizon was around two years and the inflation target was some measure of consumer prices.

[4] This is a basic implication of the Phillip's curve relationship. Absent supply side shocks, this relationship also implies there is no conflict between pursuing an unemployment target and an inflation target.

[5] To the degree central bankers were concerned with such issues, it was felt that regulatory agencies were primarily responsible for resolving problems.

[6] See BIS Annual Reports from the mid 1990's onwards. Also, for early papers see Borio et al. (2001), Borio and Lowe (2002) and White (2003).

[7] As always, there are exceptions to the rule. The Swiss National Bank has always preferred to pursue price stability over a medium-term horizon.

## Some Facts: How "Bubbles" Have Created "Bigger Bubbles"

Since roughly the latter part of the 1980s, the economies of the major countries have been characterized by three major trends. First, there was persistent downward pressure on wages and prices in advanced economies. In part, this was due to a growing labour force of baby boomers and the rising participation rate of women. Even more important, was the return of China and Eastern Europe to the global trading system. Not only could they provide lower priced goods but workers in advanced countries were faced with credible threats to move production to these countries. Second, there was widespread deregulation of financial systems facilitating faster credit growth from ever more diverse sources. Third, central banks became ever more committed to the pursuit of a low, positive inflation objective, an objective generally (and wrongly) referred to as "price stability".

In pursuing this last objective, central banks ignored the broader implications of the other two major trends. In effect, by adopting an over simplified model of the world, one that abstracted from both supply side and financial shocks, central bank policies have created the instability they were seeking to avoid.[8] Moreover, as the underlying problems have become worse, the capacity of monetary policy to respond has also become increasingly attenuated.

A particular shortcoming was ignoring the likelihood that an increasingly deregulated financial system might prove capable of creating destabilizing levels of credit and associated debt. Indeed, the first three of the four interest cycles we have seen since the late 1980s-ending in 1990, 2001, 2008 and 2020–ended with a financial crisis, while the fourth upturn was cut short by the covid pandemic. Each crisis had its origins in monetary stimulus intended to foster recovery from the previous recession, but each ended in financial "bust" and recession. Moreover, although the pace and magnitude of the monetary easing increased over successive cycles, the magnitude of the following recessions still became increasingly severe. This could indicate that the monetary cure for the downturn has been aggravating underlying problems the more frequently it has been used. If so, the implication would be that past "bubbles" might eventually culminate in still more intractable problems looking forward.[9]

Because monetary easing after the bust was always more aggressive than the subsequent tightening, peaks and troughs in policy rates also ratcheted down over time, eventually reaching zero or even slightly below zero. When rates did hit the "effective lower bound", yet central banks thought even lower rates were required, the monetary authorities responded with such unconventional measures as forward guidance, Quantitative Easing (QE) and, in the case of the Bank of Japan, yield curve control. This progression leads to the conclusion that, should the next bubble burst and cause a deep recession, monetary easing might not provide even the temporary

---

[8] In his recent autobiography, Paul Volcker (2018, p 227) makes a similar point. Also see Hannoun et al. (2019).

[9] White (2023) raises the possibility that future economic crises could trigger crises in a number of related systems, although he focuses most intently on the link between economic difficulties and turmoil in democratic political systems.

support it was able to provide in the past. This could imply a deflationary outcome, or even a highly inflationary one if monetary expansion were to be vigorously pursued regardless.

Arguably, the first of these expansionary interventions was the global easing required to support the US dollar after the Louvre agreement of 1987.[10] Further easing came in response to the global stock market crash that came in the fall of that year, a policy increasingly referred to as the "Greenspan put" limiting asset price declines. These actions might well have contributed to the Savings and Loan crisis in the United States in 1989, and also the deep financial crises that affected Japan, all the Scandinavian countries, and many other countries at around the same time.

The global reduction in interest rates that followed the 1990 contraction was promptly reversed as the economy recovered, but that reversal was then attenuated by another set of financial crises. As rates rose and the US dollar strengthened, many highly indebted countries in Latin America were hit by capital outflows during the "peso crisis" of 1994. In 1997, similar problems hit many Asian countries that had also previously enjoyed massive capital inflows. Then in 1998, the prospective failure of LTCM, a large US hedge fund, actually led to reductions in US policy rates which further fuelled an ongoing equity boom focussed on the technology, media and telecommunications sectors. When policy rates did tighten again, this boom collapsed, and a recession then followed.

As before, central banks began to lower policy rates in 2001, but did so even more aggressively than in the early 1990s and to a lower trough. Again, the global economy recovered while inflation stayed quiescent. Indeed, the post-2002 recovery was so strong, and inflation was so low and stable, that a new phrase was created to describe the economy's performance–the Great Moderation. While policy rates were raised from 2005 onwards, generally in "measured" steps, evidence once again began to accumulate of developing imbalances. In the English-speaking countries, household saving rates fell to record lows. This was accompanied by sharp increases in credit, private debt, leverage and asset prices in many large countries, as well as a number of emerging markets and important countries on the periphery of Europe.

House price increases and mortgage lending had been particularly strong in the United States with loans to "subprime" borrowers especially noticeable.[11] Moreover, in a new financial innovation, these loans had been securitized and then distributed widely to lenders in the broader economy. While US house prices first began to fall early in 2007, there was no generalized economic moderation until 2008 after the failure of a number of important American financial institutions. A financial crisis was then triggered in the United States, and the turmoil subsequently spread to Europe as many European financial institutions struggled to find short-term dollar

---

[10] The rest of this section on "Some Facts" is based on a rereading of successive Annual Reports of the Bank for International Settlements. I wrote the Introduction and Conclusions of that Report from June 1995 to June 2008, covering the largest part of the period under review.

[11] In part this was due to government support and mortgage guarantees.

financing for longer-term dollar assets.[12] In 2010 Europe was plunged into outright crisis as previous capital inflows into Italy, Spain, Ireland and Greece were reversed and the bond rates in those countries rose sharply against Bunds.

As in earlier cycles, policy rates were quickly lowered,[13] and still more aggressively than ever before. Indeed, a number of countries imposed negative rates on reserves held with them by commercial banks. In Europe, the President of the ECB vowed to do "whatever it takes" to stabilize financial developments in the Eurozone. Moreover, to help stabilize financial markets, central banks used aggressively a number of instruments of monetary expansion that had only been used rarely or more moderately before. Forward guidance about future policy rate moves was used to influence medium-term rates while central bank purchases of longer-term bonds helped push down longer-term rates. Fiscal expansion was also used to soften the downturn, although this was quickly reversed. In the Eurozone, the countries most affected by the crisis were eventually forced into outright fiscal austerity.[14]

Perhaps most important, policy rates were kept close to zero and unconventional monetary measures were maintained in use throughout the subsequent, long expansion extending to early 2020.[15] Nevertheless, in most advanced countries, the recovery was unusually slow and inflation targets were generally undershot, which provided the principal rationale for the decision not to tighten policy.

Yet, at the same time, there were many indicators of the further growth of financial imbalances. Debt ratios and asset prices rose, almost continuously and almost everywhere, while credit quality continued to deteriorate. There was also a significant shift in the source of credit. As banking regulation tightened, post-crisis, less well-regulated financial markets and non-bank financial institutions increasingly provided substitute sources of credit. Unfortunately, from a financial stability perspective, this also implied a growing lack of transparency about credit and other exposures within the financial system.[16] The growing use of derivative products to hedge portfolio exposures, often by opaque counterparties, was a particular source of uncertainty about the systemic implications of economic and financial shocks.[17]

---

[12] The crisis became known popularly as the Great Financial Crisis. However, some thoughtful commentators suggest it should rather be known as the North-Atlantic Financial crisis. See Fender and McGuire (2010) and Tooze (2019).

[13] An important if temporary exception was the ECB which, for a time, continued to raise rates in response to continuing inflationary pressures.

[14] This policy subsequently attracted criticism. See White (2015).

[15] The initial expansion of central bank balance sheets was an entirely justified response to market disorder and fears of financial instability. Subsequently, however, central bank purchases of longer-term securities (Quantitative Easing or QE) had a quite different objective; namely, to lower longer term interest rates to stimulate aggregate demand. Forward guidance was intended to lower medium term interest rates with the same objective in mind.

[16] See International Monetary Fund (2024).

[17] That there was valid reason for concern became evident in a bout of disorder and sharply higher rates in the UK gilt-edged market late in 2021. A new Prime Minister brought in a budget that for many reasons was deemed "highy imprudent" and gilt rates rose sharply. Unfortunately, many UK pension funds had followed portfolio strategies using derivatives which resulted in their facing large margin call as gilt rates rose. They were then forced to sell gilts to raise cash which exacerbated the

These were the prevailing circumstances when the covid pandemic hit the advanced countries in March of 2020. "Lockdowns", waves of infections and fears of infection then interacted to cause both aggregate demand and economic supply to fall massively. The former led to a steep recession while the latter contributed to a marked increase in inflation, particularly for goods.[18] Monetary policy responded with still lower policy rates, where possible, and an unprecedented increase in the use of unconventional instruments. Fiscal easing was also used much more aggressively than previously, with a much greater reliance on direct payments to households and companies. In combination, these policy measures constrained the contraction and contributed to a very sharp economic recovery. However, they also contributed to further, marked increases in both private debt and public debt.

The pandemic-induced increase in inflation was initially ignored as a "transitional" phenomenon and monetary policy remained highly expansionary until near the end of 2021. However, as inflation accelerated even as supply blockages eased, central bankers finally concluded they had to respond to constrain a possible wage-price spiral. Policy rates were then raised at an unprecedented pace, and with unprecedented correlation across major countries. Inflation then fell sharply as the negative supply shocks dissipated, but core inflation generally remained well above target levels through to the summer of 2024.

From the spring of 2023 onwards, some central bankers argued that enough had been done to reduce inflation back to the two per cent target. They generally suggested that monetary restraint had mostly to do with the **change** in stimulus, which had been massive, and the full effects of tightening to date remained to be seen. They concluded that, as inflation fell and real (ex post) rates rose, nominal rates should be lowered. However, others who shared that disinflationary objective felt that still higher nominal rates might be required since the **level** of real rates generally remained negative. In this eventuality, some in the former group also worried that still higher rates might trigger another private sector financial crisis.[19] By the summer of 2024, a compromise view seemed to be emerging in the United States that nominal policy rates should stay "higher for longer". Elsewhere, where inflationary pressures seemed more subdued, the appetite for further rate cuts was somewhat greater.

Moreover, and for the first time in recent years, worries began to surface about the effects of higher rates on the debt service capacities of major governments. Not only had higher deficits during the pandemic significantly raised the stock of

---

original problem and forced the Bank of England to step in. A number of commentators expressed concern that the UK experience might prove to be a "canary in the coal mine" for other countries. Fiscal imprudence could not only trigger a market reaction but in wholly unexpected ways.

[18] The demand for services, which generally involves human contact, fell particularly sharply. In contrast, the demand for goods rose sharply as fiscal easing increased household disposable income and orders for goods could be placed over the internet.

[19] Moreover, given that repeated use of monetary stimulus after previous financial crises seemed to have made the next crisis worse, supporters of lower policy rates worried that the next financial crisis might be worse still.

debt,[20] but central bank policies had raised the sensitivity of debt service to higher rates. Quantitative Easing, which replaced long-term government debt with overnight financing (reserves at the central bank), effectively shortened the duration of that debt. Moreover, the losses from higher rates were first recorded on the balance sheet of the central banks, raising fears of reputational implications.[21] Finally, the magnitude of the expansion of central bank balance sheets during the pandemic almost exactly matched the increased size of the government debt. This coincidence raised fears of "fiscal dominance" and, were it to continue, possibly much higher inflation in the future. These fears were amplified, in the United States in particular, by continuing high deficits even at full employment and political deadlock over how they might be reduced.

## Some Theory: How "False Beliefs" Contributed to "Bad Policy"

The Introduction to this paper listed a number of the negative consequences arising from the conduct of monetary policy over the last few decades. These developments occurred because central bankers in the advanced economies generally shared a set of "false beliefs". They overestimated the **need** for easy money. They overestimated its **effectiveness** in stimulating aggregate demand. They underestimated the **unintended consequences** and, finally, they underestimated how difficult it would be to **exit** from such policies.

### *The Need for Easy Money*

As noted above, the last few decades have been characterized by large, positive supply shocks in the global economy that led to persistent downward pressure on prices. There is a large, now largely forgotten literature, that suggests these initial price declines should have been allowed to happen.[22] For example, lower prices arising from positive productivity trends initially spread the benefits to consumers and workers. This would have helped avoid the worsening income inequality that has become so pervasive in many countries. Further, periods of falling prices to offset

---

[20] In contrast, higher but unexpected inflation during the pandemic lowered the ratio of debt to nominal GDP. This benefit could not be repeated if further inflation were to be anticipated and interest rates were to rise in consequence.

[21] The recorded losses of the Federal Reserve were almost $1 trillion by the end of 2023Q2. The Swiss National Bank recorded losses equal to 18 per cent of Swiss GDP in 2022.

[22] See Selgin (2018). Connolly (2023) makes a similar point, noting that the Fed's "original sin" was to lower policy rates in the face of the productivity surge of the late 1990s. This created an intertemporal disequilibrium which has continued to resonate until the present time.

rising prices at other times would have helped avoid the sharp upward trend in prices we have seen since the end of the Bretton Woods system in the early 1970s.

These arguments for allowing deflation were subordinated to the argument that deflation would lead to prices cascading downward and would culminate in depression. These latter arguments were largely based on the experience of Western countries in the 1930s. However, numerous historical studies indicate this experience was essentially unique.[23] Most periods when prices were falling were characterized by rising productivity and rising real GDP. As for cascading price declines, the experience of Japan is instructive. They have had gentle deflation since the early 1990s without any evidence of this phenomenon.

Unfortunately, once easy money has led to a significant rise in debt, the argument for not worrying about deflation loses a great deal of its force. These arguments were put forward by Irving Fisher[24] in the 1930s, and should concern us today. Nevertheless, Paul Volcker still put the ultimate blame for such problems on central bankers when he said[25] "Ironically, the 'easy money' striving for a 'little' inflation as a means of forestalling deflation, could, in the end, be what brings it about". In effect, central bankers now find themselves caught in a "debt trap". Failing to tighten policy encourages still more debt accumulation, but tightening could trigger unexpected consequences.

## The Effectiveness of Easy Money

Coming out of the 2009 recession, central banks (and the IMF and the OECD) for ten years in a row overestimated the growth rate of real GDP in the following year. Similarly, inflation was consistently forecast to rise faster than it actually did. An underlying problem was that the stimulus expected to arise from easy monetary policies failed to materialize. As discussed below, this problem might have been anticipated. At the least, it should have led to a fundamental reconsideration of the analytical (forecasting) framework that was producing such errors. Sadly, this has not happened.

John Maynard Keynes, in the General Theory (1936) warned against the efficacy of the expansionary monetary policies that he himself had recommended in the Treatise On Money (1930). "If we are tempted to assert that money is the drink that stimulates the system to activity, we must remind ourselves that there may be several slips between the cup and the lip". Plausible arguments support the view that low

---

[23] See Atkeson and Kehoe (2004) and Borio and Filardo (2004).

[24] Fisher (1933).

[25] Volcker (2018).

interest rates might not stimulate either consumption[26] or investment.[27] Indeed, these arguments imply low rates might even lead to less consumption and investment. The idea that lower rates increase wealth and therefore spur consumption also suffers from a fundamental analytical flaw.[28] Finally, experimental monetary policies could raise private unease, constraining Keynes' "animal spirits", and this could also lead to less spending rather than more.

Perhaps even more important than these static arguments, the effectiveness of monetary stimulus declines with repeated use. That is, there is a fundamental intertemporal inconsistency. To the extent lower rates do encourage spending, it is by bringing intended spending forward in time often through the vehicle of increased debt. If that spending does not generate the returns required to service the debt, then over time the debt becomes a burden reducing future spending. This is the feedback effect once referred to by Alan Greenspan as "headwinds". In fact, global debt ratios (to sectoral revenues or GDP) have been rising steadily since the 1980s, and this continued even after the onset of the recession of 2009. According to the Institute of International Finance, the global ratio of debt was 280% in 2008, 321% at the beginning of the pandemic in 2020 and then rose to a peak of 360% subsequently. Given that investment spending has declined in recent years, the presumption that a heavier debt load will eventually constrain spending seems increasingly plausible.[29]

## The Unintended Consequences of Easy Money

The **unintended accumulation of debt** is perhaps the most important of the unintended consequences, but by no means the only one.

**Inequality** of income, wealth and opportunity has been rising in many countries for a variety of reasons including technological change and globalization. However, easy monetary policies have worsened these trends to a significant degree. Richer people own most of the riskiest assets whose prices have been supported by low interest rates. While those who have benefitted the most have responded by increasing consumption, higher-income deciles still have higher saving rates than lower-income deciles. Thus, redistribution effects lower aggregate consumption and support arguments for continued easy money.

---

[26] See White (2016). For example, suppose people have a savings target which will allow them to buy an annuity of a certain size when they retire. If the rate at which their savings accumulate falls, as interest rates decline, then people must save more not less.

[27] See White (2016). For example, If future consumption is expected to be constrained, because current consumption has been financed with debt, why invest more today to meet future demand that will not materialize. As well, defined benefit pensions are a liability of the corporations that offer them. Lower returns on pension fund investments require a corporate top- up which reduces the cash flow available for investment.

[28] White (2006).

[29] This is the basic logic of a "Balance Sheet Recession". See Koo (2009) who analyses the causes and consequences of Japan's post 1990 economic performance.

**Financial instability** has also been encouraged in a variety of ways. Many financial institutions saw their lending margins squeezed by lower rates. Given the various competitive challenges already threatening banks (Fintech), insurance companies and pension funds (climate-related claims and longer living pensioners) some institutions even came to feel that their business model was under threat.[30] Not surprisingly, many financial institutions have reached for yield, and in consequence have taken on both more credit risk and more liquidity risk. The relative expansion of less traditional financial vehicles (like private equity and asset management firms) has led to the Financial Stability Board to raise still other concerns about potential financial instability.[31]

While an upward movement in asset prices was actually desired as part of the transmission process of monetary easing, it is hard to believe that an "everything bubble" was fully intended. Prior to some reversals in 2022, there was a relentless upward movement in the prices of almost all financial assets including commercial property and houses. The McKinsey Global Institute notes that these price increases were largely responsible for a new phenomenon. Since 2000, the rate of growth of "measured wealth" has for the first time ever greatly exceeded the growth of nominal GDP.[32] At the same time, credit spreads, duration spreads and measures of volatility all sank. While these developments set the stage for recent reversals, there remain considerable doubts as to whether the new downward phase in asset prices is over. What the implications of still larger losses might be for corporate insolvencies and economic stability more generally remains to be seen.

Finally, the absorption of bonds by central bank purchases (Quantitative Easing) might have contributed to the significant deterioration of market functioning seen over the last decade or so.[33] Continuing market "anomalies"[34] have been complemented by recurring "flash crashes" in various markets. Most important, there was a bout of massive disorder in the market for US Treasuries in September of 2019 which then recurred in March of 2020. In late 2021 a similar bout of disorder was observed in the market for UK gilt-edged securities, with long rates rising suddenly at an unprecedented rate.

---

[30] This too has further repercussions. For example, some companies are no longer willing to provide insurance coverage for houses in California and Florida.

[31] Financial Stability Board (2019). Also see International Monetary Fund (2024).

[32] The McKinsey Global Institute (2021) also points out that only seven percent of "measured wealth" (financial and real assets) are actually productive real assets like infrastructure, machinery and equipment and intangibles like software. The picture they paint is one of a huge, inverted and potentially unstable, financial pyramid resting on a tiny productive base. Also see White (2006) who had earlier raised similar concerns about the growing gap between "real wealth" and "measured wealth".

[33] Both tighter regulatory requirements and Quantitative Easing reduced the availability of collateral for market trading. This occurred at the same time that increased repo trading was demanding the use of more collateral and the size of the underlying markets was also growing rapidly. All of these developments threatened market liquidity.

[34] Borio et al. (2016).

While the Federal Reserve and the Bank of England stepped in to restore order, their interventions had at least two downsides.[35] First, they marked a transition from central banks being a "lender of last resort" to a "buyer of last resort", thus effecting a major extension of the financial safety net with an associated increase in moral hazard.[36] Second, they demanded an increase in the size of central bank balance sheets when the central banks were already committed to reducing them. This issue of "exit" is returned to below.

It might seem counterintuitive to suggest that easy money, and lower interest rates, promoted **fiscal unsustainability**. However, persistently low borrowing rates led governments, as well as other borrowers, to believe that their debts were sustainable and to put off needed measures of fiscal restraint. In association with the debt duration issues noted above,[37] many governments found themselves looking at a very challenging profile of future debt service requirements when interest rates did begin to rise in late 2021.

The way monetary policy has been conducted has also had implications for the **"independence" of central banks.** Many of their actions have had distributional implications and distributional issues are fundamentally political. Easy money and the associated increase in the price of assets overwhelming favour those who held the assets in the first place. Thus, wealth inequality has been added to long standing concerns about inequality of both income and opportunity. As well, quantitative easing and the effects on government debt service raise questions about central banks usurping fiscal policy,[38] while purchases of privately issued liabilities raise the issue of who has been favoured and why? All of the above considerations could imply closer political oversight of central banks than has been the case in recent years.[39] This comes on top of the need for ongoing cooperation between central banks and other government agencies in the pursuit of systemic financial stability.[40]

Another unintended consequence for central banks was that they had to change radically their **operating procedures for controlling short-term interest rates**. Previously, this was done through a "scarce reserve or corridor system" in which rates responded to differences between the level of reserves supplied by the central bank and the bank demand for such reserves implied by their clearing needs only. With reserves having expanded enormously, given Quantitative Easing, a new "ample

---

[35] The UK incident had a further complication. See footnote 17 above.

[36] Safety net provisions for financial firms have in fact been widening for decades, with deposit insurance and access to central bank lending increasingly widespread and lending terms less penal.

[37] What is also surprising is that more governments did not make a more determined attempt to increase the duration of their debt when long-term interest rates were low. Perhaps it is because short term rates were lower still, and this situation was expected to continue for the foreseeable future. In this regard, central bank "forward guidance" was distinctly unhelpful.

[38] Allen (2021).

[39] Sedgewick (2023).

[40] Central banks have generally been charged with responsibility for changing macroprudential polices to preserve the systemic stability of the financial system. However, many of the policy instruments used to do this are under the direct control of other government agencies like financial regulators.

reserve or floor" operating system was thought to be required. Borio (2023) argues convincingly that this new system is inferior to the old one and that we could and should return to it.[41] The new system also poses challenges for "exit" as will be discussed below.

**The potential growth rate** of the advanced economies might also have been reduced by past monetary policy. While neoclassical models say demand fluctuations and monetary policy have no lasting real effects on the economy, the facts seem to say otherwise.[42] A low interest rate environment has supported the survival of "zombie" companies" whose loans have been evergreened by poorly capitalized banks in particular.[43] These "zombies" absorbed resources that might have supported other more productive companies, but their continuing competition also helped keep down prices.

In addition, low borrowing costs contributed to a massive increase in the availability of financing for "high risk" but potentially "very high return" projects. Many well-established firms (especially in high tech industries) spent heavily on such "malinvestments", while the increased availability of venture capital led to the emergence of many companies that remained profitless for an abnormal number of years.[44] Finally, a low interest environment supported mergers and acquisitions and encouraged a degree of consolidation that many now find a cause for concern.[45] Should worsening market conditions force a shakeout of unviable companies, prices (or inflation) might fall less than might normally be expected. Indeed, there is some evidence for this in the recent rise of corporate profit margins in a number of countries.

Finally, some consideration needs to be given to the unintended implications for **emerging market countries**. As policy has ebbed and flowed in the advanced countries, short-term capital flows have created problems for emerging markets, both when capital has flown in and when it has flowed out. Albeit due in part to a "fear of floating", the emerging markets now suffer from many of the same unintended consequences as the advanced countries. The increase in debt ratios from 2008 to 2019 was described in a recent World Bank report[46] as "the largest, fastest and most broad based increase of debt" in the last 50 years. As a consequence, the IMF

---

[41] Borio argues that the scarce reserve system did not have to be replaced after QE since central banks retained the capacity to alter the composition of their liabilities. He also notes that the new system is far more costly since it requires central banks to pay interest on reserves to reduce the likelihood of excessive monetary and credit growth. Finally, the scarce reserve system reflects the principle that central bank balance sheets should be as small and as risk free as possible. See also Calomiris (2023).

[42] Cerra et al. (2023).

[43] See Acharya et al. (2010), Andrews et al. (2017) and Banerjee and Hoffman (2018). Poorly capitalised banks fear that recognizing losses could lead to their own bankruptcy.

[44] The business model was to subsidize prices to gain market share and eventual industry dominance. Evidently, if several firms in the same industry are behaving in this fashion, most of their hopes must be disappointed.

[45] See for example Lynn (2009) and the research work of the Open Market Institute which he previously headed. More recently, the Biden administration and the European Commission have been rethinking the criteria previously used for accepting mergers and acquisitions.

[46] See Koh and Yu (2020) as well.

estimated in 2022 that over 60 per cent of low-income countries were either "in distress" or at "high risk" of distress".

## *The Difficulties of "Exit" from Easy Money*

There are many political economy arguments for thinking that central banks will generally tighten too late after a period of monetary expansion.[47] Indeed, the way in which the unintended consequences of easy money have built up over time shows that this is a chronic tendency. Post pandemic, the delayed response of central banks to rising inflation provides further evidence of this tendency.[48] While higher inflation during and after the pandemic did eventually lead to significant monetary tightening, there are grounds for belief that further monetary tightening will be (and perhaps should be) impeded by a number of considerations.

Higher policy rates (or perhaps even "higher for longer") could trigger a crisis due to tensions generated by the unintended consequences of earlier policies. In this regard, fears of financial instability in the private sector should be a key consideration. So too should concerns about the implications for capital flows and emerging market economies.[49] Fears of fiscal unsustainability have also sharpened recently, which will surely raise further doubts about the "independence" of central banks.[50] Moreover, looking forward, the trade-off between allowing higher inflation, and the dangers of resisting it, are likely to become much worse as negative supply shocks replace positive ones.[51] Should "financial repression" be the strategy chosen to improve this trade-off,[52] "exit" would be even further delayed.

"Exiting" from Quantitative Easing has its own difficulties. Against a backdrop of increasing market disorder, the withdrawal of excess bank reserves could have unintended consequences. Acharya et al. (2023) argue that banks given excess bank reserves have made new commitments to clients to provide liquidity when needed. In effect excess reserves have been transformed into needed reserves. The implication is that Quantitative Tightening should likely be conducted even more prudently than raising policy rates.

---

[47] Group of Thirty (2015).

[48] Wheeler and Wilkinson (2022). An important consideration is that central banks gave "forward guidance" that rates would not be raised and therefore hesitated to negate their own advice. When rates did rise, borrowers who had acted in accordance with the "forward guidance" were understandably angry. The full implications for trust in government institutions remains to be seen.

[49] UNCTAD (2023) called for the Fed to eschew further tightening on the grounds that the emerging market economies would be disproportionately harmed by it.

[50] Sedgewick (2023).

[51] White (2023).

[52] Reinhart and Sbrancia (2015). "Financial repression" was used after WWII to deal with the overhang of sovereign debt. It involved letting inflation rise moderately while using administrative means to keep interest rates down. Bond holders suffered negative, real rates of return for a number of years before the debt overhang problem was resolved at their cost.

## Some Observations: How to Improve the Monetary Policy Framework?

If "bad policy" outcomes are largely due to the "false beliefs" of central bankers, then it is tempting to say the solution is to replace those false beliefs with a more realistic set of assumptions. BIS publications, dating back decades, have attempted to do so. They suggested the joint use of monetary and macroprudential instruments to lean against the financial cycle. In effect, this means adopting a longer horizon in the pursuit of price stability to take account of the unintended consequences. However, even these relatively modest[53] suggestions for change to the policy framework have received virtually no support from the central banks of the advanced economies. Even the Great Financial Crisis, which extant models said could not happen, failed to stop central banks from applying "more of the same" policies that caused the crisis in the first place.

Perhaps what is needed is a more fundamental attack on the philosophical under-pinnings of the current system of "false beliefs". The underlying assumption made by central bankers is that they understand how the financial and economic system works. It is linear and deterministic, and they can control it in consequence. Unfortunately, there are very plausible reasons to believe this fundamental assumption is not true. A philosopher would say the central bankers have made a profound epistemological[54] error. They have misunderstood the nature of the system they are trying to control.

Rather than being deterministic and linear in its properties, economies are complex, adaptive systems having very different properties.[55] Such systems are ubiquitous in nature and society and have been well studied by other disciplines. This work can be interpreted to draw some quite simple lessons to guide the monetary authorities in their conduct of monetary policy.[56] It has implications for the choice of objectives for monetary policy, for assessing and reacting to deviations from objectives, and for preventing and managing crises. Proceeding down this path would be a clear improvement on the current approach. Note, however, that it would still leave ample room for discretionary behaviour on the part of the authorities.

One of the many lessons to be drawn from the study of other complex, adaptive systems is that structure matters for systemic stability and that structure can be chosen

---

[53] For a more recent discussion of how the existing monetary and regulatory framework might be altered to help minimize the costs of "boom-bust" cycles, see White (2020). He contends that a change in how policy is conducted is a more "modest" (easier to do politically) proposal than changes to the incentive system driving lending or legislated changes to the structure of the financial system itself.

[54] A dictionary definition of epistemological is "relating to the theory of knowledge, especially with regard to its methods, validity, and scope, and the distinction between justified belief and opinion".

[55] For an introductory reference see Buchanan (2001). For a more direct application to economics, see Arthur (2014) and Arthur (2021). Complexity is also a major assumption underlying the economic research being carried out by INET (the Institute for New Economic Thinking) at the Oxford Martin School at the University of Oxford, as well as the work of the NAEC Group (New Approaches to Economic Challenges) at the OECD.

[56] See White (2018) and White (2021).

to produce more stability. Building in modularity (to isolate shocks), redundancy (to improve resilience) and negative feedback mechanisms are standard in engineering systems. So too is the desire to remove unnecessary complexity. Against this backdrop, the suggestions made in the 1930s by the "Chicago School" to introduce a "narrow money" regime should be carefully reassessed.[57]

By eliminating the capacity of private agents to create assets that can substitute for money created by the public sector, there could be a greater potential for controlling the upward drift in prices and for reducing the harmful "boom-bust" cycles that have become increasingly common in recent years.[58] As well, much (perhaps all) of financial regulation and public safety nets might be made redundant within such a framework. Finally, by restricting the creation of money to public sector entities, the demand for that money would increase sharply. Commensurately, the cost of debt service for non-money public sector debt would be significantly reduced. All of these would be positive developments.

Evidently, a regime change of this magnitude would need careful assessment and even more careful implementation. However, the recent suggestion that central banks might introduce Central Bank Digital Currencies raises the possibility of extending that initiative to introduce a "narrow money" framework. That possibility should not be ruled out of hand, given the difficult circumstances bequeathed to us by the current monetary regime.

# References

Acharya V, Pedersen L, Phillipon T, Richardson M (2010) Measuring systemic risk. NYU Stern Working Paper

Acharya VV, Chauhan RS, Rajan R, Steffe S (2023) Liquidity dependence and the waxing and waning of central bank balance sheets. NBER Working Paper 3105, March

Allen W (2021) Managing the fiscal risk of higher interest rates. NIESR Policy Paper 025, March

Andrews D, McGowan MA, Millot V (2017) Confronting the zombies: policies for productivity revival. Economic Policy Paper No 21, OECD, Paris

Arther WB (2021) Foundations of complexity economics. www.nature.com/natrevphys

Arthur WB (2014) Complexity and the economy. Oxford University Press

---

[57] See Benes and Kumhof (2012) and Macmillan (2015) for recent assessments of these possibilities. Switzerland actually had a referendum in 2018 which proposed the introduction of a "narrow money" regime in that country. The proposal was voted down, in part because of the fears of Swiss voters of "going it alone". However, it did lead to a serious discussion of the fundamental problems with the current monetary system that a narrow money regime would address.

[58] Crypto currency is another form of privately created "money" that might substitute for money created by the public sector. However, the expanded use of crypto would go in the opposite direction of introducing a "narrow money" regime. In fact, crypto currency has none of the characteristics normally attributed to money. It has not become a widely used medium of exchange, in part because of problems faced in scaling up to a large volume of transactions. Nor is it a reliable store of value, given large fluctuations in the value of many crypto currencies measured in more traditional currencies. The potential attractiveness of crypto currencies has also been diminished by operational irregularities as well as regulatory and legal challenges.

Atkeson A, Kehoe PJ (2004) Deflation and depression: is there an empirical link? Am Econ Rev 94(2):99–103

Banerjee R, Hoffman B (2018) The rise of zombie firms: causes and consequences. BIS Q Rev

Benes J, Kumhof M (2012) The chicago plan revisited. IMF Working Paper 12/2012, Washington DC.

Borio C, Filardo A (2004) Back to the future: assessing the deflation record. BIS Working Paper No. 152

Borio C, Lowe P (2002) Asset prices, financial and monetary stability: exploring the nexus. BIS Working Paper No. 114

Borio C, Furfine C, Lowe P (2001) Procyclicality of the financial system and financial stability: issues and policy options. BIS Papers No. 1

Borio C, McCauley RN, McGuire P, Sushko V (2016) Covered interest parity lost: understanding the cross-currency basis. BIS Q Bull

Borio C (2023) Getting up from the floor. BIS Working Paper 1100

Buchanan M (2001) Ubiquity: the science of history…or why the world is simpler than you think. Crown Publications

Calomiris CW (2023) Fiscal dominance and the return of zero-interest bank reserve requirements. Fed Reserv Bank St. Louis Rev 105(4)

Cerra V, Fatas A, Saxena SC (2023) Hysteresis and business cycles. J Econ Lit 61(1):181–225

Connolly B (2023) You always hurt the one you love: central banks and the murder of capitalism. Unicorn Publishing Group, Lewes UK

Fender I, McGuire P (2010) European banks' dollar funding pressures. BIS Q Bull

Financial Stability Board (2019) Global monitoring report on non-bank financial intermediation 2018. Basel

Fisher I (1933) The debt-deflation theory of great depressions. Econometrica 4:337–357

Group of Thirty (2015) Fundamentals of central banking: lessons from the crisis. Washington DC

Hannoun H, Issing O, Liebscher K, Schlesinger H, Stark J, Wellink N, de Larosiere J, Noyer C (2019) The great debate. Int Econ, Fall 35–36

International Monetary Fund (2024) Financial stability report. Washington DC

Keynes JM (1930) The treatise on money. Macmillan and Company, London

Keynes JM (1936) The general theory of employment, interest and money. Macmillan and Company, London

Koh WC, Yu S (2020) A decade after the 2009 global recession: macroeconomic developments. Policy Research Working Paper; No. 9290. World Bank, Washington, DC

Koo RC (2009) The holy grail of macroeconomics: lessons from Japan's great recession. Wiley

Lynn BC (2009) Cornered: the new monopoly capitalism and the economics of destruction. Trade Paper Press

Macmillan J (2015) The end of banking: money, credit and the digital revolution. Zero/One Economics

McKinsey Global Institute (2021) The rise and rise of the global balance sheet: how productively are we using our wealth?

Reinhart CM, Sbrancia MB (2015) The liquidation of government debt. IMF Working paper 15/7

Sedgewick P (2023) Towards an overhaul in treasury-bank of England relationship. OMFIF, The Daily Update

Selgin G (2018) Less than zero: the case for a falling price level in a growing economy. Cato Institute

Tooze A (2019) Crashed. Penguin Books

UNCTAD (2023) Development prospects in a fractured world. 2022 Trade and Development Report, Geneva

Volcker P, Harper C (2018) Keeping at it. Public Affairs, New York

Wheeler G, Wilkinson B (2022) How central bank mistakes after 2019 led to inflation: with a foreword by William White. New Zealand Initiative

White W (2016) Ultra-easy monetary policy: digging the hole deeper? Bus Econ 51(4):188–202

White (2003) International financial crisis: prevention, management and resolution. In: Speech at the annual congress of the swiss society of economics and statistics. Berne

White W (2006) Measured wealth, real wealth and the illusion of saving. Irving Fisher Committee Bulletin No 26

White W (2013) Is monetary policy a science? The interaction of theory and practice over the last 50 years. Federal Reserve Bank of Dallas, Globalisation and Monetary Policy Institute, Working Paper No. 155

White W (2015) How false beliefs about exchange rate systems threaten global growth and the existence of the Eurozone. In: The political economy of the Eurozone. Cambridge University Press

White W (2018) Recognizing the economy as a complex, adaptive system: implications for central banking. In: Hartmann P, Huang H, Schoenmaker D (eds) The changing fortunes of central banking. Cambridge University Press

White W (2020) Why international financial regulation still falls short. Institute for New Economic Thinking, Working Paper 131

White W (2021) Simple lessons for policymakers from embracing complexity. In: New approaches to economic challenges: the financial system. OECD, Paris

White W (2023) What next for the post-covid global economy: could negative supply shocks disrupt other fragile systems?. Institute for New Economic Thinking, Working Paper 199

# Money, the State and the Market

**Miguel Fernandez Ordoñez**

We need banking, but we do not need banks anymore

−Bill Gates

The most important decision when reforming any economic sector is to determine the role that the State and the Market should play. It is essential to get it right as to what should be left to the free decision of individuals and what should need the interventions of the State.

The history of economic regulation since the end of World War II can be explained from this point of view. *"All the Market that is possible, as much State as necessary"* has been the guideline that has inspired most of the regulatory changes that have occurred throughout these decades in many economic sectors.

The changes in the assignment of roles to the State and the Market during this period have had positive effects. The first of these reforms was the liberalization of international trade guided by the GATT, now the WTO. But the list of regulatory changes is long: the privatization of public companies, the liberalization of regulated or monopolized sectors such as telecommunications or the different forms of transport, labor markets, the reduction of barriers to the creation of the internal market in the European Union, etc. Without forgetting the great change produced at the end of the twentieth century in most communist countries with the introduction of market mechanisms in the production of goods and services.

These reforms contrast with the legacy of the first half of the twentieth century, which was disastrous from the point of view of economic regulation. Both the left, with the temptation of the planned economy, and the right of the totalitarian countries, were implanting systems in which the State had a preponderant and unnecessary role in the functioning of the economy.

M. F. Ordoñez (✉)
Principe de Vergara 29, 28001 Madrid, Spain
e-mail: despachomadrid2014@gmail.com

© The Author(s), under exclusive license to Springer Nature Switzerland AG 2024
M. Rangeley (ed.), *The Age of Debt Bubbles*, Professional Practice in Governance and Public Organizations, https://doi.org/10.1007/978-3-031-66473-1_5

103

## Regulation of the Financial System

And how has the financial sector evolved? To understand the evolution of financial sector regulation, it is essential to distinguish the two parts of the financial system. On the one hand are the deposit entities (banks, savings banks, and the like) and on the other, the rest of the financial system (stock markets, investment funds, hedge funds, venture capital, derivatives, etc.). This distinction is important because the evolution of financial sector regulations has had two totally opposite developments.

In the non-banking financial system, regulatory changes have been taking place in the sense of allowing consumers, users, and companies to decide freely and allowing the State to intervene only in those areas in which its role is useful or necessary, such as the protection of consumers and investors, competition defense policies, the requirement of transparency and audits, etc. Today the non-banking financial system functions fundamentally under the discipline of the Market and only with justified State interventions.

And how has the regulation of the other part of the financial system evolved, that is, the banking system? Curiously, it has gone in the opposite direction, increasing the role of the State and restricting the role of the Market. At this moment, once the communist countries have already introduced competition in the production of goods and services, the banking sector is the sector most intervened and protected by the State of all economic sectors in all countries of the world.[1]

This is not perceived by the population because they think that, since the banks are private, they deduce that they work according to the market economy. But it's not like that. It is true that today most banks are privately owned, but the banking system is a system fundamentally penetrated by State interventionism and protectionism.

In the book Adios a los Bancos (2019) I explained in detail the list of protections, privileges, and state aid that prevent competition in payment and financial services. A summary of these privileges can be seen in the Box of this chapter. But in recent years the possibility of reassigning the role of the State and the Market in regulating the banking system has opened.

There has been a big change in the field of ideas. Thanks to the possibilities offered by the new technologies for the provision of payment services, a debate has been opened that is questioning the current monetary and banking system.

And, in addition to the ideas, concrete initiatives of alternatives to the current monetary and banking system have emerged. Some of these proposals have emerged from the world of cryptocurrencies, such as Stablecoins,[2] and others have been raised

---

[1] IT is possible that this strong interventionism in banking activities explains why that part of the financial system that works according to the market economy has been expanding more and more. In the United States, 85% of financial assets are already generated by the Market and only 15% by banks. If the importance of bank liabilities in the balance sheets of non-financial companies is measured, in Europe they are still 30% of total liabilities while in the United States, they are only 8%.

[2] The comparison of Stablecoins with bank deposits deserves a separate text. This chapter only compares CBDCs with bank deposits.

by the economic authorities themselves, such as the proposal to allow all citizens access to digital money issued by central banks, known as CBDC.

## The Origin of the Problems of the Current Monetary and Banking System

Those interested in analyzing the roles of the State and the Market in the functioning of an economic sector can have a feast if they spend some time analyzing how money and the payment system work in our economies today.

The justification for this gigantic state intervention in the banking sector is the fragility of bank money. Indeed, the incessant accumulation of regulations "against the market" is explained because most of the money we use now, bank deposits, are not real money but "promises" to repay the money. They are financial assets with the risk that can go into crisis and, to avoid catastrophes, State intervention becomes absolutely necessary.

Banks use the money deposited to lend or invest it, and the difference between the interest rates of these investments and those of the deposits is (or better, was) its fundamental source of income. Cash withdrawals have a certain regularity and that normally allows banks to respond to depositors' demands without major complications. But the problem arises, not only when the bank is insolvent, but much earlier, when it is unable to quickly convert the investments into money.

At first, the normal result of this financial fragility was what was considered a hallmark of the banking industry: continued bankruptcies and payment collapses. But given the damage that this produced in the economies, the States sought formulas to avoid banking crises and reduce their consequences by increasing protections and privileges for banks and by demanding certain requirements to limit excessive risk-taking by banks.

In the nineteenth century, when most of the paper money was notes issued by private banks, the frequency with which banks caused collapses in the flow of money by not fulfilling the promises of their notes increased. And it was then that the first major debate arose about the need to avoid these problems.

Two proposals were then debated to solve these problems. On one side were those in favor of maintaining the banknotes issued by private banks and reducing their problems by increasing State intervention.

The other proposal came from those who thought that the best way to solve the problem of using a risky asset should not be to increase the privileges and protections of banks, but rather to use a risk-free asset. Specifically, they proposed that all citizens use physical money issued by central banks as a means of payment.

This proposal is the one that won the debate and the reform consisted of prohibiting private banks from issuing banknotes. But this was the last time that progress was made in monetary reform, not by protecting fragile bank money, but by using the same "fiat" money as a means of payment. Fiat money's face value does not vary and therefore does not need State protection.

Today, in all countries of the world, banknotes are issued by the central bank and not by private banks and, of course, central bank notes never collapse, especially when the monetary systems are already a totally "fiat" system.

Unfortunately, from that moment and to date, all the changes in the monetary banking system were in the sense of increasing the protections and privileges of the State to the banks. Also, State interventionism in the economic decisions of the banks was increasing, fundamentally, in the assumption of risks. And central bank Interventionism in financial markets also increased to the point of producing aberrations such as the appearance of negative interest rates.

In the same nineteenth century, it was proposed to introduce one of the most important state protections, that of using central banks to lend to private banks when they had liquidity problems. Another step on the path of adopting regulations against the Market was the creation of deposit insurance, one of the State interventions that most clearly prevents Market discipline from working.

The policies of increasing the privileges of banks to try to correct the instability problems created by bank deposits have been maintained to this day. In this same year of 2023, in view of the collapse of Credit Suisse and the US regional banks, governments and central banks have begun once again to study how to further increase the protections for bank deposits and how to increase prudential regulations to avoid problems that Basel III had not foreseen.

This spiral of "banking crisis-more protectionism and interventionism-banking crises-more protectionism and interventionism…" was also the way in which economic authorities reacted to the great banking crisis at Lehman Brothers. Then there was an incredible unanimity in the diagnosis of the origin of the crisis. Everyone repeated that "the market had failed." And this diagnosis was defended not just by the usual suspects on the left but by liberal conservatives such as Alan Greenspan, who said that while they had advocated bank deregulation before, the crisis had convinced him that, in the case of banks, it was necessary to increase the protection of the State, as well as its interventionism in business risk-taking decisions.

This erroneous diagnosis gave rise not only to the increase in the volume of insured deposits (in the United States it went from $100,000 to $250,000) but also justified the immense work of the Financial Stability Board (FSB) that approved the regulatory change that It received the name of Basel III and was incorporated into different national legislations such as the Dodd-Frank law of the United States or the Capital Directive of the European Union. More state agencies were also created to expand supervision.

No economic sector has a similar state interventionism. The regulatory development of Basel III occupies around two million words. If we compare it with the length of the Bible, it can be said that if a banker wanted to know the rules that he must comply with, he should read approximately two and a half Bibles. But this so-called "prudential regulation" is not a singular intervention only because of its volume but above all because of its content, since it assumes that regulators know better than businessmen (in this case, bank managers) how they should manage their risks.

## CBDCs are Essential to Liberalize Payment and Credit Services

Now it can be understood why the first step for payment and credit activities liberalization is for all citizens to be able to access the CBDC. What at first seems only a measure to increase stability and avoid crises is an essential measure to liberalize and introduce competition in this sector.

The explanation is that to liberalize a sector it is essential to level the playing field for all competitors, and this is done by removing the protections or privileges some may have. And the only way that protections can be removed is to use a safe asset (CBDC) since this one does not need any of those protections.

In the same way, in a monetary system where CBDCs are the normal means of payment, the enormous prudential regulation that applies to banks today can be completely abolished. This hyperregulation makes it extremely difficult for banks to compete with non-banks in the lending market. In the United States, non-banks are already the main providers of mortgages, which were previously the typical product of banks.

Another example of State interventionism is the current monetary policy that, instead of controlling the amount of money, is devoted to manipulating interest rates. This interventionism is also explained because the banks are responsible for an important part of the creation of money through the creation of deposits through the granting of credit.

This privilege of creating money prevents central banks from being able to manage monetary policy through the quantity of money. They can only carry out an indirect monetary policy, that is, a policy that does not directly modulate the amount of money in the economy; rather, it tries to indirectly influence the amount of money created by the banks, by manipulating the interest rate.

The advantage of a system based on CBDCs is that increases in the amount of money could be perfectly controlled by central banks. It could deliver to the citizens the increase in the quantity of money, and it would not be necessary for the central banks to manipulate the interest rates. The market would be allowed to work, and the interest rate would be a result of the wishes of savers and borrowers and not a decision of the State as of now. The provision of the money created to citizens instead of it being available to the banks, means a return to the citizens of the financing decisions that the banks now centralize. And it would have positive effects insofar as part of that financing would surely be done in the form of equity. Now the banks are practically prohibited from financing the companies with equity and this leads to debt having a greater weight in the system than if it were decided by the market.

The assignment of the roles of the State and the Market in the current monetary and banking system is sheer nonsense. It is the opposite of what should be done to take advantage of what the State does best and what the Market does best. In effect, now the private sector is assigned the function of creating the means of payment, bank deposits, instead of leaving the State to deal with creating safe money, which cannot vary in value. A risky asset that is produced by the private sector is chosen as a means of digital payment instead of using a CBDC as a means of payment. CBDC is fiat money, which is a safe asset and which, by definition, does not vary in value.

By letting private banks issue means of payment, microeconomic stability is lost, and crises may occur. Furthermore, "uniqueness" is lost since the value of each means of payment issued by each one of the banks has a different value. In this way, one of the typical functions of the State is wasted, which is to determine the unit of measurement such as weight, length, etc. In this case, the means of payment cannot be the measure of value because bank deposits have a different value. This diversity of value explains that, when banks want to transact with each other, they resort to using risk-free assets, public digital money, issued by central banks (CBDCs) which we call "reserves."

What should be left to the state, such as money, is left in the hands of the private sector. But instead, activities that could be subject to a competition regime such as the provision of payment or credit services are so heavily intervened and protected by the State that they prevent full competition. Today there is no payment service that is not forced to go through a bank account. And it is hard to compete with the banks in credit when they have financing guaranteed by the State at close to zero cost.

On the other hand, if, as happened with physical money, CBDC (digital money issued by central banks) were to become the generally used means of digital payment, all protections and privileges of banks could be easily removed, thereby payment and credit services could be provided by the private initiative in full competition and without any relevant State intervention.

## The Role of the State in the Transition

In a system based on CBDCs, the Market takes on all its leading role, leaving financing and payment decisions to individuals, and the State simply appears as the issuer of safe money. The State no longer protects any of the payment service providers with CBDCs or any of the many intermediaries that will appear in a liberalized credit market.

However, the role of the State in the transition from a system based on bank deposits to a system based on CBDCs is very important. The reason is obvious, and it is that the main task in the transition is to end all the protections, privileges, and interventions of the State and this, precisely, is a task that only the State can do.

Indeed, if we could press a button that would allow us to move from the current system to a system in which the means of payment were CBDCs, we would find a system without a crisis in payment flows, full competition in payment and credit services, and a direct monetary policy without bubbles or slow recoveries, with interest rates that would no longer be manipulated by the State and would be the result of market forces.

But that button does not exist, just as it has not existed in any liberalization reform that has been carried out in the world over the last 70 years.

All liberalization reforms have losers, and the liberalization of payment and banking activities also have losers, they are no exception. And the best reforms take care of the losers so that the transition is smooth.

If access to safe money such as the CBDC were offered and the protections and privileges of banks were removed, as unnecessary, all banks around the world would fail. Bank protectionism is existential. If their privileges are removed the banks will immediately cease to exist.

For this reason, the State must play an essential role in the transition from the current system to a safe money system and liberalization of banking activities. The State must help banks to transform and start providing payment services and credit services without protections or privileges, under the discipline of the Market.


## The Future


I have outlined what should be a reform of the current monetary system that defends the public interest. But it is difficult to predict how this debate will end since important private interests are also at stake, as always happens when you want to end monopolies or suppress protectionism.

Parallel to the debate on the public objectives of money and banking reform, there is a fierce defense of private interests. It is logical that the banks try to prevent the privileges they still have from disappearing. But there are also other private interests, such as those of the Stablecoins promoters, who have realized the enormous profit possibilities that exist if the regulators let them provide some services with quality and cost that banks today are unable to offer. They are also against the existence of safe public money because it would be very difficult for them to compete with payment service providers with CBDC.

It is not easy to predict the result of the debate on the liberalization of payment services and credit. But, in view of what has happened in other sectors, it is to be expected that the reconsideration of the regulation of money and banking activities will be done with a pragmatic vision when deciding the role that the Market and the State.

Most likely, in the end, the provision of goods and services will remain in the hands of the Market because it knows how to do it better than the State. Instead, the State will be in charge of doing what it knows how to do best, such as issuing a means of payment that is a safe asset and that does not need protections or privileges, or intrusive prudential regulation to maintain its face value.

Pragmatism is the best guide to designing the best reforms. As Deng Xiao Ping, the communist leader who introduced the Market in China, said when he was accused by his co-religionists that what he was doing was Capitalism and not Communism: *"I don't care if the cat is black or white, what interests me is that it catches mice."*

# Appendix: 1

## Main Banking Privileges and Protections

1.  Only banks have the privilege of creating money
2.  Only banks can have CBDCs current accounts at the Central Bank
3.  The State assures the banks a very cheap financing
4.  Banks can obtain liquidity from the State when they need it
5.  General bankruptcy laws do not apply to them. They have special resolution systems
6.  Competition laws do not apply to them
7.  Taxpayers' money is used to save the banks
8.  Seigniorage resulting from the creation of bank deposits is not transferred to the State or to citizens.
9.  Banks are required to hold lower levels of capital than the market would require.

# Monetary and Fiscal Policy Challenges in Europe Since 2000: A Comprehensive Analysis

Barbara Kolm

## Introduction

The economic climate in Europe over the last 23 years has endured various calamities, examples of mismanagement, and government intervention. Many policymakers have found solace in increasing policy measures when confronted with an economic crisis. In contemporary economics, the reliance on policy measures to ensure stability in the market was engendered by John Maynard Lord Keynes. Keynes, attributed as the favorite economist of the twentieth century, was heavily in favor of increased government intervention in economic operations and believed that a stable market was the key to success (Davis et al. 2011, pp. 134–135). Policymakers in the US, being faced with a recession and an inflation crisis in the 1970s, became more skeptical of government intervention in the economy. This led to heterodox thinkers like F.A. Hayek and Milton Friedman being endorsed by mainstream intelligentsia. However, recent years would indicate that a gradual shift back towards Keynes and his beliefs in highly controlled monetary and fiscal authorities has been steadily increasing in the twenty-first century, especially in Europe. This chapter analyzes the economic policies and crises that have plagued Europe for the last 20 years and provides relevant context. By defining and explaining the exact policies enacted in the European Union since 2000, this chapter is able to examine their consequences with regard to the 2008 crisis, the Greek debt crisis, and the Covid-19 pandemic. In short, the rise of Unconventional Monetary Policy, EU bailouts, and lack of fiscal responsibility has led to a rapidly destabilizing economic environment within Europe, and unless policymakers are willing to make bold steps, this could have drastic consequences.

B. Kolm (✉)
Grünangergasse 1/15−1, 1010 Vienna, Austria
e-mail: b.kolm@austriancenter.com

© The Author(s), under exclusive license to Springer Nature Switzerland AG 2024
M. Rangeley (ed.), *The Age of Debt Bubbles*, Professional Practice in Governance and Public Organizations, https://doi.org/10.1007/978-3-031-66473-1_6

## Policy Delegation

Monetary and Fiscal policy are two tools governments and central banks use to manage the economy. While monetary and fiscal policy both work to serve the overall economy, each does so in distinct ways. The European Union (EU) is composed of individual member states, each with its own fiscal policies, while monetary policy in the EU is primarily managed by the European Central Bank (ECB).

The Eurozone comprises the group of EU member states that have adopted the Euro as their official currency and united under a monetary union. In addition to using the same currency, these countries share a common authority, the European Central Bank (ECB). Currently, 20 of 27 EU member states are part of the Eurozone. Within the Eurozone, the Eurosystem is the monetary authority responsible for managing monetary policy. At a basic level, the responsibilities of the Eurosystem are to: Define and implement the monetary policy of the eurozone, conduct foreign exchange operations, hold and manage the official foreign reserves of the Member States, and promote the smooth operation of payment systems (Europian Union 2022).

The European Central Bank (ECB) is a key of the Eurosystem, serving as the central bank for the entire Eurozone. The official mandate of the ECB is "the primary objective of maintaining price stability and the secondary objective of supporting the general economic policies in the Union" (European Union, European Central Bank 2023). The national central banks of the Eurozone member states work together in executing monetary policy measures effectively, following the guidance and framework provided by the European Central Bank (ECB). These national central banks—such as the Oesterreichische Nationalbank (OeNB) in Austria—contribute to the implementation of monetary policy and carry out specific tasks within their respective countries (Oesterreichische Nationalbank 2023).

The Eurosystem, consisting of the ECB and the national central banks of the Eurozone, utilizes various approaches to achieve price stability through monetary policy. One key aspect of Monetary Policy in the Eurosystem is that the ECB is responsible for controlling the money supply. The ECB's primary objective is to maintain an inflation rate close to but below 2% over the medium term (Oesterreichische Nationalbank 2023). To achieve this objective, the ECB has various tools at its disposal, including the ability to control the money supply. Expansionary monetary policy alone is rarely the sole solution, so the ECB often uses increased monetary expansion as part of a broader set of monetary policy tools to influence the economy and achieve its policy objectives.

The second regulatory tool used by the ECB is controlling interest rates. The ECB uses interest rates in monetary policy to influence the cost of borrowing money, stimulate or slow economic activity and maintain price stability. The ECB sets three primary types of interest rates. First, the *Main Refinancing Rate* is the interest rate commercial banks incur to borrow from the ECB. Second, the *Deposit Rate* is the interest rate banks receive on their overnight deposits to the ECB. Lastly, the *Marginal Lending Rate* is imposed on banks to borrow additional funds from the ECB, usually in the short term. Marginal lending rates act as the price ceiling for short-term interest rates (Oesterreichische Nationalbank 2023). Together, these various interest rates create economic shifts that, in theory, work to achieve the goal of price stability.

Fiscal policy refers to the use of government expenditure, revenue, borrowing, and taxation to achieve specific outcomes in an economy (European Union 2023). Although the European Union has a monetary union, it does not have a fiscal union. As a result, fiscal policies look much less homogeneous than monetary policies implemented by the ECB because individual countries maintain the autonomy to set their own Fiscal Policies. Due to states' autonomy in shaping their fiscal policy, each country can determine its fiscal policy to achieve its desired ends. EU member states are responsible for setting their own national budget, and countries can decide the best way to allocate resources for their citizens and establish budgetary priorities.

In Austria, fiscal policy is primarily set by the federal government, specifically the Ministry of Finance. Once the Ministry of Finance drafts a proposed budget, the government presents it to Parliament for review. In review, members of Parliament can criticize and propose modifications before Parliament eventually passes a budget. Other government bodies and institutions, such as the OeNB, may provide input or advice on fiscal policy matters. The working relationship between a central bank and the government is paramount in allowing for social cohesion of regulatory agencies. However, the ultimate decision-making authority lies with the federal government.

However, Autonomy is not absolute. The EU has enacted multiple guidelines and regulations that member states must adhere to in their fiscal policies. For example, the Stability and Growth Pact (SGP) requires that member states aim for a balanced or surplus budget and set a limit on government debt. Another example is the Fiscal Compact, which imposes budget rules and coordination mechanisms, such as the requirement to introduce national fiscal rules into legislation. Further, a shared surveillance mechanism called the Macroeconomic Imbalance Procedure (MIP) identifies and prevents imbalances that could affect economic stability (European Central Bank 2023). Among other mechanisms, these safeguards are in place to help ensure that EU member states' fiscal policies can coordinate with the goals of the ECB.

Of course, the interaction of monetary and fiscal policy creates the undercurrents for the tide of the economic environment. For example, consider a scenario where a country is experiencing an economic recession. To stimulate the economy, the nation's government decides to implement expansionary fiscal policy by increasing government spending on infrastructure projects such as the construction of roads or schools. Increased government spending puts upward pressure on inflation, and the nation's central bank assesses this as a potential risk, so they choose to implement a contractionary monetary policy that increases interest rates and reduces spending. In theory, their policy would moderate aggregate demand and counteract the potential inflationary impact of expansionary fiscal policy.

As Newton's third law of physics states, "For every action in nature, there is an equal and opposite reaction." In some cases, it seems that the ECB's role is to act as the opposite—yet not always equal—economic force to EU member states fiscal decisions. The delicate economic balance the ECB aims to achieve inevitably lends to the loss of sovereignty EU member states have to pursue their economic stake (Klooster

2022). Additionally, the ECB's role as a counterbalancing force to member states' fiscal decisions unmasks the complex interplay between supranational economic governance and national sovereignty within the European Union. In any case, a nation's prosperity in the EU largely depends upon the optimal synchronization of national economic policies with the goals of the EU.

The interplay between the European Central Bank (ECB) and the member states of the European Union (EU) exhibits a game-theoretical dynamic, where strategic coordination shapes the execution of monetary policy measures. In pure coordination games, all players have identical preferences for equilibria and incentives, making it relatively straightforward for them to coordinate on a single equilibrium point. The relationship between the ECB and EU states is more analogous to impure coordination games, where players have both shared interests and conflicting incentives. In impure coordination, there can be multiple equilibria, which makes it harder for the ECB and EU member states to navigate the decision space and arrive at favorable equilibria. Consequently, the interplay between the two resembles a sort of intricate dance, where careful strategic choices and effective communication are essential to achieve optimal outcomes.

## Post-2008 European Central Bank Unconventional Monetary Policy

After the inflationary crises of the 1970s, the developed world underwent a period known as the Great Moderation. Characterized by milder recessions and stable prices, central banks kept rates low to stimulate the economy with little concern about inflation (Klooster 2020, p. 587). This period was expected to continue barring a major economic catastrophe—that catastrophe arrived in 2008. As the subprime mortgage crisis roiled US markets, the ripples exacerbated Europe's own debt problems. Out of ammunition due to zero-bounded lower rates, the European Central Bank (ECB) resorted to Unconventional Monetary Policy (UMP). This section will examine the actions taken by the ECB, as well as the ramifications of UMP, and then provide a critique from the viewpoint of Austrian Business Cycle Theory (ABCT). It is evident that these policies not only impeded recovery but have had enduring repercussions on the economic environment of Europe.

Confronted with the constraints of a zero lower bound on interest rates during the financial crisis, the ECB resorted to a remarkable expansion in its balance sheet through UMP. Starting in October 2008, the ECB cut its main rate from 4.25 to 1% by May 2009 (Febrero et al. 2015, p. 718). By the time the European debt crisis had commenced, the Central bank had no space to continue to lower rates. The Taylor rule—a rate targeting model utilized by central banks to determine short-term interest rates for various policy objectives—would have recommended further slashing rates into the negative realm to adequately stimulate the economy; but as most savings could be held in cash without negative rates—this is hardly possible (Joyce et al. 2012,

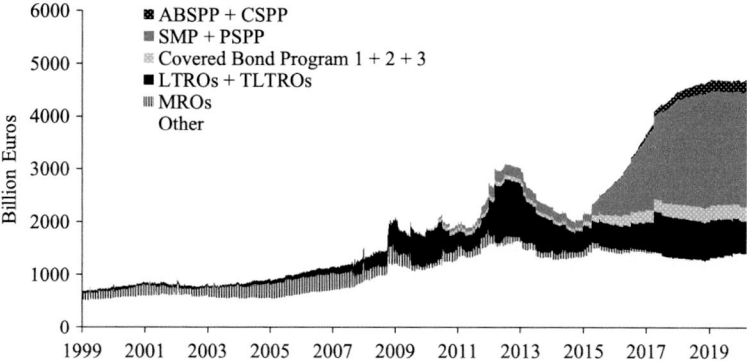

**Fig. 1** Structure of the balance sheet of the European system of central banks. *Source* European central bank (Schnabl et al. 2020, p. 14)

p. 272). Consequently, the ECB expanded its balance sheet dramatically through these UMP programs. Between 2007 and 2019, the ECB extended its holdings by €3.3 trillion, from €1.4 trillion to € 4.7 trillion (Radić 2019, p. 1073). This expansion is often referred to as Quantitative Easing (QE), a policy that had been exercised by the Japanese central bank in the 1990s in the face of deflationary pressures. The ECB employed a broader range of tools than had been activated by any other central bank up until that point (Fig. 1).

The ECB used six main policies starting in 2011. Firstly, the Fixed-Rate Tender, Full-Allotment Programs (FRFAP) involved the provision of reserves to EU banks at a fixed rate, a significant shift from the previous use of marginal rates. This policy imparted more certainty to borrowing institutions regarding the cost of acquiring reserves. Secondly, the ECB initiated the Securities Markets Program (SMP), which involved the direct purchase of corporate and government bonds. This program aimed to ensure liquidity and stability within the bond markets and indirectly stimulate economic activity through lower borrowing costs. Thirdly, the Covered Bond Purchase Programme (CBPP) resulted in an investment of €76.4 billion. The ECB's acquisition of these debt securities, backed by a separate pool of assets, was intended to support the covered bond market, further providing liquidity to banking institutions. The ECB also implemented Outright Monetary Transactions (OMT), which involved purchasing government debt in the secondary market. The primary objective of this policy was to address severe distortions in government bond markets that impeded the effective transmission of monetary policy. Additionally, the ECB utilized Longer-Term Refinancing Operations (LTRO). This strategy infused one trillion euros into the banking system by granting financial institutions access to three-year liquidity. It was crafted to avert a potential credit crunch and maintain stability in the banking sector. Lastly, the ECB issued forward guidance on its key interest rates. The objective was to communicate its intention to maintain an extended period of lower-level inflation. This forward looking approach sought to shape market expectations and influence the longer-term trajectory of inflation and interest rates

(Šetková, 2016, pp. 22–24). These policies were unprecedented to a formerly hesitant central bank mostly preoccupied with price stability. While not as hawkish as the US Federal Reserve, the UMP of the ECB had lasting effects.

While the UMP of the ECB, such as the Outright Monetary Transactions (OMT) program, helped stabilize the banking sector by indirectly recapitalizing European banks through positive impacts on peripheral sovereign bonds, they did not translate into robust economic growth. Mario Draghi, the president of the ECB, later acknowledged that the "positive developments in the financial sphere have not yet fully transferred into the economic sphere" (ECB 2014, quoted in Acharya et al. 2019). The underlying growth momentum remained weak and unemployment fell very slowly. Additionally, evidence suggests that zombie lending by weakly capitalized banks contributed to the slow economic recovery. Zombie lending is when firms receiving loans do not use funds for real economic activity such as employment and investment, but rather to build cash reserves. Notably, in 2013, a significant percentage of debt in Portugal, Spain, and Italy was owed by firms which were not able to cover their interest expenses from their pretax earnings, indicating a scenario similar to Japan's zombie lending experience in the 1990s (Acharya et al. 2019).

Austrian Business Cycle Theory posits that two factors contribute to a credit boom: Positive economic outlook and cheap credit (Hoffmann et al. 2017, p. 104). This was precisely the environment that preceded the European economic crisis. A growing and strengthening European Union presented a particularly strong economic outlook, especially for smaller countries. This, coupled with an extended period of near-zero rates, undeniably impacted credit supply. Without delving into the specific debt crises in individual countries, this cheap credit from low rates and UMP had an extended adverse effect on recovery by its hindrance of creative destruction as theorized by Austrian Economist Joseph Schumpeter. Creative destruction is the process by which innovation and recovery occur at the bottom of the business cycle by incentivizing profitable ideas and clearing out inefficient zombie companies. This malinvestment is expounded by Hayek (1931, p. 98, quoted in Schnabl et al. 2017, p. 15), "If voluntary decisions of individuals are distorted by the creation of artificial demand, it must mean that part of the available resources is again led into a wrong direction and a definite and lasting adjustment is again postponed." Here he suggests that policies intending to aid the economy recover may temporarily boost output, but they will leave the core issues that caused the crisis, allowing them to resurface in the future. Hayek (1933, p. 20, quoted in Schnabl et al. 2017, p. 15) further states, "To combat the depression by a forced credit expansion is to attempt to cure the evil by the very means which brought it about." This is exactly what the ECB did, and the results are more than mere future credit worries. Schnabl et al. (2017, p. 19) have evaluated the policies of the European Central Bank and found that excessively accommodating refinancing circumstances in times of economic growth can lead to an increase in investment projects that are less likely to provide high returns. They theorize that this happens because the general effectiveness of investments decreases during prosperous periods and persists at these lower levels with the additional monetary help, allowing businesses with less promising returns to stay afloat. In a similar way to zombie companies creating a drag on recovery, the ECB has other member states' individual credit problems to manage.

The UMP implemented by the ECB marked a shift towards a more active European monetary policy, providing trillions of Euros of liquidity. As Joyce et al. (2012, p. 271) wrote in their summary of UMP, "Central banks now have a much greater focus on financial stability in addition to targeting inflation. But by Tinbergen's Law, if an authority has N policy targets it needs at least N policy instruments, so we have seen central banks augment their arsenal of policy instruments with macroprudential tools." The consequences of this can be seen not only in less efficient market operations but future credit issues that arise from sovereign debt issues and COVID-19. ABCT provides a resolution, though not without financial discomfort: The EU should permit the markets to set interest rates and abstain from pumping money into the economy. This would preclude future credit issues and allow the market's natural forces to operate—ultimately fostering a more prosperous and free Europe.

## The Greek Debt Crisis of 2010

As exchange becomes more globalized, the great achievements of mankind are increasingly promulgated across the world. At the same time, globalism aggravates costly oversights in large markets causing catastrophic damage for the rest of the world. In the last 20 years, the global economy has gone through two different major economic recessions, with many economists predicting that there will be another downturn in the next few years. As the previous chapters mentioned, both twenty-first-century recessions were caused by errors made by a combination of Central Banks deciding how to execute monetary policy and governments legislating on fiscal policy. Having the world's largest economy, the US holds enormous economic influence over the rest of the world. The situation in the European Union (EU) is unique due to its supranational jurisdiction, lording over individual member states' governments. This effectively shares the blame of fiscally irresponsible countries with countries who acted prudently. One of the more famous examples of this is Greece during the mid-2000s and early 2010s when its national economy was on the brink of collapse due to a debt bubble.

Greece has been no stranger to unusual and extremely criticized economic policies in the twenty-first century. Throughout the span of 11 years, its government raised the minimum wage to an unprecedented level, from €457 a month in 2000 to €751 a month in 2011, a near 60% increase (Karamanis and Naxakis 2014). Additionally, pensions and social transfers grew by 7% of the national GDP in about 9 years, which alone caused the domestic debt to rise by 15% (Thomsen 2019). Policies like these instituted in a relatively small country with a shallow economy and small population allow for government oversight and degraded economic logic. After Greece joined the eurozone in 2001, its economy received an immediate boost in investments from most European countries in the hopes of being the first to take advantage of an economy full of opportunity. Poul Thomsen, the Director of the European Department at the International Monetary Fund (IMF), mentioned publically that this wave of unrealistically optimistic investors from other countries in the EU was one of the early stages of the Greek economic downfall (Thomsen 2019).

In the mid-2000s, the Greek economy expanded, experiencing economic prosperity they had not yet encountered. As a result, the Greek government was inclined to invest more into its economy, including public, corporate, and residential investments (Gourinchas et al. 2016). However, when looking at how these investments were financed, it becomes exceedingly obvious that the Greek government was primarily using debt to support the financial burden, causing the debt to grow past national GDP even with the economic growth. A study published in the National Bureau of Economic Research identified this problem by saying "Budget discipline became looser after EZ (eurozone) entry, and especially after 2007. As a consequence, debt to GDP increased—to 103.1% in 2007 and 126.8% in 2009—despite the fast growth in GDP during the period 2001–2008" (Gourinchas et al. 2016). This steep incline in debt to GDP ratio created a debt bubble which put the Greek economy in a position where it was heavily reliant on foreign entities for funding. Not only was the Greek government burdened with debt, but the private sector was as well. In 1998, the Greek private sector had a lower debt-to-GDP ratio than Spain, Ireland, Italy, and Portugal; only 34.1%. After Greece's entry into the eurozone, their private sector loans to GDP spiked, reaching 103% just 10 years later (Gourinchas et al. 2016). Risky methods of financing and increased monetary and fiscal expenditures turned Greece's economy into a shadow of its former self caused by a large-scale economic crisis: the Great Recession of 2008.

Just two years after the US financial crisis, investors that once were cheering on the Greek economy no longer felt safe with the amount of their money going into a country whose condition was worsening by the day. In 2010, the Greek economy experienced several shocks simultaneously, creating the now infamous debt crisis. With investors losing faith in the economy, foreign banks began losing faith in Greek banks and started to withdraw their loans. Coupled with the enormous amount of money they were spending on government expenditures, the Greek economy started to lose billions of euros. The first response from the European Central Bank was to blame Greek policymakers for their incompetence and inability to properly manage their economy. However, the response from many economists outside of the EU recognized that the Greek debt crisis was just a part of the massive crisis the EU was facing as a whole (Lapavitsas 2019). It soon became apparent that monetary policy pushed by the EU, namely the very relaxed required reserve ratios, extremely low interest rates, and cavalier lending rates were causing several countries economic troubles. However, Greece stood out as an interesting case particularly because its debt was outrageously high and the initial responses to solve the crisis made things even worse (Fig. 2).

Immediately, the Greek government and treasury were doing everything they could to bail out themselves and the large private sector banks. This sank the economy much further into debt and did almost no good. The IMF intervened to help slow the spread of these issues, however they too misjudged the resistance from the populace

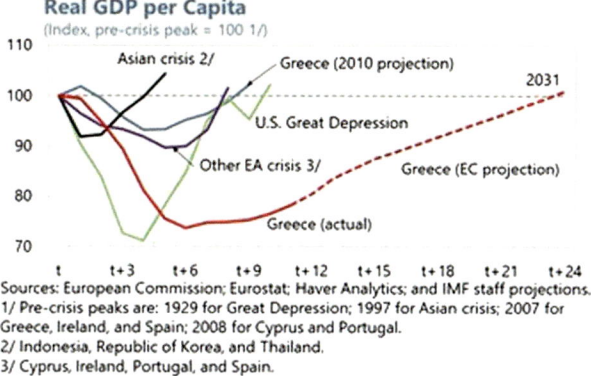

**Fig. 2**  Real GDP per capita

and government to accept monetary assistance to pull their country out of debt. The fiscal policies were among the first to be addressed. Even with the IMF's insistence that the Greek government cut down on the size of their pensions, Greece has denied any and all attempts to do so. Since Greek politics were keeping fiscal policy from being fixed, the IMF turned towards creating monetary policy that would decrease the debt with the aid of other European countries. They concluded the best response was to significantly lower interest rates, making them less than 1.8% on average; an attempt to lessen the debt burden on Greece (Thomsen 2019). Yet again, this solution was plagued with political interference. In the same speech given by Thomsen, he admits that this solution was not the IMF's first choice to solve the problem. The IMF wanted to do "haircut" loans in an attempt to get money from their own populace, however the eurozone rejected the idea of haircuts which would have allowed Greece to solve the debt issue more internally. Political forces in the eurozone took precedence and pressured the IMF to make this decision, essentially making the debt crisis in Greece a political issue rather than an economic issue (Thomsen 2019). While the claims of eurozone politicians and IMF officials that lowering interest rates lessened the debt burden might be true in the short run, the long-run effects are beginning to show.

Germany has been a very large trading partner with Greece for years, but their investments in Greece's economy began to surge once these historically low interest rates were introduced. As of 2022, German investments in Greece made up well over 18% of all investments made in the country, totaling approximately €6.8 billion (GTP 2023). What was a great deal for Germany in the short run is now causing them to be thrust into debt as they continue to bail out their investments in Greece. A study from the OECD shows that a likely reason for these continuous bailouts stems from Greece's relatively unproductive workforce (OECD 2018). The monetary efforts of continuous Quantitative Easing (QE), low interest rates, and bailouts have led to an incredibly prolonged debt recession in Greece. If left unchecked, these policies have the potential to extend this period of economic hardship and dependency for decades. It is imperative that Greece restrain its fiscal authority and begin a process of Quantitative Tightening if its economy has any chance of sustainably recovering. As stated by Nobel Laureate winning economist F.A. Hayek almost 100 years before this crisis occurred, the use of monetary policy to stabilize an economy will put a halt to economic progress, causing the economy to never fully recover. Rather, it is important to remove or reduce large amounts of money being spent through fiscal policy as a means of economic revitalization (Hayek 2008, pgs. 102–103).

Greece is a perfect modern example of how short-sighted monetary policy can be heavily politicized and cause adverse damage in the long term. While there have been other shocks to the world's economy since 2010, the corroborative evidence would suggest that the monetary policy enacted in Greece has delayed current economic problems. In recent years, Greece's prime minister since 2016, Kyriakos Mitsotakis, has made large strides in trying to bring down the GDP to debt ratio. While the economic problems caused by government intervention during the pandemic have hindered Greece's economy, Mitsotakis's victory in the recent election has shown that his policies of keeping the interest rate steady have caused inflation to remain stagnant at 3% (Economist 2023).

## COVID-19 Fiscal Policy

The COVID-19 pandemic in 2020 posed substantial economic challenges; prompting governments to respond with a range of monetary and fiscal measures. Additionally, the health issues resulting from the pandemic compelled governments to implement many protective measures such as mandatory lockdowns, social distancing, forced masking, and quarantining in the interest of public well-being. These public health measures, aimed at protecting the general populace from infection, posed severe problems for the world economy. As the pandemic forced many business closures and thus left millions without jobs, governments responded with expansionary monetary and fiscal policies they hoped would limit the negative impacts brought by unemployment and economic productivity losses. In order to safeguard against severe economic downturns akin to the recessions of 2008, 1973, or the infamous Great Depression of the 1930s, governments implemented these policies to facilitate swift economic recovery. While expansionary monetary and fiscal policy protected global economies in the short term and thus may have been necessary, they certainly contributed to the widespread inflation worldwide seen today.

Governments across the world implemented a range of restrictive measures on their citizens, including full-scale lockdowns, quarantines, and mandated social distancing in an effort to mitigate and contain the spread of COVID-19. These restrictions made it difficult, if not impossible, for many companies to perform at normal levels. The introduction of lockdowns and social distancing measures forced businesses to run at lower capacities with fewer workers. The European Economic Forecast 2023, conducted by the European Commission, shows that labour productivity (real GDP occupied per person, percentage change in the preceding year) dropped almost across the board for every country between the end of the year 2019 and 2020. For example, the EU fell from 0.7% in 2019 to −3.0% in 2020. The biggest drops recorded from 2019 to 2020 were in the UK and Malta, which both experienced over 10% drops in labour productivity over the preceding year. Almost universal negatives in labour productivity between 2019 and 2020, brought by restrictive public health measures, naturally led to decreases in firms' ability to produce, thus, leading to supply reductions and a supply shock.

However, lockdowns and global travel restrictions also decreased demand. Two-thirds of businesses "experienced a decline" in demand as a result of restrictions (Stemmler 2023). Lockdowns and global travel restrictions kept people in their homes and away from travel. Combined with forced business closures in recreational industries, the governments disincentivized consumer spending through rest restrictions; driving down demand.

Moreover, in response to concerns that economic shocks brought by the pandemic would lead to a global recession, governments scrambled to implement unprecedented stimulus packages. The EU passed a record-setting €750 billion stimulus plan, known as NextGenerationEU, aimed at allocating significant relief to businesses and individuals experiencing financial hardship (Riegert 2021). Similarly, the US passed a massive $5 trillion stimulus plan, the largest in recorded history. $1.8 trillion of the stimulus package went to households and individuals (Parlapiano et al. 2022). The EU, US, and other countries implementing the biggest expansionary fiscal stimulus plans in history hoped that unemployment and large-scale business closures would be kept at bay. The evidence suggests that the EU plan worked exceptionally well in the short term, while the US plan was semi-ineffective. The 2023 European Economic Forecast suggests that the EU's unemployment rate only increased by 0.4%, while the US rate increased by 4.4% between 2019 and 2020.

The disparity in unemployment rate percentages between the EU and the US lies in the amount of stimulus provided and the qualifications to receive the stimulus. A US Chamber of Congress survey found that "almost a quarter [of unemployed persons] (24%) say government aid packages during the pandemic have incentivized them not to work" (Ayala et al. 2022). Additionally, an economic analysis conducted by the San Francisco Fed corroborates this in its conclusion: "When one properly controls for local demand shifts, the disincentive effects of UI turn out to be sizable" (Hornstein et al. 2022). Thus, the stimulus packages brought by expansionary fiscal policy in the US must have exceeded the level that would still incentivize work. F.A. Hayek's theory on unemployment benefits and expansionary fiscal policy concurs with this conclusion in an interview on the TV show Firing Line. Hayek suggested, "but once of course you make it more attractive to employ on employment compensation than to work … it [is] a temptation to remain unemployed, as unemployment compensation is very large … I suspect that a comparatively large part of the unemployment, which we call this statistically, isn't even unemployment. It's just a preference of people to draw unemployment compensation rather than to work" (Hayek 1977). The preference to remain unemployed rather than seek work in the US certainly increased the already existing supply shock. Due to the global influence of the American market, most countries around the world felt these additional supply shocks.

As a result of the stimulus payments, lockdowns of businesses and individuals, and global travel restrictions—the household saving rate increased. The 2023 Economic Spring Forecast shows that the savings rate of households increased a staggering 6.1% in the EU and 7.7% in the US between 2019 and 2020. Stimulus payments gave households additional income, which they saved because they could not spend as frequently on their usual daily purchases. Inflation rates in the EU and the US fell to levels close to 0% during this time. However, once governments began to lift Covid restrictions in 2021 and 2022, the inflation rate soared, reaching a peak of 11.5% in October 2022 (EUROSTAT 2023). The inflation rate increases emerged from the higher-than-usual dispensable income; increasing demand once consumers could spend at their usual levels after many restrictions were lifted. The inability of supply to meet the new demand was primarily caused by pre-existing economic shocks that had already reduced the available supply. Consequently, a new demand shock emerged, where demand surpassed the available supply, leading to substantial inflation. Prices elevated to a point where supply could meet demand. Therefore, expansionary fiscal policy, which pumped trillions into the global economies, led to widespread inflation.

As already introduced previously, the significant rise in inflation rates and subsequent economic imbalances in the global economy can be attributed to the imprudent utilization of expansionary fiscal policy, particularly through the United States' excessive stimulus payments. The US stimulus payments, or EIPS (Economic Impact Payments), were afforded to households whose incomes vastly exceeded the medium income. In fact, 93% of households with incomes between $100,000 and $150,000 reported receiving or expecting to receive stimulus checks. In combination with this, "over roughly a year, EIPs provided the equivalent of more than 125 percent of median monthly income for a four-person household with two married adults and two children" (Gelman et al. 2022). The US and some European countries made stimulus payments to households that were not in severe need. This ultimately increased disposable income for higher-earning households. Due to their relatively large wealth, these households had a higher propensity to spend this money once restrictions were lifted; further contributing to the demand shock that substantially increased the inflation rate.

The COVID-19 pandemic presented various economic shocks that forced governments worldwide to react with monetary and fiscal policy action. The EU and the US, two of the major economic governing bodies in the world, employed record-setting expansionary fiscal and monetary policies to keep the global economy out of a deep recession. While some would say that the employment of expansionary fiscal policy was likely necessary, the resulting inflation rate was substantial. Historically, high inflation rates lead to various undesirable consequences in the economy. Therefore, as shown in earlier chapters, the high inflation rates from the expansionary fiscal policy seen during the COVID-19 pandemic are likely to result in some form of economic contraction.

## Political Implications

As previously discussed, European monetary and fiscal policy risk has been building up for decades. In the case of Britain, inflation was a ticking time bomb that ignited amidst Liz Truss's fledgling government. Like many political leaders worldwide, Truss came into office hoping to grow the economy, but was forced out of office because of the broken economic situation she inherited (Salmon 2022). In addition, the Bank of England harshly opposed Truss since her inaugural day in office, refusing to compromise and allowing financial regulation to go unchecked. This underlying risk was the result of decades of bad monetary and fiscal policy. Covid stimulus packages and lockdowns only triggered the inevitable.

The European Central Bank has confidently stated that inflation is not here to stay, but Europeans have angrily watched basic goods and services continue to climb as inflation shows no signs of stopping (Tamma 2020). Not being able to afford the same basic necessities is a strong motivator for voters to try to change their situation. Isabella Weber, professor of economics at the University of Massachusetts Amherst, noted that: "When essential prices explode in ways that people can't pay them anymore, it's like some basic social contract breaks" (Zahn 2022). When that basic social contract breaks, or at least appears to, individuals support changes to their political and economic system. This is in part because they feel as if they don't have a moral imperative to uphold their side of a bargain any more. Last year in Colombia, the people elected the country's first-ever leftist president, and Brazil swore in President Lula da Silva at the beginning of 2023, his third time in office (PBS 2022, Kahn et al. 2023).

Political turnover is to be expected with inflation. Eurasia Group managing director Robert Kahn and CEO Maziar Minovi conducted a study on the effect of inflation on elections by looking at more than fifty inflation shocks around the world since 1970. They found a 58% government turnover, demonstrating the importance of inflation to voters (Zahn 2022). If inflation hits within two years of an election, there was a change in three out of every four governments. This can have serious implications for the market. The change of power between different political parties means unpredictable and at times conflicting economic policy. As one IMF staff discussion handout stated: "Policy consistency assists policy effectiveness" (Gaspar et al. 2016, p. 7). Governments which are bestowed power amidst economic turmoil won't be consistent—precisely because the people elected something different from what they had before—which means the effectiveness of new policies combating inflation would only worsen. Producers and consumers can better adjust themselves to a consistent economic policy, whereas inconsistent policy shocks the economy, distorting underlying pricing mechanisms.

The implications of economic turmoil go beyond political consequences for individuals or parties. Inaccurate predictions for the future create a weighty problem for European political institutions: a decline in trust. People want to believe that the government works on their behalf, but the government's intentions are irrelevant when their decisions fail to create better economic outcomes. A recent study found a "fixed decline in trust across all institutions, including national governments, the EU and healthcare systems" since the Covid lockdowns (Ahrendt et al. 2022, p. 10). The study suggests that the major factors that caused the widespread decline in trust are the war in Ukraine, the proceeding energy crisis, and inflation.

A society without high trust does not function properly. Frayed social fabric leads to less trust in markets and between individuals that undergird the free market. A 2015 study by Kim Sønderskov and Peter Dinesen described the relationship between institutional and social trust. The authors discussed the findings of numerous studies which show that trust increases important indicators of social well-being, including volunteering, donating to charity, and paying taxes. The authors also note that "fair and efficient state institutions form the basis for trusting others by signaling that untrustworthy behavior is uncommon, and will be sanctioned regardless of who commits the exploit" (Sønderskov et al. 2015, p. 181).

Trust between individuals in a society and between individuals and their institutions is the glue that holds a body politic. Humans enter into political associations with one another in politics because they trust that their fellow citizens will respect their rights and that the government will protect them if need be. When people stop trusting institutions, they stop trusting one another. Aside from lowering trust, inflation also affects corruption, which slows the economy and further undermines trust. A 2004 study published in the Harvard Business School found a positive relationship between inflation and corruption in 75 countries. The study explains: "A one standard deviation increase in inflation variance from the median increases corruption by 12 percent of a standard deviation and reduces growth by 0.33 percentage points" (Braun et al. 2004, p. 77). This cycle can continue to spiral out of hand. While corruption itself can hurt the economy, causing hiccups in the system and increasing fees and regulations, corruption also attracts less foreign investment, especially in developing countries (Wei 1999).

A 2019 study by Johan Graafland, an economics professor at Tilburg University in the Netherlands, explained that "free market institutions foster human development only in high trust societies, not in low trust countries" (Graafland 2019, p. 271). Graafland also discusses previous research which showed how human development depends on institutions, and how economic growth depends on generalized trust. Economic growth requires social trust. Societies cannot achieve prosperity if individuals don't have foundational trust in each other and in their institutions. Inflation destroys this trust, thus halting human development and reversing positive economic development.

A decline in trust in institutions has downstream effects on European society. The United Nations explained why trust is important: "[Trust] allows public bodies to plan and execute policies and deliver services. Greater public trust has been found to improve compliance in regulations and tax collections, even respect for property rights. It also gives confidence to consumers and investors, crucial to creating jobs and the functioning of economies more broadly" (Perry 2021). In other words, trust is the foundation for a prosperous society. Inflation breaks down that trust and weakens the economic promise of the free market.

**Acknowledgements** The author would like to acknowledge the contributions of Leo Koerner, Stuart Anker, Zach Bauder, Sam Hooton, and Burkley McCarthy. Austrian Economics Center, July 2023.

# References

Acharya V et al (2019) Whatever it takes: the real effects of unconventional monetary policy. Rev Financ Stud 32(9):3366–3411. https://doi.org/10.1093/rfs/hhz005. Accessed 21 June 2023

Ahrendt D, Consolini M, Mascherini M, Sandor E (2022) Fifth round of the living, working and Covid-19 e-survey: living in a new era of uncertainty. Eurofound. https://www.eurofound.europa.eu/sites/default/files/ef_publication/field_ef_document/ef22042en.pdf. Accessed 21 June 2023

Ayala M et al (2022) A current snapshot of those unemployed during the COVID 19 pandemic. U.S. Chamber of Commerce, https://www.uschamber.com/workforce/the-pandemic-unemployed-survey-why-americans-are-staying-out-of-the-workforce. Accessed 21 June 2023

Braun M, Di Tella R (2004) Inflation, inflation variability, and corruption. Econ & Polit 16(1):77–100. https://www.hbs.edu/ris/Publication%20Files/Braun%20et%20al%202004%20Economics_b1e37cad-d510-48e8-92ed-6fe2bced6a5f.pdf. Accessed 21 June 2023

Cavounidis J (2018) The migration experience of Greece and the impact of the economic crisis on its migrant and native populations. Eur J Public Health 28(5):20–23. https://academic.oup.com/eurpub/article/28/suppl_5/20/5196845. Accessed 21 June 2023

Chan K (2022) Inflation protests across Europe threaten political turmoil. The Hill, 22 October. https://thehill.com/homenews/ap/ap-business/ap-inflation-protests-across-europe-threaten-political-turmoil/. Accessed 21 June 2023

Davis W, Figgins B, Hedengren D, Klein D Economics Professors' favorite economic thinkers. Journals, and Blogs (along with Party and Policy Views). Econ J Watch, (8)(2):126–146. https://econjwatch.org/File+download/487/DavisMay2011.pdf?mimetype=pdf. Accessed 23 June 2023

European Central Bank (2014) Verbatim of the remarks made by Mario Draghi, Speech at the Frankfurt European Banking Congress Frankfurt am Main, 21 November. https://www.ecb.europa.eu/press/key/date/2014/html/sp141121.en.html. Accessed 21 June 2023

European Central Bank (2023) European system of central banks (ESCB). https://www.ecb.europa.eu/ecb/orga/escb/html/index.en.html. Accessed 21 June 2023

European Commission (2023) Spring 2023 economic forecast. https://economy-finance.ec.europa.eu/economic-forecast-and-surveys/economic-forecasts/spring-2023-economic-forecast-improved-outlook-amid-persistent-challenges_en#:~:text=Upward%20revisions%20for%20the%20euro,0.3%25%20higher%20than%20in%20winter. Accessed 21 June 2023

European Union (2023) European central bank. https://european-union.europa.eu/institutions-law-budget/institutions-and-bodies/search-all-eu-institutions-and-bodies/european-central-bank-ecb_en. Accessed 21 June 2023

EUROSTAT (2023) Annual inflation rates down to 6.1% in the Euro area. https://ec.europa.eu/eurostat/documents/2995521/16965667/2-16062023-AP-EN.pdf. Accessed 21 June 2023

Febrero E, Uxó J, Dejuán Ó (2015) The ECB during the financial crisis. Not so unconventional. Metroeconomica 66(4):715–739. https://doi.org/10.1111/meca.12088. Accessed 21 June 2023

Gaspar V, Obstfeld M, Sahay R (2016). Macroeconomic management when policy space is constrained: a comprehensive, consistent, and coordinated approach to economic policy. Int

Monet Fund. https://www.imf.org/external/pubs/ft/sdn/2016/sdn1609.pdf. Accessed 21 June 2023

Gelman M, Stephens M (2022) Lessons learned from economic impact payments during COVID-19. Brookings Institute. https://www.brookings.edu/essay/lessons-learned-from-economic-impact-payments-during-covid-19/. Accessed 21 June 2023

Gourinchas PO, Philippon T, Vayanos D (2016) The analytics of the Greek crisis. NBER Macroecon Annu 3. https://www.journals.uchicago.edu/doi/full/10.1086/690239. Accessed 21 June 2023

Graafland J (2019) Contingencies in the relationship between economic freedom and human development: the role of generalized trust. J Inst Econ 16(3):271–86. https://www.cambridge.org/core/services/aop-cambridge-core/content/view/455C6214E32F50EF20C3F7BFA83E675A/S1744137419000705a.pdf/contingencies-in-the-relationship-between-economic-freedom-and-human-development-the-role-of-generalized-trust.pdf. Accessed 21 June 2023

GTP editing team (2023) IOBE: Germany leading investor in Greece. Greek Travel Pages. https://news.gtp.gr/2023/03/29/iobe-germany-leading-investor-in-greece/. Accessed 21 June 2023

Hayek FA (1931) Prices and production. Kelly Publishers, New York, August M

Hayek FA (1933) Monetary theory and the trade cycle. Jonathan Cape, London

Hayek FA (2008) Prices and production and other works. In: Salerno JT (ed) Ludwig von Mises Institute. https://cdn.mises.org/prices_and_production_and_other_works.pdf. Accessed 21 June 2023

Hayek FA (2012) FA Hayek-unemployment and the free market. YouTube. https://www.youtube.com/watch?v=Qz9TzbyIHFw. Accessed 21 June 2023

Hlupić Radić D (2019) Unconventional monetary policy of the European central bank. EU Comp Law Issues Chall Ser (ECLIC) 3(June):1064–1079. https://doi.org/10.25234/eclic/9045. Accessed 21 June 2023

Hoffmann A, Cachanosky N (2017) Unintended consequences of ECB policies. SSRN Electron J. https://doi.org/10.2139/ssrn.2898276. Accessed 21 June 2023

Hornstein A, Karabarbounis M, Kurmann A, Lalé E, Ta L (2022) Disincentive effects of pandemic unemployment benefits. San Francisco Fed. https://www.frbsf.org/wp-content/uploads/sites/4/10-21-2022-Karabarbounis-paper.pdf. Accessed 21 June 2023

Hayek FA (1977) Unemployment And The Free Market. YouTube, November 28, 2012. https://www.youtube.com/watch?v=Qz9TzbyIHFw

Joyce M, Miles D, Scott A, Vayanos D (2012) Quantitative easing and unconventional monetary policy—an introduction. Econ J 122(564):271–88. http://www.jstor.org/stable/23324224. Accessed 21 June 2023

Kahn C, Bowman E (2023) Leftist Lula da Silva is sworn in as president to lead a divided Brazil, NPR. https://www.npr.org/2023/01/01/1146518711/leftist-lula-brazil-sworn-in-president. Accessed 21 June 2023

Karamanis K, Naxakis C (2014) Minimum wage and unemployment in Greek labour market: a descriptive analysis. Int J Hum Resour Stud. https://www.researchgate.net/figure/The-nominal-evolution-of-the-minimum-wage-in-Greece-NGCA-2000-2012-Law-4046-2012_fig1_268386673. Accessed 21 June 2023

Klooster J (2020) The ethics of delegating monetary policy. J Polit 82(2):587–99. https://doi.org/10.1086/706765. Accessed 21 June 2023

van 't Klooster J (2022) The ethics of delegating monetary policy. European University Institute. Accessed June 19 2023

Lapavitsas C (2019) Political economy of the Greek crisis. Rev Radic Polit Econ 51(1):31–51. https://journals.sagepub.com/doi/10.1177/0486613417730363. Accessed 21 June 2023

OECD Jobs Strategy (2018) How does GREECE compare? https://www.oecd.org/greece/jobs-strategy-GREECE-EN.pdf. Accessed 21 June 2023

Oesterreichische Nationalbank (2023) Monetary policy. https://www.oenb.at/en/Monetary-Policy.html. Accessed 21 June 2023

Parlapiano A, Solomon DB, Ngo M, Cowley S (2022) Where $5 Trillion in pandemic stimulus money went. The New York Times. https://www.nytimes.com/interactive/2022/03/11/us/how-covid-stimulus-money-was-spent.html. Accessed 21 June 2023

PBS NewsHour (2022) In historic shift, Gustavo Petro sworn in as Colombia's first leftist president. https://www.pbs.org/newshour/world/in-historic-shift-gustavo-petro-sworn-in-as-colombias-first-leftist-president. Accessed 21 June 2023

Perry J (2021) Trust in public institutions: trends and implications for economic security. United Nations, Department of Economic and Social Affairs. https://www.un.org/development/desa/dspd/2021/07/trust-public-institutions/. Accessed 21 June 2023

Riegert B (2021) EU launches coronavirus stimulus program–DW–06/23/2021, Deutsche Welle. https://www.dw.com/en/eu-launches-coronavirus-stimulus-program/a-58020515. Accessed 21 June 2023

Salmon F (2022) U.K.'s Liz Truss inherits an economic nightmare. Axios. https://www.axios.com/2022/09/07/liz-truss-uk-economy-inflation-pound. Accessed 21 June 2023

Schnabl G, Sonnenberg N (2020) Monetary policy, financial regulation and financial stability: a comparison between the fed and the ECB. https://doi.org/10.2139/ssrn.3571200. Accessed 21 June 2023

Schnabl G (2017) The failure of ECB monetary policy from a Mises-Hayek perspective. SSRN Electron J. https://doi.org/10.2139/ssrn.2951044. Accessed 21 June 2023

Šetková L (2016) Unconventional monetary tools adopted by ECB and FED from 2008 until 2014. Vysoká škola ekonomická v Praze

Sønderskov KM, Dinesen PT (2015) Trusting the state, trusting each other? The effect of institutional trust on social trust. Polit Behav (38):179–202. https://doi.org/10.1007/s11109-015-9322-8. Accessed 21 June 2023

Soyres F, Santacreu AM, Young H (2022) Demand-supply imbalance during the COVID-19 pandemic: the role of fiscal policy. Board Gov Fed Reserv Syst. https://www.federalreserve.gov/econres/ifdp/files/ifdp1353.pdf. Accessed 21 June 2023

Stemmler H (2023) The effects of COVID-19 on businesses: key versus non-key firms. International Labour Organization. https://www.ilo.org/legacy/english/intserv/working-papers/wp077/index.html. Accessed 21 June 2023

Tamma P (2020) Politicians sweat as Europe's inflation time bomb ticks, Politico. https://www.politico.eu/article/europe-inflation-time-bomb/. Accessed 21 June 2023

The Economist (2023) A stunning election result for Greece's prime minister. https://www.economist.com/leaders/2023/05/25/a-stunning-election-result-for-greeces-prime-minister.    Accessed 21 June 2023

Thomsen P (2019) The IMF and the Greek crisis: myths and realities. Speech Deliv Lond Sch Econ. https://www.imf.org/en/News/Articles/2019/10/01/sp093019-The-IMF-and-the-Greek-Crisis-Myths-and-Realities. Accessed 21 June 2023

Wei SJ (1999) Corruption in economic development: economic grease, minor annoyance, or major obstacle? Harv Univ Natl Bur Econ Res. https://doi-org.ezp-prod1.hul.harvard.edu/10.1596/1813-9450-2048. Accessed 21 June 2023

Zahn M (2022) Inflation has helped decide elections worldwide. Here's what that means for the midterms. ABC News. https://abcnews.go.com/Business/inflation-helped-decide-elections-worldwide-means-midterms/story?id=92808587. Accessed 21 June 2023

# Politics and the Monetary and Banking System

**Syed Kamall**

During my time as a member of the European Parliament, I saw two main issues relating to monetary policy. The first was the era of cheap money. The second was the battle between the politicians and the markets over the sustainability of the single European currency. In this chapter, I will focus on the first issue.

## The 2008 Financial Crisis

In my first parliamentary term, the global finance crisis of 2008 occurred when banks collapsed and at one stage it looked like the whole global financial system might go into meltdown. There were debates between those who urged government intervention and others who argued we should leave it to the markets to resolve. However, governments intervened to restore confidence in the financial system. Many blamed free market capitalism, while free marketeers argued that it was a lack of market mechanisms that led to the crisis in the first place. In addition, free marketers argued that markets had not been allowed to operate due to three distortions:

1. Some banks were considered too big to fail, whereas in a true free market they would be allowed to fail to enable existing competitors to take market share and for new competitors to emerge. This is often referred to as Schumpeterian creative destruction.
2. The existence of taxpayer-funded deposit guarantee schemes created a moral hazard since depositors did not consider how stable or viable a bank was when opening an account, since they would get their money back if the bank failed.

S. Kamall (✉)
Professor of Politics and Internatonal Relations, St Mary's University, Waldegrave Rd, Twickenham TW1 4SX, UK
e-mail: syed.kamall@stmarys.ac.uk

© The Author(s), under exclusive license to Springer Nature Switzerland AG 2024
M. Rangeley (ed.), *The Age of Debt Bubbles*, Professional Practice in Governance and Public Organizations, https://doi.org/10.1007/978-3-031-66473-1_7

3. The lack of accountability and director liability. If directors were held liable for their banks failing, they would be more cautious and considerate in making decisions, but since they were not held liable there was no incentive for them to seek out and prevent risky behaviour.

In the event, some banks were bailed out with taxpayers' money, no directors were prosecuted, and more financial regulation was passed. However, this ignored the fact that there was plenty of financial regulation that did not prevent the crisis. As the late Queen Elizabeth II asked on a visit to the London School of Economics after the 2008 financial crisis "Why did no one see it coming?" (Giles 2008).

In the aftermath, commentators pointed to a number of potential causes including the lack of transparency of financial instruments such as Collateralized Debt Obligations (CDOs) and Credit Default Swaps (CDSs), and the move to rules-based IFRS accounting standards.

In simple terms, CDOs are created when banks pool individual loans, such as car loans, mortgages, etc., and then divide these pools of loans into different tranches depending on risk and maturity (Tardi 2024). CDOs can combine tranches of debt which have a high credit rating with more risky debt. If there is sufficient debt with a high credit rating, the whole CDO can also receive a high credit rating even though it may contain highly risky debt. Banks can then make money by selling these CDOs to investors, which allows them to spread risk and free up money (Study Master, n.d.). In the run up to the 2008 financial crisis, CDOs containing riskier subprime mortgages were rated safer than they were, since they also contained debt with higher credit ratings. When borrowers with subprime mortgages were unable to make repayments and defaulted, investors in CDOs such as insurance companies, banks, pension funds and hedge funds faced huge losses (Uzialko 2023).

A Credit Default Swap (CDS) is a financial instrument that has been compared to an insurance policy to cover a fixed income product such as a bond. The seller of the CDS receives a regular premium or fee from the buyer, but if a default occurs the seller pays out the value of the product. IFRS accounting standards were criticised for allowing banks to book the revenue from CDSs and other financial instruments up front without making provision or setting aside sufficient funds if there was a default. As Plender (2012) wrote *"IFRS requires provisions to be made only when losses are already incurred, as opposed to expected."*

In Brussels and Strasbourg, where I sat on the European Parliament's Economic and Monetary Affairs committee, we debated new financial regulations. Even though there had been many financial regulations before the crisis, in 2009 the G20 leaders announced the *"Framework for Strong, Sustainable, and Balanced Growth"* (G20 2009) at its meeting in Pittsburgh which called for:

- Responsible fiscal policies, with short-term flexibility and longer-run sustainability
- Strengthened financial supervision to prevent excess credit growth and leverage
- Macro prudential and regulatory policies to prevent credit and asset price cycles from destabilising the global economy

- More balanced current accounts, open trade, investment and a rejection of protectionism measures.
- Monetary policies consistent with price stability in the context of market-oriented exchange rates
- Structural reforms to increase economic growth and improve social safety nets.
- Balanced and sustainable economic development to narrow development imbalances and reduce poverty
- Increased private savings
- G20 Finance Ministers to work with the IMF to develop a mutual assessment process to evaluate the collective implications of national policies for the global economy

At the same summit, the G20 tasked the Financial Stability Board (FSB) to take over from the Financial Stability Forum to deliver reforms within the framework. To that end, the FSB called for the following priority reforms (Financial Stability Board 2022):

- Building resilient financial institutions
- Ending too-big-to-fail, identifying systemically important financial institutions (SIFIs)
- Effective resolution regimes and policies in the event of bank failures
- More effective supervision
- Making derivatives markets safer
- Enhancing resilience of non-bank financial intermediation
- Addressing data gaps
- A uniform global Legal Entity Identifier (LEI)
- Reducing reliance on credit ratings
- Improving risk disclosures

While these reforms might suggest global coordination, some EU officials and politicians believed that since the new US President Barack Obama was focused on healthcare reform, this presented an opportunity for the EU to set the gold standard in financial regulations. This ignored the fact that US financial regulators and supervisors would still be working on financial legislation.

One of my concerns at the time was that while we should be focusing on making sure that in future banks would no longer be bailed out with taxpayers' money, the focus of early legislation was not on banks. One of the first new directives to be considered was the Alternative Investors Fund Managers Directive (AIFMD) tackling hedge funds and private equity. This brought to mind an anecdote that when a fight breaks out in a bar you don't hit the person who started the fight, you hit the person you always wanted to hit. There were many in European Union countries who were critical or suspicious of private equity and hedge funds so were keen to target them. In fact, later research suggested that

> hedge funds were not a primary cause of the financial crisis, although some aspects of their operations contributed to the crisis. The roles played by credit-rating agencies, mortgage

lenders, and inadequately backed credit default swaps (CDSs) were far more important. (Dixon et al. 2012).

There was also broad consensus on the need to increase the capital requirements on banks, i.e. to increase the amount of money they have available to cover any losses and in theory prevent banks having to be bailed out with taxpayers' money. This need not be in the form of cash. In reality,

> capital requirements are regulatory standards for banks that determine how much liquid capital (easily sold assets) they must keep on hand, concerning their overall holdings … [are] … expressed as ratios, [and] … are based on the weighted risk of the banks" different assets (Chen 2023).

## The Era of Cheap Money

Higher capital requirements may suggest that banks have less money to lend, i.e. reduce liquidity, so to counterbalance this, central banks can reduce interest rates. As Cecchettia and Kohlerb (2014) suggest *"bank lending: an easing of monetary policy raises the level of bank reserves and bank deposits, increasing the supply of funds."*

This action by central banks to lower interest rates led to the era of cheap money. There is some dispute over when this began. Blakeley (2023) argues that *"between 2008 and 2022 … central banks cut … interest rates following the financial crisis to encourage investment by reducing financing costs."* Others trace it back to the recession of 2001. White (2009) explains that *"the Federal Reserve System, under Chairman Alan Greenspan, began aggressively expanding the U.S. money supply … [when] year-over-year growth in … M2 monetary aggregate rose briefly above 10 percent, and remained above 8 percent … [into] … 2003.* In addition the Federal Reserve reduced *"the federal funds (interbank short-term) interest rate from … 6.25 percent … [in 2001] … [to] a low in mid-2003 of 1 percent, where it stayed for a year."*

Hanke (2008) believes: *"This set off the mother of all liquidity cycles and yet another massive demand bubble."* What is interesting about these analyses is that Blakely writes as a socialist while White and Hanke write from a classical liberal perspective. Blakeley (2023) probably gives one of the most succinct analyses of loose money when she explains that:

> central bankers began pumping money into the world economy in an unprecedented display of coordinated central planning within nominally free market economies … [which] … pushed up asset prices …making asset owners extremely wealthy … It also allowed unviable businesses and impoverished working people to cover over the cracks in their balance sheets with ever greater borrowing. But this model of debt-fuelled growth was never sustainable …. As economists like Joseph Schumpeter realised, capitalism requires creative destruction to maintain its dynamism.

While classical liberals would mostly agree with Blakely's analysis, they would disagree with her assertion that *"Financial crises are critical parts of capitalist development because they clear out old, unproductive firms to make space for newer, more innovative ones."*

Classical liberals argue that it is market competition that allows creative destruction, not financial crises. However, they would agree with Blakely when she writes *"since the 1980s, central banks have intervened to ensure that large, powerful corporations and financial institutions are protected from the consequences of their own greed and recklessness."* While Blakely blames capitalism per se, classical liberals would be equally critical of this behaviour as an example of crony capitalism.

Classical liberals propose two possible explanations of why loose money is bad for the economy, i. The Austrian Business Cycle Theory and ii. Monetarism.

To consider the Austrian Business Cycle Theory, we need to think about the role of interest rates. Interest on savings may be considered as a reward for saving or an opportunity to earn money at a later date if you choose not to spend your income or savings immediately. Some economists propose complex relationships between interest rate and time, while Swedish economist Knut Wicksell, proposed the idea of a natural rate of interest, that:

> governs the allocation of resources between current consumption and investment for the future. By keeping saving and investment in balance, the natural rate guides the economy along a sustainable growth path (Garrison 2006).

Friedrich Hayek claimed that lower interest rates lead to lower savings, more spending and malinvestment, i.e. investment in assets due to the extra money available and not necessarily due to the robustness and growth potential. Hayek believed that.

> credit creation by monetary authorities would push investment beyond society's long-term willingness to save, creating a mismatch between supply and demand that would inevitably cause recession (Oppers 2002).

Tumerkan (2023) offers a simpler summary of the Austrian Business Cycle Theory suggesting that:

> when interest rates drop, it raises consumer spending power with cheaper debt … pushes prices higher amid greater consumption … [and] … creates a false signal for businesses … Thus firms … binge on debt to over-hire, over-build, over-invest, and over-produce. Fueling an economic boom ... But the crux here is that this boom was only driven because of artificially lower interest rates. Not 'real' organic consumer demand. Eventually, when growth overheats and inflation picks up, central banks will raise interest rates. And the malinvestment is exposed. [Even] if the central bank doesn't raise interest rates–the market will become saturated with excess capacity and unsustainable private sector debt. Creating a bust all on its own … Asset prices and investment returns plunge. Corporate margins erode. Unemployment rises. Debt-defaults soar. And the financial system grows unstable.

For monetarists, the problem with cheap money is that an increase in money supply without a corresponding increase in productivity leads to inflation. To explain this, let's consider a simplified example where there are 10 children in a small remote village who each receive £1 pocket money every week. Every week all 10 children spend their £1 pocket money on a chocolate bar at a sweet shop which is the only place selling these chocolate bars. If they are all suddenly given £2 pocket money, but the sweet shop is only able to supply 10 chocolate bars each week and no more, the sweet shop owner will increase the price of the chocolate bars to £2. Since the supply of money has increased but the supply of chocolate bars has not increased, this leads to inflation. Of course, this example makes lots of assumptions such as they cannot buy the chocolate bar elsewhere in-person or online, the children do not buy competing products or spend their money elsewhere or do not save, etc., but it makes the point well. This example also suggests that if the supply of chocolate bars did increase to 20 chocolate bars, then there would be no inflation. In other words, inflation occurs where there is no increase in productivity or overall demand. As Friedman (2012) said *"Inflation is caused by too much money chasing after too few goods."*

## Inflation

During the era of cheap money, consumer price inflation was kept low for time partly due to the flood of cheap imports from companies in China and perhaps elsewhere. However, some economists believe this downward pressure has been exaggerated. For example, Bai and Stumpner (2019) have found that *"Chinese imports led to a 0.19 percentage point annual reduction in the price index for consumer tradables."* The other factor that reduced consumer inflation was the increased productivity and fall in margins in the distribution sector (Nickell 2005).

But while consumers did not initially feel the impact of inflation as a result of cheap money, investors and homeowners saw the value of their assets rise, increasing the gap between the wealthy and the poor, as well as between homeowners and first-time buyers. Goodier (2023) points out that:

> [in] 1999, a median house in England cost 4.4 times the median income, according to the ONS … [and while] … the late 2000s saw a house-price boom … although house prices recovered from the subsequent crash, wages did not keep up after the global financial crisis … [so this] ratio had almost doubled to 8.4 times income in 2022.

While O'Connor (2022) describes how those:

> who weren't on the housing ladder watched the bottom rung move further away. In the UK, 55 per cent of those born between 1956 and 1960 were homeowners by the age of 30. For people like me born between 1981 and 1985, that figure was just 27%.

O'Connor also points out that *"UK real wages grew an average 33 per cent a decade from 1970 to 2007 but didn't grow at all in the 2010s."* While this wage stagnation would have been expected to reduce consumer demand, low interest rates encouraged more consumption. She cites the statistic that in 2019, 92 per cent of new car registrations were financed at the point of sale by members of the Finance & Leasing Association, up from 46 per cent in 2006. Low interest rates led to investments in loss-making start-ups and an expansion of consumer credit companies, allowing consumers to pay in instalments. She concludes: *"Money was tight but people could summon cheap rides and buy things even when they couldn't afford them."*

In 2020, there was an economic slump as most countries' economies contracted due to the COVID crisis. The UK economy shrank by nearly 10 per cent. This crisis was different since it was mainly due to a supply-side shock rather than a drop in demand or spending. As Castaneda and Congdon (2020) explained:

> the crisis is mainly due to a supply-side shock in the economy and not to a drop in aggregate demand or spending … [since] … economies have been put in 'lockdown' by governments, while international trade and world-wide supply chains have been severely disturbed. Entire sectors such as aviation, travel, hospitality and other services companies have virtually closed down. Further, this … happened in a matter of weeks, if not days. In effect, people and companies have been told not to produce.

Governments responded by increasing budget deficits to spend on keeping companies afloat and to understandably prevent job losses. However, these deficits were supported by monetising the debt. In this context monetisation is defined as *"the permanent increase in the monetary base to fund the government."* (Johnston 2023). In simple terms, central banks create new money which governments then borrow. Castaneda and Congdon (2020) warned that:

> monetisation of budget deficits, combined with official support for emergency bank lending to cash-strained corporates, is leading ... to extremely high growth rates of the quantity of money … suggesting that consumer **inflation may move into double digits** at some point in the next two or three years.

At the time, their warnings were ignored and even criticised. Brenchley (2020) quotes a number of economists who argued that warnings of double-digit inflation were *"wide of the mark"*. One Chief Investment Officer of a private bank suggested that *"Inflation is likely to remain tepid due to huge slack that occurs in recessionary times"*, while a Chief Economist of another private bank believed there would not be *"a sustained and lasting acceleration in inflation"* with the caveat *"at least for the next two or three years."*

But time proved Castaneda and Congdon correct. While the Bank of England's task was to keep inflation at 2 per cent or lower, inflation rocketed to 11 per cent in 2022 and at the time of writing (May 2024) remains above the target range. To paraphrase the late Queen "why did no one [else] see it coming?" Why were central bankers in agreement that quantitative easing would not lead to inflation? And, why were they not challenged? Baker and Rangeley (2022) suggest that:

> Central bankers benefit from the orthodoxy that has developed and have an intellectual and financial interest in maintaining it. Ultimately, this mistake of uniformity of opinion is a key reason that has led to failure among central banks … Roger Koppl's work on expert failure … [found] … that failure among experts often develops when uniformity of opinion takes hold … central bankers earn their livelihoods through their recognition as the official orthodoxy.

A House of Lords Economic Affairs Committee (2023) report found a:

> perceived … lack of intellectual diversity in many central banks, including the Bank of England. Witnesses suggested that this contributed to insufficient challenge on the MPC in 2020 and 2021 which allowed a unanimity of view to prevail about the "transitory" nature of above-target inflation.

The report recommended that the Monetary Policy Committee membership should comprise *"people of different backgrounds and economic perspectives. The Bank must be proactive in encouraging a diversity of views."*

Concerns were also raised about the *"notable absence of any detailed discussions about money supply in the Bank's published Monetary Policy Reports",* so the report recommended *"that the Monetary Policy Reports should include discussion of the main monetary aggregates, accompanied by an analysis of their relevance to the Bank's inflation outlook."*

## What Can Be Done?

However, there is another issue. Given that the remit of the bank was to keep inflation at 2 per cent or less, there appears to be no sanctions or accountability for consistently failing to meet this target. As Lynn (2023) asks *"What does it take to get fired from the Bank of England?"* On its website, the Bank of England (2024) explains that is accountable since it has to:

> … explain how and why we arrive at the decisions we make. And as a public body, we are answerable to both the UK parliament and public … [and] … are held accountable … through public meetings with the House of Commons Treasury Select Committee. These meetings typically happen when we publish our latest reports on the state of economy and the financial system.

While it appears to offer some form of accountability, it remains the fact that no-one loses their jobs when the Monetary Policy Committee fails to meet its inflation target, which it has failed to do since April 2021.[1]

The House of Lords Committee report cited above also highlighted concerns about accountability when it concluded that:

*"an independent Bank of England must be held to account effectively. A small group of appointed Bank officials, who are not part of the elected Government, exercise significant powers which have an impact on the entire UK economy".*

While it accepts that the Government should not compromise the Bank of England's independence, the committee recommends that:

> … Parliament should conduct an overarching review of the Bank's remit, performance and operations … every five years … to hold the Bank to account and to express its view on the Bank's performance and leadership. More scrutiny and accountability should strengthen confidence in operational independence.

Various economists including Walter Bagehot, Milton Friedman and Alan Greenspan over the years have proposed abolishing central banks. Walter Bagehot, the nineteenth-century journalist and editor of The Economist magazine thought

---

[1] Source: https://www.statista.com/statistics/306648/inflation-rate-consumer-price-index-cpi-uni ted-kingdom-uk/#:~:text=The%20UK%20inflation%20rate%20was,11.1%20percent%20in%20O ctober%202022.

there should not be a central bank but also believed that change would be difficult if not impossible when he argued:

> the system of entrusting all our reserve to a single board, like that of the Bank directors, is very anomalous … is very dangerous [with] … bad consequences, though much felt, have not been fully seen … But … What would be better? What other system could there be? We are so accustomed to a system of banking, dependent for its cardinal function on a single bank, that we can hardly conceive of any other Bagehot (1873).

Friedman (1994) agreed with Bagehot that while central banks are not necessary, it is unlikely they will be abolished, when he said:

> there is no need for a lender of last resort … the market is perfectly capable of providing that function … if banks go bad, it is best that they fail earlier and not later. They will do less harm if they fail early. So taken as a whole, my conclusion is: we do not need central banks, but we shall certainly continue to have them.

In 1966, Alan Greenspan, wrote in favour of a free banking system, i.e. a system where private banks are allowed to issue their own currency as opposed to a state central bank having the monopoly on issuing and regulating a national currency:

> Under the gold standard, a free banking system stands as the protector of an economy's stability and balanced growth …In the absence of the gold standard, there is no way to protect savings from confiscation through inflation. There is no safe store of value. If there were, the government would have to make its holding illegal, as was done in the case of gold (Rand et al. 1986).

By 1987, when he was appointed as Chairman of the US Federal Reserve (the US central bank), he adopted a pragmatic approach by working within the existing system. In a 2007 interview he explained that: *"there are lots of institutions which we would be better without but … compromise is a very essence of a democratic society because if we're all individuals with different ideas and we want to live together we have to do that."*

But he did add *"There are numbers of us, myself included, who strongly believe that we did very well in the 1870 to 1914 period with an international gold standard."* (Fox Business News 2007).

Critics of the current system of central banks being the lender of last resort exist across the political spectrum. When in March 2020, the Federal Reserve announced a cut in interest rates to "near zero" longtime consumer advocate and political activist, Ralph Nader warned that the Federal Reserve had *"no regard for the hundreds of billions of dollars in interest payments taken from one hundred million unorganised savers who have their savings in Treasury bonds, banks, and money market accounts."*

He criticised the US central bank for ignoring *"the largely unproductive spiral in corporate debt … [and] … the risk of a domino effect from underwater zombie companies"* and for *"printing money… to bailout … profitable corporations –not depleted savers."*

He also pointed out the lack of accountability of the Federal Reserve and for deciding *"in secret the fate of the monetary policy, which includes the interest rates paid on your savings. There are no public hearings or ... real explanations by the Fed; just dictates. It is a government of its own inside our government –the epitome of corporate socialism."* (Nader 2020).

Ellen Brown, President of the Public Banking Institute in the US, argues in favour of a public–private partnership and pre-empts critics who argue that such partnerships distort the market, when she states:

> To ask whether public banks would interfere with free markets assumes that we have free markets, which we don't ... Banks have been bailed out by the government, when in a free market they would have gone bankrupt. The Federal Reserve blatantly manipulates interest rates in a way that serves Wall Street, lending trillions at near-zero interest and pushing rates ... artificially low (Brown 2013).

Brown admires the example of state banks in Germany and Taiwan and cites the state-owned Bank of North Dakota which operates as a mini-federal reserve and *"cooperates rather than competes with local banks, aiding with capital and liquidity requirements. Its deposit base is almost entirely composed of the revenue of the state and state agencies. North Dakota has more banks per capita than any other state, because they have not been forced to sell to their Wall Street competitors. The North Dakota Bankers' Association endorses the Bank of North Dakota, which has a mandate to support the local economy."*

She argues in favour of *"publicly owned banks for a capitalist market economy to run properly ... [acting as] ... economic infrastructure, just as roads and bridges are physical infrastructure ... [that supply] ... inexpensive, accessible financing to the free enterprise sector of the economy ...[to] ... make commerce more vital and stable."*

While Nader, Brown, Bagehot, Friedman and Greenspan believe that central banks will not be abolished, the issue of abolition has not gone away completely. In 2024, US Congressman Thomas Massie introduced the "Federal Reserve Board Abolition Act (Redman 2024). He is unlikely to succeed but it demonstrates that the issue is still on the agenda for some.

While Greenspan did not seek to abolish the US Federal Reserve when he was chairman, he did point to the merits of an alternative monetary system, the gold standard. This was a monetary system where the value of a country's currency was directly linked to gold or some other metal such as silver. Lioudis (2024) explains that before World War One:

> international trade was based on ... the classical gold standard, [i.e.] trade was settled using physical gold. Nations with trade surpluses accumulated gold as payment for their exports. Conversely, nations with trade deficits saw their gold reserves decline as gold flowed out of those nations as payment for their imports.

Currencies backed by gold or silver or another physical item of value are often referred to as commodity-based currencies or commodity money (Mises, 1981).

At the Bretton Woods conference in 1944 to discuss the post-World War 2 economic and financial system, as well as establishing the International Monetary Fund and the World Bank, western powers agreed to the Bretton Woods system which valued national currencies in relation to the US dollar. In turn, the US dollar was convertible to gold at the fixed rate of \$35 per ounce. As other countries developed and became wealthier their demand for dollars increased so the Federal Reserve printed more. This led to a situation where there were four times as many dollars in circulation as there were gold in reserves (Garten 2021).

In August 1971, the French and British governments stated their intention to convert the dollars they held into gold. Since the US government did not have sufficient gold available, President Nixon announced a suspension of the convertibility of dollars into gold. This later became permanent. In addition, since the value of the dollar relative to gold had not changed since 1944, it was considered overvalued leading to cheaper imports, but more costly exports which in turn led to the first US trade deficit since the nineteenth century. In the 1960s, the US Federal Reserve ended its focus on controlling the monetary supply and adapted to the Kennedy and Johnson administrations' increased focus more on full employment even though this would lead to increased inflation (Bordo 2017).

Some economists have argued for a return to the gold standard or a commodity-based currency since they believe it would limit the Federal Reserve's ability to print money and increase inflation, while critics suggest a return to the gold standard would lead to economies becoming vulnerable to shocks in supply and demand for gold (Lioudis 2024).

Since the end of the Bretton Woods system, central banks of countries that had signed up to the gold standard have issued currencies that are no longer convertible into or backed by gold or silver or another physical commodity. Such currencies are known as "fiat money" and are based on the creditworthiness of the issuing government. In Latin, "fiat" means "let it be done or it shall be done". As Rozsa (2022) explains:

> fiat money has value because the government says it does-there is no physical backing behind them … It means that a currency's value is based on faith from lenders and investors that the government will repay its debts.

Hayek predicted that the end of the Bretton-Woods system and the move to fiat money would tempt central banks to pursue a policy of cheap money when he wrote that: *"we cannot hope that any authority which has power to determine the quantity of money will long resist the pressure for, or the seduction of, cheap money."*

However, Hayek also believed that a return to the gold standard was unrealistic suggesting that *"any attempt now to re-instate the gold standard by international agreement would break down within a short time and merely discredit the ideal of an international gold standard for even longer."*

Instead, he proposed ending a government's or central authority's monopoly on issuing currencies, when he wrote:

> I have no objection to governments issuing money, but I believe their claim to a monopoly, or their power to limit the kinds of money in which contracts may be concluded within their territory, or to determine the rates at which monies can be exchanged, to be wholly harmful.

He believed that under a system of competing currencies:

people will be very quick indeed to refuse to use the national currency once it depreciates noticeably, and they will make their dealings in a currency they trust. Employers … would find it in their interest to offer, in collective agreements, not wages anticipating a foreseen rise of prices but wages in a currency they trusted and could make the basis of rational calculation. This would deprive government of the power to counteract excessive wage increases, and the unemployment they would cause, by depreciating their currency. It would also prevent employers from conceding such wages in the expectation that the national monetary authority would bail them out if they promised more than they could pay.

He also dismissed concerns that this would make it would be impractical since if *"shopkeepers knew that they could turn it instantly at the current rate of exchange into whatever money they preferred, they would be only too ready to sell their wares at an appropriate price for any currency."* (Hayek 1976).

The idea of competing issuers of currency was not a new idea. Dowd (2023) refers to this idea as free banking i.e. *"a banking system in which banks issue their own notes under competitive conditions while typically operating on a commodity standard, in the absence of a central bank and in a legal environment in which the public are free to accept or reject bank currency as they choose."*

He points to historical episodes of free banking in Australia, Belgium, Canada, Chile, Colombia, China, France, Ireland, Italy, Peru Scotland, Sweden, Switzerland and the USA.

In 1990, the then British Chancellor (finance minister), John Major proposed the idea of a new currency the hard ecu (European currency unit) to compete with national currencies in European Community countries *"as a 'gradualist' alternative to going for the 'Big Bang' solution of full monetary union."* He believed that countries needed *"differing levels of interest rates in order to eliminate inflation before even thinking about anything as radical as full monetary union."* (The Guardian Archive 2016).

The idea was dismissed, but the European Union adopted a two-phased approach to adopting the European single currency, launching the euro for accounting purposes and electronic payments on 1 January 1999 followed by a switchover to euro notes and coins on 1 January 2002.

## The Digital Future

Given that it is unlikely that governments will abolish central banks or reintroduce commodity-based currencies, some critics of fiat money suggest that the answer could be cryptocurrencies. A cryptocurrency is a virtual digital currency which is made safe by cryptography. Cryptography is a method of hiding information in messages using codes, so that only the intended recipient can read it (Richards, n.d.). The use of cryptography makes it almost impossible to counterfeit cryptocurrencies or accidentally or deliberately spend them more than once. Most cryptocurrencies exist on decentralised networks using blockchain technology. The Economist (2021) explains that:

A blockchain is a database that contains the history of whatever information it was designed to store. It is made up of a string of "blocks" of information that build on top of one another in an immutable chain. Bitcoin, one of the first blockchains, was built in 2009. It stores data on transactions in bitcoin, providing proof of who owns what at any time. What distinguishes a blockchain from other databases is that its ledger is distributed, publicly available and replicated on thousands of computers —or "nodes"—around the world. Rather than a centralised entity, like a bank or a tech platform, ensuring that the ledger is accurate, it is verified by a decentralised network of individuals.

In simple terms, units of cryptocurrency are created through a process referred to as mining. In this context, mining refers to the process of validating cryptocurrency transactions and creating new units of cryptocurrency. The mining process uses powerful computer hardware and software to solve complex mathematical problems that generate coins (Geeks for Geeks 2022).

For the critics of fiat money, the main advantage of cryptocurrencies is that they are not issued by any central authority making them theoretically immune to interference from central banks or governments. Other advantages include the potential for *"cheaper and faster money transfers and decentralized systems that do not collapse at a single point of failure."*

However, critics of cryptocurrencies point to their price volatility, impact on the environment due to consuming lots of energy in mining or creating them, as well as their use in criminal activities (Investopedia Team 2024).

Central banks have been fighting back in issuing Central Bank Digital Currencies (CBDCs) which are essentially a digital version of a country's national currency issued and backed by the central bank. They are being promoted as *"an alternative to cash, ... [a] more secure ... means of payment, ... less prone to loss or counterfeiting."* (Muradzikwa et al. 2023). However, there are concerns over the minority of people who do not trust new digital technology and prefer to continue using cash.

Supporters of the current system of fiat money issued by central banks believe that inflation can be controlled if central banks are held accountable, especially when they consistently miss their inflation targets. While many of those who support the abolition of central banks and a return to the gold standard, or commodity-based currencies, believe that both are unlikely or impossible.

However, all is not lost for the latter group. Given the rise of cryptocurrencies and Central Bank Digital Currencies (CBDCs), we may well be on the path to a system of competing currencies, where those central banks and private issuers of cryptocurrencies who irresponsibly expand the supply of their currencies are punished as consumers switch to digital currencies they trust. In other words, we may well find ourselves living in a world of competing digital currencies leading to more responsible and accountable central banks and an era of sound money.

# References

Bagehot W (1873) Lombard street: a description of the money market, 3rd edn. Henry S. King, London. https://oll.libertyfund.org/titles/bagehot-lombard-street-a-description-of-the-money-market

Bai L, Stumpner S (2019) Estimating US consumer gains from Chinese imports. Am Econ Rev: Insights 1(2):209–24. https://www.aeaweb.org/articles?id=10.1257/aeri.20180358

Baker S, Rangeley M (2022) Are we in the largest bubble in history? An Austrian school analysis. Cobden Centre. https://www.stevebaker.info/2022/07/are-we-in-the-largest-bubble-in-history-an-austrian-school-analysis-by-steve-baker-mp-max-rangeley/

Bank of England (2024) How is the bank of England independent of the government? https://www.bankofengland.co.uk/explainers/how-is-the-bank-of-england-independent-of-the-government

Blakeley G (2023) The end of cheap money is bad news for workers. Tribune. https://tribunemag.co.uk/2023/10/capitalism-is-losing-its-crutches-interest-rates#:~:text=As%20a%20recent%20editorial%20in,accustomed%20to%20extraordinarily%20cheap%20money

Bordo M (2017) The operation and demise of the Bretton woods system: 1958 to 1971. Vox.eu. Centre for Economic Policy Research 23 April. https://cepr.org/voxeu/columns/operation-and-demise-bretton-woods-system-1958-1971

Brenchley D (2020) Economists: post-covid double-digit inflation warnings wide of the mark. Investment Week. https://www.investmentweek.co.uk/analysis/4021088/economists-post-covid-double-digit-inflation-warnings-wide-mark

Brown E (2013) Public banks are essential to capitalism. New York Times. 2 October. https://www.nytimes.com/roomfordebate/2013/10/01/should-states-operate-public-banks/public-banks-are-essential-to-capitalism

Castañeda J, Congdon T (2020) Inflation: the next threat? IEA Covid briefing 7. June. Institute of Economic Affairs, London. https://iea.org.uk/publications/33536/#

Cecchettia SG, Kohlerb M (2014) When capital adequacy and interest rate policy are substitutes (and when they are not). Int J Cent Bank. https://www.ijcb.org/journal/ijcb14q3a6.pdf

Chen J (2023) Capital requirements: definition and examples. Investopedia.com. https://www.investopedia.com/terms/c/capitalrequirement.asp#:~:text=Capital%20requirements%20are%20regulatory%20standards,of%20the%20banks'%20different%20assets

Dixon L, Clancy N, Kumar KB (2012) Hedge funds and systemic risk. RAND Corporation, Santa Monica, CA. https://www.rand.org/pubs/monographs/MG1236.html

Dowd (2023) The experience of free banking, 2nd edn. Institute of Economic Affairs, London. https://iea.org.uk/wp-content/uploads/2023/12/Dowd-Free-Banking-Interactive.pdf

The Economist (2021) What are blockchains? 18 September. https://www.economist.com/briefing/2021/09/18/what-are-blockchains

Financial Stability Board (2022) Post-2008 financial crisis reforms. Last updated: 13 June 2022. https://www.fsb.org/work-of-the-fsb/market-and-institutional-resilience/post-2008-financial-crisis-reforms/#:~:text=Following%20the%202008%20financial%20crisis,social%20damage%20that%20it%20caused

Fox Business News (2007) Alan greenspan on FOX business network. [online] YouTube. https://www.youtube.com/watch?v=ZjMQG3qUFKo. Accessed 24 May 2024

Friedman M (1994) Do we need central banks? In monetary management in Hong Kong. In: Proceedings of the seminar on monetary management. 18–19 October 1993. pp 44–47. Hong Kong Monetary Authority. https://miltonfriedman.hoover.org/internal/media/dispatcher/215005/full

Friedman M (2012) Milton Friedman in his own words. Becker Friedman Institute for Research in Economics, Chicago, IL. https://mfidev.uchicago.edu/about/tribute/mfquotes.shtml

G20 (2009) Leaders' statement: The Pittsburgh summit September 24–25 https://www.g20.org/en/about-the-g20/previous-summit?activeAccordion=73814cd9-ed16-4890-aca8-232da5793466%2C1f9fb67e-c869-4b8a-8ff7-f9d61735f5db

Garrison RW (2006) Natural and neutral rates of interest in theory and policy formulation. Q J Austrian Econ 9(4) (Winter 2006):57–68. https://mises.org/quarterly-journal-austrian-econom ics/natural-and-neutral-rates-interest-theory-and-policy-formulation

Garten JE (2021) When America remade the world economy. Project syndicate. August 13. https:// www.project-syndicate.org/onpoint/nixon-dollargold-standard-end-of-bretton-woods-by-jef frey-e-garten-2021-08

Geeks for Geeks (2022) How are cryptocurrencies created? 5 May. https://www.geeksforgeeks.org/ how-are-cryptocurrencies-created/

Giles C (2008) The economic forecasters' failing vision. Financial Times. November 25. https:// www.ft.com/content/50007754-ca35-11dd-93e5-000077b07658

Goodier M (2023) How UK house prices left the middle class behind. The Guardian. 28 July. https:// www.theguardian.com/money/2023/jul/28/how-uk-house-prices-left-the-middle-class-behind

Hanke SH (2008) Greenspan's bubbles. Finance Asia. 5 June. Available at https://www.cato.org/ pub_display.php?pub_id=9448

Hayek F (1976) Choice in currency. A way to stop inflation. Institute of Economic Affairs, London. https://iea.org.uk/publications/research/choice-in-currency-a-way-to-stop-inflation

House of Lords Economic Affairs Committee (2023) Making an independent bank of England work better. Authority of the House of Lords. 27 November. https://committees.parliament.uk/public ations/42289/documents/210852/default/

Investopedia Team (2024) Cryptocurrency explained with pros and cons for investment. Investo-pedia.com 26 May. https://www.investopedia.com/terms/c/cryptocurrency.asp

Johnston M (2023) How central banks Monetize government debt. Investopedia. September 13. https://www.investopedia.com/articles/investing/032516/how-central-banks-monetize-govern ment-debt.asp#:~:text=Monetization%20occurs%20when%20central%20banks,conducts% 20to%20achieve%20policy%20targets.

Lioudis N (2024) What is the gold standard? Advantages, alternatives, and history. Investopedia, 5 April. https://www.investopedia.com/ask/answers/09/gold-standard.asp

Lynn M (2023) What does it take to get fired from the bank of England? Daily Tele-graph. 23 December. https://www.telegraph.co.uk/business/2023/12/23/what-does-take-get-fired-bank-england-andrew-bailey/

Mises L (1981) The theory of money and credit, translated by HE Batson. Indianapolis: Liberty Fund. https://oll.libertyfund.org/titles/mises-the-theory-of-money-and-credit

Muradzikwa T, Kazmierczak A, Jungreis M (2023) Unpacking central bank digital currency and the future of monetary policy. Plug and Play. 7 March. https://www.plugandplaytechcenter.com/ resources/unpacking-central-bank-digital-currency/

Nader R (2020) The federal reserve dictatorship runs amok against savers. Common dreams. March 18. https://www.commondreams.org/views/2020/03/18/federal-reserve-dictat orship-runs-amok-against-savers

Nickell (2005) Why has inflation been so low since 1999? Speech given by Stephen Nickell. Bank of England 27 January. https://www.bankofengland.co.uk/-/media/boe/files/speech/2005/why-has-inflation-been-so-low-since-1999.pdf

O'Connor S (2022) How will we remember the age of cheap money? Financial Times, November 1. https://www.ft.com/content/1d2af214-caf6-4326-916d-b597577186c8

Oppers ES (2002) The Austrian theory of business cycles: old lessons for modern economic policy? IMF Working Paper No. 2002/002. January 1. https://www.imf.org/en/Publications/WP/Issues/ 2016/12/30/The-Austrian-Theory-of-Business-Cycles-Old-Lessons-for-Modern-Economic-Policy-15480

Plender J (2012) Banks, bonuses and bad accountancy. Financial Times, March 25. https://www.ft. com/content/ed4033ce-7275-11e1-9c23-00144feab49a

Rand A, Branden N, Greenspan A, Hessen R (1986) Capitalism. Penguin

Redman J (2024) US lawmaker introduces bill to dismantle fed's board of governors and abolish the central bank. Bitcoin.com 17 May. https://news.bitcoin.com/us-lawmaker-introduces-bill-to-dismantle-feds-board-of-governors-and-abolish-the-central-bank/

Richards K (n.d) What is cryptography? TechTarget Network. https://www.techtarget.com/search security/definition/cryptography

Rozsa A (2022) What is fiat money? Definition & more. Wise.com 30 May. https://wise.com/us/blog/what-is-fiat-currency

Study Master (n.d) Collateralized debt obligations. Study Smarter. https://www.studysmarter.co.uk/explanations/macroeconomics/economics-of-money/collateralized-debt-obligations/

Tardi C (2024) Collateralized debt obligation (CDOs): what it is, how it works. Investopedia. February 13. https://www.investopedia.com/terms/c/cdo.asp

The Guardian Archive (2016) John major champions new European currency–archive. The Guardian, 12 June. https://www.theguardian.com/business/2016/jun/21/john-major-ecu-european-currency-unit-monetary-union

Tumerkan A (2023) Why the Austrian business cycle theory matters more than ever in today's global economy. Speculators anonymous. May 15. https://speculatorsanonymous.com/articles/austrian-business-cycle-theory/

Uzialko A (2023) The return of CDOs: is another economic crisis on the horizon? Business News Daily. October 20. https://www.businessnewsdaily.com/10353-cdo-financial-derivatives-economic-crisis.html

White LH (2009) Housing finance and the 2008 financial crisis. Downsizing the Federal Government. August 1. https://www.downsizinggovernment.org/hud/housing-finance-2008-financial-crisis